Communication and Citizenship

This book addresses a question which is increasingly at the centre of academic and journalistic debate: to what extent are the media in modern societies able to help citizens learn about the world, debate their responses to it and reach informed decisions about what courses of action to adopt? Can the media play a role in the formation of a 'public sphere' at a time when public service broadcasting is under attack, and the popular press plays to the market with an output of celebrity gossip and sensationalized reporting?

The contributors to this collection of new essays each concentrate on one aspect of the role and future of the public sphere in the United States and Europe, both East and West. Topics under discussion include American politics and television news, feminist perspectives on the public sphere, the Polish media after Stalinism and the popular press and television in the United Kingdom.

The Editors:

Peter Dahlgren is Principal Lecturer in the Department of Journalism, Media and Communication at Stockholm University, Sweden.

Colin Sparks is Principal Lecturer in the School of Communication at the Polytechnic of Central London.

The Contributors:

Ian Connell, Ann N. Crigler, James Curran, Peter Dahlgren, Klaus Bruhn Jensen, Karol Jakubowicz, Todd Gitlin, Michael Gurevitch, Suzanne Hasselbach, Mark R. Levy, Paolo Mancini, John M. Phelan, Vincent Porter, Itzhak Roeh, Colin Sparks, Liesbet van Zoonen.

Communication and Society
General Editor: James Curran

Communication and Citizenship

Journalism and the Public Sphere

Edited by
Peter Dahlgren and Colin Sparks

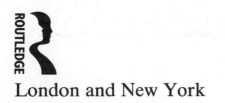

London and New York

First published 1991
by Routledge
11 New Fetter Lane, London EC4P 4EE
29 West 35th Street, New York, NY 10001

First published in paperback 1993
by Routledge

Collection © 1991 Peter Dahlgren and Colin Sparks
Individual chapters © 1991 the respective authors

Typeset by Selectmove Ltd, London
Printed in Great Britain by T.J. Press (Padstow) Ltd,
Padstow, Cornwall

British Library Cataloguing in Publication Data
Communication and citizenship: journalism and the public sphere in
the new media age. – (Communication and society)
1. Society. Role of mass media
I. Dahlgren, Peter – II. Sparks, Colin – III. Series
302.234

Library of Congress Cataloging in Publication Data
Communication and citizenship: journalism and the public sphere in
the new media age/edited by Peter Dahlgren and Colin Sparks.
p. cm. – (Communication and society (New York, N.Y.))
Includes index.
1. Journalism – Social aspects. 2. Journalism – Political aspects –
United States. 3. Journalism – Political aspects – Europe.
I. Dahlgren, Peter –. II. Sparks, Colin –.
III. Series.
PN4749.C65 1991
302.23'0973 – dc20

ISBN 0–415–100674

Contents

Part III Journalistic practices

A note on contributors

Ian Connell is Professor of Media Studies at Wolverhampton Polytechnic, England.

Ann N. Crigler is Assistant Professor in the Department of Political Science, University of Southern California, USA.

James Curran is Professor of Communications at Goldsmiths' College, University of London, England.

Peter Dahlgren is Principal Lecturer in the Department of Journalism, Media and Communication at Stockholm University, Sweden.

Todd Gitlin is Professor of Sociology and Director of the Mass Communications Programme at the University of California, Berkeley, USA.

Michael Gurevitch is a professor in the College of Journalism at the University of Maryland, USA

Suzanne Hasselbach is a research fellow in the Centre for Communication and Information Studies at the Polytechnic of Central London, England.

Karol Jakubowicz is the Editor of the journal *Przekazy i Opinie* at the Centre for Public Opinion and Broadcasting Research of Polish Radio and TV, Warsaw, Poland.

Klaus Bruhn Jensen is Associate Professor in the Department of Film, Television and Communication at the University of Copenhagen, Denmark.

Mark R. Levy is a professor and Associate Dean in the College of Journalism at the University of Maryland, USA.

Paolo Mancini is Professor of Communication at the University of Perugia, Italy.

John M. Phelan is Professor of Communication and Director of the Donald McGannon Communication Research Center at Fordham University, New York, USA.

Vincent Porter is Professor of Communication and Deputy Director of the Centre for Information and Communication Studies at the Polytechnic of Central London, England.

Itzhak Roeh is a senior lecturer in the Department of Communication at the Hebrew University of Jerusalem, Israel.

Colin Sparks is a lecturer in the School of Communication at the Polytechnic of Central London, England.

Liesbet van Zoonen is a lecturer in the Department of Communication at the University of Amsterdam, Netherlands.

Acknowledgements

This book originates from a Colloquium organized in May 1989 at the Inter-University Centre in Dubrovnik under the auspices of the Department of Journalism, Media and Communication of Stockholm University. Without their support it would not have been possible to gather together such a range of scholars from different countries for what turned out to be a productive and enjoyable week. We must first thank the University and the Department for their generosity with time and resources. We would also like to express our appreciation to the staff of the Inter-University Centre for making available their facilities and for their work in easing the task of organizing and running the Colloquium.

In moving from a collection of papers to a book, we have been forced to leave out some of the original contributions. The demands of space and thematic unity have meant that we have excluded very valuable papers. A number of these have already been published elsewhere and others are being reworked as part of more extensive projects. We hope that in time most of the material discussed will be publicly available. The consideration of thematic unity also led us to include two papers, by Michael Gurevitch and his collaborators and by Vincent Porter and Suzanne Hasselbach, which were not presented at the Colloquium.

All the articles were specially commissioned with the exception of 'Musical chairs?: the three public spheres in Poland' by Karol Jakubowicz. It first appeared in the journal *Media, Culture and Society*, volume 12, number 2, and is reprinted here with the kind permission of the journal's editors and Sage Publications.

The production of this volume has been greatly facilitated by the generosity of the Bonnierföretagen in endowing the Albert Bonnier Visiting Professorship at the Department of Journalism, Media and Communication of Stockholm University. Both the Series Editor and one of the Editors of this volume have benefited from holding this chair and their time in Stockholm contributed greatly to the planning and organizing of this book.

Introduction

Peter Dahlgren

The public sphere is a concept which in the context of today's society points to the issues of how and to what extent the mass media, especially in their journalistic role, can help citizens learn about the world, debate their responses to it and reach informed decisions about what courses of action to adopt. The essays collected in this volume all address aspects of the relationship between the mass media and the public sphere, both in Europe and the USA. From a variety of intellectual standpoints, they all touch upon topics and debates which are central to the daily functioning of a democratic society. In the discussion which follows, I briefly trace the evolution of the idea of a public sphere, especially as it was developed by Jürgen Habermas. Delving into some issues of Habermas's conceptual framework and methodology, I will argue that despite the undeniable pathbreaking quality of his work, there remains some troublesome ambiguity at the core. I then offer some reflections on the renewal of the concept of the public sphere.

Some version of what we have come to call the public sphere has always existed as an appendage to democratic theory. As the vision of democracy has evolved historically, so has the view of the desirability and feasibility of fora where the ruled can develop and express their political will to the rulers. And clearly the view among rulers and ruled has often been at odds. The development of mass-based democracy in the west coincided historically with the emergence of the mass media as the dominant institutions of the public sphere. As the political and cultural significance of traditional and localized arenas continue to recede in the wake of social transformations and media developments, the notion of the public sphere moves to the fore and takes on a particularly normative valence. It becomes a focal point of our desire for the good society, the institutional sites where popular political will should take form and citizens should be able to constitute themselves as active agents in the political process. How well the public sphere functions becomes a concrete manifestation of society's democratic character and thus in a sense the most immediately visible indicator of our admittedly imperfect democracies.

The concept of the public sphere can be used in a very general and common-sense manner, as, for example, a synonym for the processes of public opinion or for the news media themselves. In its more ambitious guise, however, as it was developed by Jürgen Habermas, the public sphere should be understood as an *analytic category*, a conceptual device which, while pointing to a specific social phenomenon can also aid us in analysing and researching the phenomenon. For Habermas, the concept of the *bourgeois* public sphere signifies a specific social space, which arose under the development of capitalism in Western Europe. The modifying adjective is not an epithet but points rather to the particular historical circumstances and class character of the phenomenon. As an analytic category, the bourgeois public sphere consists of a dynamic nexus which links a variety of actors, factors and contexts together in a cohesive theoretic framework. It is this configurational quality, with its emphasis on institutional and discursive contingencies, which gives the concept its analytical power. Habermas's analysis incorporates, among other things, theoretical perspectives on history, social structure, politics, media sociology, as well as the nature of opinion, to give some sense of the notion's entwinement.

Habermas's study ends with his depiction of the decline of the bourgeois public sphere and its final 'disintegration' in the modern industrialized welfare states of advanced capitalism. One could in principle accept Habermas's evaluation as definitive for our own 'post-bourgeois' age and for the future as well, in which case there is little more to be said or done. But there is no point in merely going on repeating Habermas's conclusions. History is not static, and the public sphere in the contemporary situation is conditioned by other historical circumstances and is (hopefully) imbued with other potentialities. To the extent that one is concerned about the dynamics of democracy, we need an understanding of the public sphere which is congruent with the emerging realities of today, and serviceable for both research and politics. This involves coming to terms with Habermas's analysis, incorporating it and modifying it within new intellectual and political horizons.

While the full text of Habermas's *Strukturwandel der Offentlichkeit* (1962) has only recently become available in English as *The Structural Transformation of the Public Sphere* (1989), the central features of his thesis had become familiar to British and American media studies by the late 1970s, via a synoptic article by Habermas (1974) and some secondary literature. Even from these texts, one could see that with his emphasis on democracy and the role of the media, Habermas's notion of the public sphere actually has a good deal in common with prevailing liberal thought in the Anglo-American traditions. At the same time, the concept has a theoretical ambition beyond those developed within the traditions of liberal democratic theory, of which his analysis also in part presents itself as a critique.

THE AMBIGUITY OF HABERMAS

In this short presentation I can only hope to give a compressed view of Habermas's line of argument and identify some of the problematic features of his thesis. Mats Dahlkvist (1984) develops these ideas further in his excellent introduction to the Swedish translation, while a similar discussion in English can be found in Keane (1984).

The ascending bourgeois classes in Western Europe, in struggling against the powers of the absolutist state, managed to generate a new social space or field between the state and civil society. This struggle gained momentum especially during the eighteenth century. In contrast to what Habermas refers to as the 'representative publicness' of the medieval period, where the ruling nobility and its power were merely displayed before the populace, this new public sphere offered the possibility for citizens to engage in discussion on the state's exercise of power. In other words, private people using their own critical reason came together to create a public. The highpoint of the bourgois public sphere, characterized by the discussions and writings of 'men of letters' was reached in the early to mid-nineteenth century.

In tracing this development, Habermas emphasizes its positive qualities yet is quick to point out a fundamental flaw in the worldview through which the bourgeois classes came to see themselves, namely the problem of universalism. While there were specific variations in the evolution of the public sphere in Germany, Great Britain and France, in general the rights of citizenship, e.g. access to the public sphere and voting, did not include everyone, but was largely limited to property-owners. Moreover, literacy was also at least an implicit requirement and, given the social structure at this time, tended to coincide with the ownership of property. In essence, Habermas points to the contradictions between the ideal of formal equality espoused by liberal doctrine and the social inequalities generated by market relations, a state of affairs still very much with us today.

Despite these restrictions on full participation in the public sphere, by the mid-nineteenth century when *laissez-faire* capitalism was at its height, liberal philosophers like Mill and De Tocqueville were already arguing for the delimitation of the status, role and power of what had come to be called public opinion. They clearly saw dangerous possibilities to the prevailing social order if power was to be truly subordinate to popular will. But it was not so much philosophical arguments *per se* which began the disintegration of the bourgeois public sphere, but rather the rapid social developments which altered its conditions and premises. In the latter half of the nineteenth century, industrialization, urbanization, the growth of literacy and the popular press, and not least the rise of the administrative and interventionist state all contributed in various ways to its decline. The consequences of these developments included a blurring of the distinctions between public and private in political and economic affairs, a rationalization and shrinking of the private intimate sphere (family life) and the gradual shift from an (albeit limited) public of political and cultural debaters to a mass public of consumers.

With the emergence of the welfare state in the twentieth century Habermas notes the further transformations of the public sphere. Journalism's critical role in the wake of advertising, entertainment and public relations becomes muted. Public opinion is no longer a process of rational discourse but the result of publicity and social engineering in the media. At this point in Habermas's narrative the Anglo-American reader begins to recognize more familiar intellectual landscape. Indeed, in the last sections of the book Habermas uses ideas from such innovative books from the 1950s as Riesman's *The Lonely Crowd* and Whyte's *The Organization Man* to support his arguments. In the last two pages of the text Habermas cites and discusses C. W. Mills's distinction (found in his *The Power Elite*) between 'public' and 'mass' to highlight his own position. Here we find a helpful bridge. From Mills's analysis of power relations in mid-century USA the reader can then, with whatever modifications may seem necessary, connect with the various strands of media research which have come to the fore over the past two decades. And the connections are by no means limited to research with a neo-marxian profile: a book such as Postman's (1986) echoes many of Habermas's arguments.

Habermas's analysis is truly ambitious and largely compelling, yet there remain some areas of difficulty. It might be argued that he doubly overstates his case, that the discourse of the bourgeois public sphere even at its zenith never manifested the high level of reasoned discourse he suggests, and that the situation under advanced capitalism – dismal as it may be – is not as bleak and locked as he asserts. But these are questions of historical evaluation. In terms of the logic of his own argument, however, there seems to be three related and very central points of ambiguity in the analysis:

1   The ideal of the bourgeois public sphere, with its salons and literary pamphlets, is retained as a model, a vision, at the same time that its historical manifestation is found lacking and needs to be transcended. Thus his devastating critique is coloured both by a quality of romanticism verging on nostalgia as well as a pervasive pessimism. He seemingly clings to an ideal whose historical concreteness he has penetratingly found to be an ideological distortion. There is consequently a sense of a dead-end about the study. In later work, such as in the two-volume *Theory of Communicative Action* (1984, 1987), while he takes up issues on communication within the social system, he only in passing addresses the specific and concrete issues of the public sphere. Within the framework of that study, with its central distinction between system and life-world – a problematic separation, as some commentators have noted (e.g. Baxter 1987) – the public and private spheres fall within the domain of the colonized life-world. There, normatively grounded communication is subverted by the system's instrumental rationality. In short, one could say he essentially repeats his thesis at a higher level of abstraction, subsuming it under a systems-theoretic mode of exposition.

To this point should be added the observation that there is a major blind spot in Habermas's critique of the bourgeois public sphere: while he clearly reveals its class bias, he neglects to identify its patriarchal character. His ideal of a public sphere is predicated on a public–private dichotomy, but, from a feminist perspective, uncritically accepting this separation, as liberalism itself has tended to do, results in complicity in the subordination of women. The universalism and equality of democratic theory is thus subverted not only by class but also by gender. Even alternative, socialist models have failed adequately to address gender, as recent feminist writing has pointed out. However, such critics readily concede the complexity of the problems (cf. Patemen 1987). An excellent feminist analysis, much in the tradition and spirit of Critical Theory itself, of Habermas's later work, is found in Fraser (1987). In the present volume, Liesbet van Zoonen takes up the strategic uses and implications of femininity in Dutch TV newscasters.

2 He is silent on alternative, 'plebeian', popular, informal or oppositional public spheres. This leaves a big theoretic vacuum. For under both the periods of liberal and advanced capitalism there have existed other fora which have shaped people's political consciousness, served as networks for exchange of information, rumour and gossip, and also provided settings for cultural expression. Oskar Negt's and Alexander Kluge's attempts to formulate a 'proletarian public sphere' is one example of an effort to conceptualize such an alternative (see Knödler-Bunte 1975). Historically one can point to the unions and other popular political movements which combined cultural, social and informational functions and provided significant settings for debate.

3 A corollary to this second point arises from the perspectives of today's intellectual horizons and research in such areas as media reception, semiotics, cultural theory and general 'postmodern' modes of thought. In Habermas's book there seems to be an implicit understanding of how people carry on conversation and arrive at political opinions which seems strangely abstract and formalistic. References to the complexities and contradictions of meaning production, and to the concrete social settings and cultural resources at work, are absent. With almost three decades of research and hindsight at our disposal, this observation could smack of all too easy criticism. Yet it

could be argued that his later work in such areas as universal pragmatics and ideal speech situations makes explicit a highly rationalistic orientation to human communication which is only implicit here.

Lurking in the shadows at this juncture of the discussion are the debates over postmodernism, in which Habermas has been a central figure (Habermas 1987, Bernstein 1986). While this topic would take us too far from our present concerns, I do want to call attention to the importance of a domain – let us call it the process of sense-making – as central for understanding at the micro level the conditions of citizen involvement with the public sphere. Perspectives and approaches from Cultural Studies are as imperative here as those deriving from, say, traditional political science or linguistics.

FOR A RECONSTRUCTION

Any consideration of Habermas's analysis of the bourgeois public sphere must take into account that his study emanates from the Frankfurt School tradition of Critical Theory. This gives the concept its historical concreteness as well as its intellectual specificity. Methodologically, this means that Habermas's work incorporates elements of critique. By this I mean basically the analytic process whereby the seeming facticity of a phenomenon (i.e. the bourgeois public sphere), as well as the conceptual categories by which this phenomenon is grasped (e.g. 'opinion', 'citizen', 'voting'), are probed to reveal their historical conditions and limits. This is done with the aim of an emancipatory interest.

In other words, Habermas first examines the bourgeois public sphere, not by accepting its definition of itself, but by elucidating the historical circumstances which make it possible and, eventually, also impossible. Then he strives to establish the conditions which account for the social origins and functioning of the *discrepancy* between the conceptual categories used in the discourse about the public sphere and the actual social relations and value relations which are at work. In short, he highlights its illusory or ideological component; he examines both what is socially accomplished by the discrepancy and what is at stake in its revelation. It is in this sense that his method can be said to be critical.

The Frankfurt School's version of critique was an intellectual milestone, not least for the area of media analysis (cf. Negt 1980). However, this does not mean we should treat their analyses as an orthodoxy. Such canonicalness would only create an impasse and would in fact be contrary to the logic of critique itself. It is much more fruitful to integrate a general notion of critique with an overall approach to the human sciences generally and the media in particular, not least where issues of ideology arise (cf. Thompson 1990). Critique, the critical moment or dimension of analysis and research, then becomes one of several necessary dimensions, along with what can be termed the empirical, the interpretive and the reflexive. The particular research task and interests at hand must decide the ratio between these dimensions. The critical moment is thus neither exhaustive nor exclusive. Moreover, we have come to see that there are even conceptual limitations to its liberatory project (cf. Fay 1987, Benhabib 1986).

The knowledge which critique generates points to contingencies, yet also to possibilities: to change and to human intervention in a social world whose human origins are often not recognizable. (In this regard even Habermas's critical dimension here is perhaps underdeveloped: there seems to be no point of entry for such intervention.) For the public sphere, this means not letting the concept become just a flat referent, reduced to merely signifying what is, losing sight of what should and could be. The critical dimension – incorporating the other dimensions of analysis – ideally serves to scramble the existing demarcations between the manifest and the latent, between what is and what might be, such that the lines might be redrawn in a way which could take us closer to a more democratic society.

In order to reconstruct a conceptualization of the public sphere as an analytic category, with Habermas as a point of departure, it is in my view productive and even imperative to retain this critical dimension. This means of course going beyond Habermas's own analysis. It is important to be aware of his ambiguity. The romantic notion of a public sphere composed of individuals speaking face to face or communicating via small-circulation print media is not of much utility. We live in the age of electronic media and mass publics and cannot turn back the historical clock; we can only go forward. Likewise, while much in the contemporary situation is troubling to say the least, we must not let pessimism become the all-pervasive motif. The concept of the public sphere must have evocative power, providing us with concrete visions of the democratic society which are enabling rather than disabling. In other words, it must also fuel our utopian imagination, not leave us apathetic or paralytic. We need to render the public sphere as an object of citizen concern, scrutiny and intervention. The defence and expansion of the public sphere always remains a political accomplishment.

In sum, an understanding which can guide our thinking and research about the contemporary 'post-bourgeois' public sphere needs to examine the *institutional configurations* within the media and the social order as a whole and their relevance for the democratic participation of citizens. The compelling nexus quality of the concept is central here. It is important to anchor analysis in the historical realities of today, continually updating our understanding of the present. For example, while we cannot ignore the dominance of the mainstream media, we should be careful not to exaggerate unnecessarily their homogeneity or monolithic character. Such a view will blind us to other, even incipient forms of the public sphere. The social order and its political institutions, and thus the public sphere itself, are today anything but stagnant.

Further, we must also be attentive to the *sense-making processes* in daily life, especially in relation to media culture, drawing upon and contributing to both the concrete empirical investigation and theoretical development. A nuanced understanding of the limits and possibilities of meaning production and circulation is essential, if we are to avoid such pitfalls as assuming cardboard cut-out versions of 'rational man', reducing all signification to ideology or positing an unlimited polysemy in media-audience interfaces (Dahlgren 1987, 1988).

We should not forget that today we know an awful lot about the media, politics and the problems of democracy. We are by no means starting from scratch: there is a good deal of relevant and excellent work going on – empirical, interpretive, reflexive as well as critical – which is contributing to our understanding of the various dimensions of the public sphere. For instance, the sociology of news production tells us a great deal about the conditions and contingencies which shape journalistic practices and output. (See Ericson *et al.* 1987 and 1989 for a survey of this field as well as a report from a very ambitious project thus far within the area. Schudson 1989 offers a useful overview of the literature.) Indeed, all the practical concerns and debates concerning journalistic freedom – e.g. access to information, use of sources, censorship, the legal frameworks which balance privacy with the collective good – are as decisive for the public sphere today as they were in the early nineteenth century, if not more so. Yet knowledge-wise we are in a better position to confront them.

INSTITUTIONAL CONFIGURATIONS: A NEW MEDIA AGE

The institutional configurations of the prevailing social order and its media are staggering in their complexity and can be represented in innumerable ways. The category of the public sphere can help us to order these configurations in a cohesive manner from the standpoint of the criteria of citizen access and participation in the political process, as well as provide a focused political angle of vision. In the years since Habermas's book appeared, there have been many dramatic societal changes; these seem to be accelerating, not least within the area of the media. To speak of a new media age is not to engage in periodization at the level of serious historiography, but only to emphasize the profundity of the transformations in the media and society generally. Neither media institutions nor constellations of social power are exactly as they were in the early 1960s.

The political economy of the traditional mass media in western societies has evolved significantly. Research brought to our attention the dramatic developments in their ownership, control and political use. The trends of privatization, conglomeration, transnationalization and deregulation have amplified and broadened the mercantile logic of media operations, to the increasing exclusion of other norms (cf. Murdock 1990a). Public broadcasting in the USA has always been a minor voice in the otherwise fully commercial system. In Western Europe public-service broadcasting has seen the historical conditions for its existence rapidly dissolving, forcing it to capitulate further to commercial imperatives, with the state contributing to, rather than struggling against, these developments (cf. Keane 1989, McQuail and Siune 1986). The modern public sphere seemingly recalls the representative public-ness of the middle ages, where elites display themselves for the masses while at the same time using the forum to communicate among themselves, as Paolo Mancini's chapter in this book argues.

The progressive political struggle is not one to defend the present form of state-financed monopolies, which have shown themselves often to be elitist, moribund and susceptible to state intervention.

Rather, the goal is to establish structures of broadcasting in the public interest, free of both state intervention and commodification, which optimize diversity in terms of information, viewpoints and forms of expression, and which foster full and active citizenship (cf. Chapter 4 by Porter and Hasselbach in this volume; also Murdock 1990b).

In another domain, the much-heralded information society is decidedly not about to make politically useful information and cultural expression more available to more people (cf. Schiller 1989, Garnham 1990, Melody 1990). On the contrary, while technological advances have generated new interfaces between mass media, computers and telecommunication and satellites, market forces coupled with public policy have tended to opt for private gain over the public interest. From the standpoint of the citizen, access to relevant information will cost more and more, augmenting differentials in access and further eroding the universalist ideal of citizenship (Murdock and Golding 1989).

Within journalism we also find a growing class-based segmentation of the press (see the chapter here by Colin Sparks; also Sparks 1988), further accelerating the distance between the informed elite and the entertained masses. While the press accommodates its structures and operations to the imperatives of commercial logic, it does not turn a deaf ear to the wishes of the state (cf. Curran and Seaton 1989 for a discussion of the British case). In TV journalism, it would be difficult to argue that rational public discourse is enhanced as news and public affairs become more and more subordinate to audience-attracting and -maintaining commercial logic (cf. Todd Gitlin's chapter in this volume).

These developments essentially only intensify the import of Habermas's arguments concerning the modern media's contribution to the decay of the public sphere; in fact such has been the basic message from critical media research over the years. The fundamental logic of the media's political and cultural significance is quite recognizable. One could say that what was true in the early 1960s is still true today, only more so; all that is required is the ongoing updating of the specifics regarding media structures, discourses, audiences and so on. Yet there is a risk that such a totalizing move can create a distorting lens if it is not complemented with a perspective on the tensions, cracks and contradictions within the media and, perhaps more significantly, society at large. In other words, in solely emphasizing the monolithic compactness of the communications sector of society, coupled with the power nexus of state and capital, we may lose sight of other configurations which also condition the public sphere but which may be functioning to pull it in other directions. I would point to a nexus comprising four key intertwined areas to illustrate this point: the crisis of the nation-state, the segmentation of audiences, the rise of new political and social movements and the relative availability of advanced computer and communication technology to consumers.

It was within the framework of the nation-state that modern democracy had its theoretical origins. Today, the nation-state as a political entity is in deep crisis, beset not only with fiscal dilemmas but also with problems of legitimation. This crisis of course goes in tandem with the transnationalization of capital and the dispersion of production within the international economy. Economic control of the economy within the nation-state's borders increasingly resides outside those borders. Internally the state is facing a stagnation of national parliamentary politics, where the margins of administrative and political manoeuvrability are contracting and the consequent political programmes of the established parties are tending towards dedifferentiation.

Where major political initiatives have been successful, e.g. in Reagan's USA and Thatcher's Great Britain in the 1980s, the resultant social dislocations have generated still more political stresses at the popular level. Here particularly we see the emerging contours of the 'two-thirds society' – a form of societal triage where the system can seemingly provide for the well-being of approximately two-thirds of the populace while sacrificing the remaining third and allowing it to solidify into a underclass. Party loyalty and participation in the arena of official politics understandably recedes. Reagan, it should be recalled, came to power with just over one-fourth of the popular vote: about half the electorate did not feel that participation was meaningful. In such a situation, the ideological success of the powerful in the public sphere is at least being passively contested to a degree not manifested three decades ago.

In the wake of the expanding commercial rationality of the media we observe the continual segmentation of audiences according to consumption capacities and demographics. News journalism becomes targeted to different groups according to market strategies. This is a very complex process, but tends to follow the class polarization noted above. One can say that generally there is a weakening of the serious media which have attempted to serve as national fora, the case of European public service being paramount. The active segmentation in news 'packaging' is perhaps most pronounced in the realm of radio news in the USA, but can also be seen within television news and the printed media. The marked decline of literary culture and skills among younger generations is having a profound impact on the whole newspaper industry in the USA (Shaw 1989). Where this trend toward fragmentation is negated by new initiatives, the best example being the success of *USA Today* as a national paper, the utility of such initiatives as resources for political participation in the arena of national politics is limited, to say the least. The overall upshot is thus a further decline of a viable public sphere for national politics.

. In the intersection of the crisis of the national state, the sagging vitality of parliamentary politics and the segmentation of audiences we find the dramatic flowering of new political and social movements. They cover such diverse domains as the environment, disarmament, women's and sexual minorities' legal rights and social conditions, racial and ethnic groups' interests and social welfare issues such as housing and health care. These movements vary greatly in their orientation, tactics and goals; within certain movements one sees differing strands which can even be at odds with each other. On the other hand, groups focused on different concerns, such as women and the environment, may at times join forces with each other for particular campaigns. A 'post-marxist' attempt to theorize these movements can be found in Laclau and Mouffe (1985); see also Aronowitz (1988).

For the most part politically progressive, there are also conservative and reactionary movements, such as various right-wing Christian groups in the USA and racist, anti-immigration groups in Europe. What does tend to unite them is their largely middle-class character, though even this is not wholly uniform. Their political bases lie mostly outside the established political parties, though they can at times align themselves with these parties as well as with the more traditional class-based organizations such as trade unions.

One of the significant features of these movements is that many of them link the experiences of everyday life, not least those of the private sphere of family and neighbourhood, with a normative vision which is translated into political action. A major contributing factor to their success is the availability of suitable computer and communication technology at affordable prices. With desktop facilities, electronic mail and faxes, it is possible to carry out organizational, informational and debate functions in ways not possible in previous decades. The newsletter has become a cheap but effective medium in this context. At times one sees a genre blurring between newsletter, newspaper and opinion pamphlet; the capacity to turn out a book within a week of the final manuscript begins to dissolve the distinctions between journalism and book publishing.

In effect, what we have here is emergence of a plurality of dynamic alternative public spheres (see for example, Downing 1988), an inverse complement to the mainstream media's audience segmentations. While it would be a mistake to make too much of these movements (the corporate and state sectors certainly outgun them in terms of the resources to use new media) it would be an analytic blunder to ignore them.

In particular, if we now synthesize the four elements of this configuration – crisis of the state, audience segmentation, the new movements and the available communication technologies – we see the contours of historically new conditions for the public sphere, a new nexus to set in contrast to the dominant one of the corporate state and its major media. It is precisely in this interface where interesting points of tension arise. For example, the established media continually attempt to delegitimize those movements it finds threatening to the system (while one can even see attempts in the legal field to criminalize further certain forms of extra-parliamentary political action). Yet the versions of reality disseminated by the dominant media cannot be too far at odds with the experiences and perspectives of movement participants. As the movements gather size, the area of contested definitions grows. The major media must acknowledge to some extent the interpretations of the movements.

While one has seen how the movements can at times skilfully make use of the dominant media (e.g. Greenpeace), a new pattern or phase may now be emerging where the movements' own media can increasingly come to serve as news source organizations for the dominant media. In other words, movement media begin to compete with other, more established source organizations (see Schlesinger 1990), lobbying for time and space in the major media via 'news-promoting' activities. Perhaps this is the first sign of a new, two-tiered public sphere, where the alternative movement media, with their stronger link to the experiences and interpretations of the everyday lives of their members, have a growing political capacity to transmit their versions of political reality to the dominant media. This serves both to diffuse and legitimate a wider array of viewpoints and information.

If this interpretation is accurate, it would suggest that we may be approaching an historical development which parallels the one Habermas described. For him the political struggles of the emerging bourgeois classes against state powers resulted in the creation of a new public sphere, which in turn began to decay and finally disintegrate under what he terms the refeudalization of social power under the welfare state. While the new movements are not likely to dissolve or supplant the prevailing state–corporate–media power nexus, their alternative media may be ascending to a much larger complementary role *vis à vis* the dominant communications system. If such is the case, a new, more solidified two-tiered public sphere would at least be a reflection of altered social relations of power.

As a coda to this discussion I would call attention to the recent unprecedented historical events in Eastern and Central Europe. Though viable oppositional public spheres may not be able to flourish in situations where state repression is thorough and systematic, e.g. pre-1989 USSR, Czechoslovakia or Romania, a relatively benign (by comparison) repressive apparatus as found in Poland in the 1980s was sufficiently porous to allow an oppositional public sphere to function. Its relation to the dominant media was complex, as Karol Jakubowicz points out in his contribution to this volume. Where the more repressive apparatus is suddenly relaxed, we saw a veritable explosion of alternative media (e.g. the Baltic republics), despite having little of the financial and technological resources available to movements in the west. With a sort of political stability – though perhaps temporary – now emerging in, for example, Hungary, Poland and Czechoslovakia, the high intensity politicization of society reaches a watershed. A 'normalization' is achieved. Yet the turn to versions of western style political democracy is also followed by vast and rapid investments from western media entrepreneurs. No doubt new configurations of dominant and alternative media will take shape, giving rise to new struggles over the public sphere.

THE REALM OF SENSE-MAKING

The institutional configurations of the public sphere grasp the phenomenon at the macro-level of structures. However, an understanding of its dynamics requires that we also consider the processes and conditions of sense-making, whereby subjects link experience and reflection to generate meaning (political or otherwise). This involves considering the interactions between members of the public, the media–public interface, as well as media output itself.

If we begin with the idea of a public, Habermas, much like John Dewey – who can be seen as his American counterpart in this regard – underscores the importance of conceptualizing the public as a process within the framework of a community. (See Dewey 1927 and also Carey 1989 and Rosen 1986 for discussions of Dewey's relevance.) Habermas was reacting against technocratic rationality, especially prevalent in the contexts of the major media, which reduces the idea of publics to that of media-consuming audience. The public thus becomes a commodity to be delivered to advertisers or an object of social engineering, potential buyers for advertised products or voters whose behaviour is to be steered. Escalating commercial and instrumental logic contributes to mutual cynicism between media and audiences, further corroding the public sphere (cf. Miller 1987). The very idea of opinion, for example, becomes increasingly vacuous in the context of polling (cf. Bourdieu 1979).

Such constricted perceptions of the public, often reinforced and reproduced by discourses in commercial, political and academic contexts, have an obvious ideological valence. Also they deflect sociological awareness away from a number of very salient issues. Among them are how publics are constituted, the media's role in the process, the nature of the social bonds between members of the public and the ways in which journalism and other media output help or hinder in stimulating dialogue and debate. Publics, in other words, have specific socio-cultural traits and contingencies – they do not consist of abstract collectives of 'talking heads' – and the media in turn are central agents in the shaping of publics. It is important to underscore that the media's centrality here has not just to do with its journalism and current affairs output, but with their overall logic and strategy. Journalism is embedded in and largely contextualized by the other media output with which it appears. The public sphere, in other words, is enmeshed with discourses from entertainment and advertising; the maintenance of boundaries becomes somewhat artificial, not least when the media themselves are so adept at blurring them. This is very important in understanding the media-based conditions of sense-making in the public sphere.

While the loosening of the boundaries between journalism, entertainment, public relations and advertising is precisely the type of trend which Habermas lamented, he may have overlooked the importance of the general media culture in providing shared interpretive frameworks. It may often be that the social bonds between members of the public sphere and their overall interaction fall short of the ideal of an active polity, yet, for better or worse, the media themselves are an important factor in creating the shared cultural perceptions which do exist. Whether such 'communities' are 'authentic' or not is another matter, but media-based interpretive communities are a precondition for sense-making in a modern public sphere. One may be critical of the meanings which are shared, but a model which would strive for a public 'uncontaminated' by media culture is both illusory and counter-productive. Analysis must begin with the realities of the contemporary situation.

To note one important trend in this regard: one can see how especially commercial broadcasting has traditionally created 'markets' which did not necessarily coincide with the political boundaries within a nation. Today we witness how satellite TV may be generating international communities. If audience segmentation within nations is contributing to differentiated interpretive communities, the internationalization of TV news production is perhaps helping to construct inchoate international networks of shared meaning, as Michael Gurevitch and his colleagues describe in this volume. While such constellations have no formal political base, they may well be of significance for international opinion formation.

If publics emerge in the discursive interaction of citizens, then audiences (that is to say, the position of being an audience member) should be realistically seen as a moment, a step in the process of being a member of the public. It constitutes the encounter with media output within the immediate social ecology of reading/viewing/listening. The 'publicness' can be said to emerge in the social practices which emanate beyond that interface. Recent debates have brought to the fore the complex and problematic character of audiences (cf. Allor 1989 and the responses to him in the same issue, and Erni 1989). All the same, it may well be easier, both conceptually and empirically, to deal with audiences, rather than publics, but we should be clear about the relationship between them.

The last decade has witnessed an enormous development in media reception studies and other forms of qualitative audience research, which helps to fuse the moment of being an audience member with other social practices which may be relevant for the constitution of publics. This work, falling mostly within the broad field of Cultural Studies, has had the encouraging consequences of emphasizing the active sense-making processes of audience members, both in terms of social interaction and media decoding. Such research has intertwined the domains of social and cultural practices together with the textual, via an emphasis on language, consciousness and subjectivity as constitutive elements of social reality. (For some recent surveys of this large literature, and overviews of the theoretical and methodological issues, see Morley 1989, Moores 1990, Höijer 1990, Silverstone 1990, Jensen and Jankowski 1991.)

In terms of understanding media output and the media audience interface, these developments, together with current lines of inquiry in the humanities generally, help us get beyond some of the rationalistic premises of Habermas. We see now a strong tendency to problematize and emphasize such issues as – to indulge in an orgy of alliteration – representation, realism, ritual, reception and resistance. To this we can add polysemy and the pluralistic subject. These concerns are often associated with postmodernist positions, but it seems that by now the debates are beginning to lose some of their character of trench warfare and that these developments are contributing to the further refinement of critical and interpretive orientations (e.g. Hall 1986, Wellmer 1986, Kellner 1989a, b). For example, such themes as pleasure and resistance (De Certeau 1984 and Fiske 1987a, b), combining critical and postmodern sensibilities, now move to the fore, even in relation to such ostensibly rational discourses as news programmes.

The a priori distinction between, say, information and entertainment becomes highly problematic from the standpoint of audience sense-making. (Media culture itself seems to be catching up with media theory, as we witness an increasing *mélange* of traditional genres, e.g. the pervasive 'infotainment'.) These newer intellectual currents alert us to important considerations such as the subject as a site of negotiation and contestation. Meaning is thus never fully fixed. Incorporating this insight with the polysemic character of media discourses and audience interpretations has important consequences (cf. Jensen 1990, Streeter 1989) which cannot be explored here. Suffice to say that among the more challenging questions to which these currents give rise is to specify the possibilities and limits of the 'free play' of sense-making in relation to the systemic character of social structure and ideology.

These trends – conceptual, theoretical, methodological – within Cultural Studies (cf. Real 1989 for a useful synthesis) have great relevance for understanding the dynamics of sense-making in the public sphere. A problem here has been that most of this work has emphasized fiction rather than journalism and news, and that while TV news has been studied rather extensively and the television medium as such has been ambitiously theorized (cf. Collins 1989), the other media of the public sphere have been relatively neglected. Traditional empirical studies of newspapers and their content, for example, have told us a good deal about their sociology, but have not probed very deeply into readers' sense-making processes. The agenda for journalism research (cf. Dahlgren 1989 for a programmatic statement) needs to be augmented by insights from Cultural Studies.

In this presentation I have emphasized an understanding of the public sphere which is at once subtle and ambitious. This requires that we set our horizons on its intricate institutional nexus and the equivocal processes of sense-making. Yet our understanding of the public sphere must also be of a practical nature, atuned to the flow of the relevant discourses in the media. Close familiarity with what is said and not said, and how it is said – the topics, the coverages, the debates, the rhetoric, the modes of address, etc. – are a prerequisite not only for an enhanced theoretical understanding but also for concrete political involvement within – and with – the public sphere. Nobody promised that citizenship would be easy.

The essays in this collection are grouped into three parts: Institutional Logics, Politics and Journalism and Journalistic Practices. In Chapter 1, James Curran explores the major problems arising out of the two major models of the public sphere: the market-based pluralist version and the state-dominated marxist alternative. He argues for a third path, with autonomy from both state and market forces, structured by a system of careful balances. Colin Sparks (Chapter 2) takes up the question of to what extent the British press has functioned and continues to function as a public sphere. He argues that not only is the decline of seriousness widespread and growing, but also that the notion of a single concept of what is a 'newspaper' becomes more untenable as the class character of their form, content and readerships becomes more pronounced. In the American context, John M. Phelan (Chapter 3) demonstrates how marketing logic shapes the strategies of TV journalism, including public-service and community campaigns, which were heralded as an effort genuinely to serve the public. In the West German setting, Vincent Porter and Suzanne Hasselbach (Chapter 4) chart the political and economic forces which have shaped the regulation of broadcasting and the consequences for television as a citizen resource.

In the second part, on Politics and Journalism, Todd Gitlin (Chapter 5) looks at recent developments on US network election campaign coverage and considers the implications of the increasingly sophisticated news-management strategies. For Gitlin, the US media are inviting its audiences to join in a celebration of their powerlessness. Looking at the Italian situation, Paolo Mancini (Chapter 6) argues that the media do not empower citizens to participate in the public sphere. Rather, they provide a mechanism for elites to speak to each other and conduct their own closed debates about the future of society. In the profoundly different Polish context, Karol Jakubowicz (Chapter 7) discusses the rise of two alternative public spheres which came to challenge the official one dominated by the state and party. One of the alternatives was dominated by the Church, the other associated with Solidarity. He focuses on the struggle for legitimacy between the three. Turning to the audiences, Ann Crigler and Klaus Bruhn Jensen (Chapter 8) compare how, in the USA and Denmark, the content of the media itself is responsible for the ways in which citizens actually constitute the concerns and ideas which make up the public sphere. They do this by actively imposing thematic structures on the news stories they encounter.

The third part of the book, Journalistic Practices, begins with an essay by Michael Gurevitch, Mark R. Levy and Itzhak Roeh on the internationalization of TV news (Chapter 9). They look at both the topics covered in different countries as well as the meanings which national cultures mobilize to frame these topics. As the subtitle of their essay suggests, both convergence and diversities are at work. Liesbet van Zoonen's article (Chapter 10) considers the fact that Dutch TV news is now predominantly presented by female newscasters. In assessing the feminist critiques of the public sphere she finds that this development in Dutch television news does not necessarily constitute a step beyond the patriarchal order. Ian Connell (Chapter 11) closes the volume by examining how the popular press and television entertainment intersect and overlap, constituting a form of mythic image world. This image world provides a significant yet politically problematic perceptual framework for making sense of public issues.

REFERENCES

Allor, M. (1988) 'Relocating the site of the audience', *Critical Studies in Mass Communication*, vol. 5, pp. 217–33.

Aronowitz, S. (1988) 'Postmodernism and politics', in A. Ross (ed.), *Universal Abandon? The Politics of Postmodernism*, Edinburgh: Edinburgh University Press.

Barker, D. (1988) ' "It's been real": forms of televisual representation', *Critical Studies in Mass Communication*, vol. 5, no. 1, March.

Baxter, H. (1987) 'System and life-world in Habermas' *Theory of Communicative Action*', *Theory and Society*, vol. 16, no. 1.

Benhabib, S. (1986) *Critique, Norm and Utopia: A Study of the Foundations of Critical Theory*, New York: Columbia University Press.

Bernstein, R. (ed.) (1986) *Habermas and Modernity*, Cambridge, Mass.: MIT Press.

Bourdieu, P. (1979) 'Public opinion does not exist', in A. Mattelart and S. Siegelaub (eds), *Communication and Class Struggle*, New York: International General.

Carey, J. (1989) *Communication as Culture*, London: Unwin Hyman.

Collins, J. (1989) 'Watching ourselves watch television, or who's your agent?', *Cultural Studies*, vol. 3, no. 3 (Oct.).

Curran, J. and Seaton, J. (1988) *Power Without Responsibility: The Press and Broadcasting in Britain*, London: Routledge.

Dahlgren, P. (1987) 'Ideology and information in the public sphere', in J. D. Slack and F. Fejes (eds), *The Ideology of the Information Age*, Norwood, NJ: Ablex.

Dahlgren, P. (1988) 'What's the meaning of this? Viewers' plural sense-making of TV news', *Media, Culture and Society*, vol. 10, no. 3 (July).

Dahlgren, P. (1989) 'Journalism research: tendencies and perspectives',

The Nordicom Review of Nordic Mass Communication Research, no. 2.
Dahlkvist, M. (1984) 'Jürgen Habermas' teori om "privat" och "offentligt"'. Introduction to the Swedish edition of Habermas's *Structural Transformation of the Public Sphere*, Bogerlig offentlighet, Lund: Arkiv.
De Certeau, M. (1984) *The Practice of Everyday Life*, Berkeley: University of California Press.
Dewey, J. (1927) *The Public and its Problems*, Chicago: Swallow Press.
Downing, J. (1988) 'The alternative public realm: the organization of the 1980's anti-nuclear press in West Germany and Britain', *Media, Culture and Society*, vol. 10, no. 2 (Apr.).
Ericson, R. V., Baranek, P. M. and Chan, J. B. L. (1987) *Visualizing Deviance: A Study of News Organization*, Toronto: University of Toronto Press.
Ericson, R. V., Baranek, P. M. and Chan, J. B. L. (1989) *Negotiating Control: A Study of News Sources*, Toronto: University of Toronto Press.
Erni, J. (1989) 'Where is the "audience"?: discerning the (impossible) subject', *Journal of Communication Inquiry*, vol. 13, no. 2 (Summer).
Fay, B. (1987) *Critical Social Science*, Cambridge: Polity Press.
Ferguson, M. (ed.) (1990) *Public Communication: The New Imperatives*, London: Sage.
Fiske, J. (1987) *Television Culture*, London: Methuen.
Fiske, J. (1989a) *Understanding Popular Culture*, London: Unwin Hyman.
Fiske, J. (1989b) *Reading the Popular*, London: Unwin Hyman.
Fraser, N. (1987) 'What's critical about critical theory? The case of Habermas and gender', in S. Benhabib and D. Cornell (eds), *Feminism as Critique*, Cambridge: Polity Press.
Garnham, N. (1990) *Capitalism and Communication*, London: Sage.
Habermas, J. (1974) 'The public sphere', *New German Critique*, no. 3.
Habermas, J. (1984, 1987) *The Theory of Communicative Action*, 2 vols, London: Polity Press.
Habermas, J. (1987) *The Philosophical Discourses of Modernity*, Cambridge, MA: MIT Press
Habermas, J. (1989) *The Structural Transformation of the Public Sphere*, Cambridge: Polity Press.
Hall, S, (1986) 'On postmodernism and articulation: an interview with Stuart Hall', *Journal of Communication Inquiry*, vol. 10, no. 2 (Summer).
Höijer, B. (1990) 'Studying viewers' reception of television programmes: theoretical and methodological considerations', *European Journal of Communication*, vol. 5, no. 1 (Mar.).
Jensen, K. B. (1990) 'The politics of polysemy: television news, everyday consciousness and political action', *Media, Culture and Society*, vol. 12, no. 1 (Jan.).
Jensen, K. B. and Jankowski, K. (eds) (1991) *A Handbook of Qualitative Methodologies for Mass Communication Research*, London: Routledge.
Keane, J. (1984) *Public Life and Late Capitalism*, New York: Cambridge University Press.

Keane, J. (1989) ' "Liberty of the press" in the 1990's'. *New Formations*, no. 8 (Summer).

Kellner, D. (1989a) *Critical Theory, Marxism and Modernity*, Baltimore: Johns Hopkins University Press.

Kellner, D. (ed.) (1989b) *Postmodernism/Jameson/Critique*, Washington, DC: Maisonneuve Press.

Knödler-Bunte, E. (1975) 'The proletarian public sphere and political organization: an analysis of Oskar Negt's and Alexander Kluge's *The Public Sphere and Experience*', *New German Critique*, no. 4.

Laclau, E. and Mouffe, C. (1985) *Hegemony and Socialist Strategy: Towards a Radical Democratic Politics*, London: Verso.

McQuail, D. and Siune, K. (eds) (1986) *New Media Politics*, London: Sage.

Melody, W. (1990) 'Communication policy in the global information society: whither the public interest?', in M. Ferguson (ed.), *Public Communication: The New Imperatives*, London: Sage.

Miller, M. C. (1897) 'Deride and conquer', in T. Gitlin (ed.), *Watching Television*, New York: Pantheon.

Moores, S. (1990) 'Texts, readers and contexts of reading: developments in the study of media audiences', *Media, Culture and Society*, vol. 12, no. 1 (Jan.).

Morley, D. (1989) 'Changing paradigms in audience studies', in E. Seiter *et al.*, *Remote Control: Television, Audiences and Cultural Power*, London: Routledge.

Murdock, G. (1990a) 'Redrawing the map of the communication industries: concentration and ownership in the era of privatization', in M. Ferguson (ed.), *Public Communication: The New Imperatives*, London: Sage.

Murdock, G. (1990b) 'Television and citizenship: in defence of public broadcasting', in A. Tomlinson (ed.), *Consumption, Identity and Style*, London: Routledge.

Murdock, G. and Golding, P. (1989) 'Information poverty and political inequality: citizenship in the age of privatized comunication', *Journal of Communication*, vol. 39, no. 2 (Summer).

Negt, O. (1980) 'Mass media: tools of domination or instruments of liberation? Aspects of the Frankfurt School's communication analysis', in K. Woodward (ed.), *The Myths of Information*, London: Routledge.

Pateman, C. (1987) 'Feminist critiques of the public/private dichotomy', in A. Phillips (ed.), *Feminism and Equality*, Oxford: Basil Blackwell.

Real, M. (1989) *Supermedia: A Cultural Studies Approach*, London: Sage.

Schiller, H. (1989) *Culture, Inc.: The Corporate Takeover of Public Expression*, New York: Oxford University Press.

Schlesinger, P. (1990) 'Rethinking the sociology of journalism: source strategies and the limits of media-centrism', in M. Ferguson (ed.), *Public Communication: The New Imperatives*, London: Sage.

Schudson, M. (1989) 'The sociology of news production', *Media, Culture and Society*, vol. 11, no. 3 (July).

Seiter, E. *et al.* (eds) (1989) *Remote Control: Television, Audiences and*

Cultural Power, London: Routledge.

Shaw, D. (1989) 'For papers, generation is missing', *Los Angeles Times*, 15 March.

Silverstone, R. (1989) 'Let us then return to the murmuring of everyday practices: a note on Michel de Certeau, television and everyday life', *Theory, Culture and Society*, vol. 6, no. 1 (Feb.).

Sparks, C. (1988) 'The popular press and political democracy', *Media, Culture and Society*, vol. 10, no. 2 (Apr.).

Streeter, T. (1989) 'Polysemy, pluality, and media studies', *Journal of Communication Inquiry*, vol. 13, no. 2 (Summer).

Thompson, J. B. (1990) *Ideology and Modern Culture*, Cambridge: Polity Press.

Wellmer, A. (1986) *Dialektiken mellan det moderna och det postmoderna*, Stockholm: Symposion.

Part I

Institutional logics

Chapter 1

Rethinking the media as a public sphere

James Curran

Classic liberal theories of the media have been advanced so often that their central arguments seem almost wearisomely familiar. The traditional communist and marxist approaches are also well-established reference points in terms of contemporary debate. The same is not true, however, of radical democratic[1] perspectives of the media, at least in Britain. These surface in critiques of the capitalist media and advocacy of public-service broadcasting, in the working assumptions of radical journalists and, in a fragmentary form, in speeches, articles and academic commentary. When collated, these represent nevertheless a coherent and fruitful way of looking at the role of the media, which should take its place alongside the better-known liberal and marxist perspectives.

This chapter seeks therefore to pull together the eclectic elements of the radical democratic tradition, and present it as a formal 'theory'. It does this by setting out in a schematic way the differences between the radical approach and its principal rivals. (See Table 1 for a summary.)

This schema cuts across the best-known modern representation of the media and the public sphere – the historical analysis advanced by Jürgen Habermas. His study has rightly triggered widespread debate, and this essay follows a detour by evaluating his arguments in the light of subsequent historical research. This digression is hopefully justified in that it casts light on a seminal study; and it also brings out the way in which historical research – the neglected grandparent of media studies – can contribute to the debate about the role of the media in liberal democracies.

Implicit in rival theories and historical accounts of the media are alternative prescriptions for organizing the media. Both liberal and marxist approaches have major pitfalls. The essay concludes with

Table 1.1 Alternative perspectives of the media

	Liberal	Marxist critique	Communist	Radical democratic
Public sphere	Public space	Class domination	——	Public arena of contest
Political role of media	Check on government	Agency of class control	Further societal objectives	Representation/counterpoise
Media system	Free market	Capitalist	Public ownership	Controlled market
Journalistic norm	Disinterested	Subaltern	Didactic	Adversarial
Entertainment	Distraction/ gratification	Opiate	Enlightenment	Society communing with itself
Reform	Self-regulation	Unreformable	Liberalization	Public intervention

an attempt to define a third route, which avoids the shortcomings and builds on the strengths of both liberalism and marxism.

LIBERAL AND RADICAL APPROACHES

According to classical liberal theory, the public sphere (or, in more traditional terminology, 'public forum') is the space between government and society in which private individuals exercise formal and informal control over the state: formal control through the election of governments and informal control through the pressure of public opinion. The media are central to this process. They distribute the information necessary for citizens to make an informed choice at election time; they facilitate the formation of public opinion by providing an independent forum of debate; and they enable the people to shape the conduct of government by articulating their views. The media are thus the principal institutions of the public sphere or, in the rhetoric of nineteenth-century liberalism, 'the fourth estate of the realm'.

Underlying the traditionalist version of this theory is a simplistic view of society as an aggregation of individuals, and of government as 'the seat of power'.[2] The key social relationship that needs to be policed by an ever-vigilant media is therefore the nexus between individuals and the state. Indeed, in some presentations of liberal theory, the media are on permanent guard duty patrolling against the abuse of executive power and safeguarding individual liberty.

However, one problem with this approach is that it fails to take adequate account of the way in which power is exercised through capitalist and patriarchal structures, and consequently does not consider how the media relate to wider social cleavages in society. It also ignores the way in which interests have become organized and collectivized, and so does not address the question of how the media function in relation to modern systems of representation in liberal democracies. Consequently, it has nothing useful to say about the way in which the media can invigorate the structures of liberal democracy.

The starting-point of the radical democratic approach is that the role of the media goes beyond that defined by classic liberalism. The media are a battleground between contending forces. How they respond to and mediate this conflict affects the balance of social forces and, ultimately, the distribution of rewards in society.

A basic requirement of a democratic media system should be, therefore, that it represents all significant interests in society. It should facilitate their participation in the public domain, enable them to contribute to public debate and have an input in the framing of public policy. The media should also facilitate the functioning of representative organizations, and expose their internal processes to public scrutiny and the play of public opinion. In short, a central role of the media should be defined as *assisting the equitable negotiation or arbitration of competing interests through democratic processes*.

However, there is a basic ambiguity within the radical democratic tradition. The less radical strand argues that the media should reflect the prevailing balance of forces in society: a 'representative' media system is tacitly defined in terms of existing structures of power. This has led to the construction of broadcasting systems which, in different ways, have sought to reflect the balance of social or political forces in society. In Sweden, this has taken the form of incorporating representative popular movements into the command structure of broadcasting; in Germany and Finland, a system of making broadcasting appointments informed in part by the principle of proportional political representation; in the Netherlands, allocating airtime and technical facilities to representative organizations; and, in Britain and elsewhere, imposing a public duty on broadcasting to maintain a political balance between the major political parties.

But there is another strand within the radical democratic tradition which believes that the media should be a 'countervailing' agency (though within a framework that ensures representation of all interests). This is sometimes articulated in politically neutral, ethical terms: the media should expose wrongdoing, correct injustice, subject to critical public scrutiny the exercise of power (whether this be by trade unions or business corporations). Alternatively, it is formulated in more overtly radical terms: the media should seek to redress the imbalance of power in society. Crucially, this means *broadening access to the public domain* in societies where elites have privileged access to it. It also means compensating for the inferior resources and skills of subordinate groups in advocating and rationalizing their interests by comparison with dominant groups. Although this formulation can be made to sound elitist and opposed to a 'representative' media system, it has an underlying rationale. Since no 'actually existing' liberal democracy is a polyarchy in which power is evenly diffused or in perfect equipoise, it is legitimate for the media to function as an equilibrating force.

The radical approach also differs from the traditional liberal one in the way it conceptualizes the role of the media in modern democracies. In traditional liberal theory, the media are conceived primarily as vertical channels of communication between private citizens and government: they inform individual choice at election time, and they influence governments by articulating the collective view of private citizens. In contrast, radical revisionism advances a more sophisticated perspective in which the media are viewed as a complex articulation of vertical, horizontal and diagonal channels of communication between individuals, groups and power structures. This takes account of the fact that individual interests are safeguarded and advanced in modern liberal democracies partly through collective organizations like political parties and pressure groups, and at a strategic level through the construction and recomposition of alliances and coalitions. The role of the media is to facilitate this intricate system of representation, and democratize it by exposing intra-organizational decision-making to public disclosure and debate.

This can be illustrated by considering the media in relation to one small aspect of the contemporary system of representation – decision-making in a trade union. A trade union journal should provide a channel of communication between the union's leadership and rank and file:[3] it should inform members of decisions taken in their name, reveal the processes of power broking in the union and relay union members' reactions. More generally, it should facilitate a debate within the union about how best to advance members' broadly defined interests, so that initiatives and ideas can emerge from the grass roots and be the subject of collective debate. And since solidarity is vital to the welfare of union members, the journal should also project symbols of collective identification. Yet the union journal, along with circulars and union videos, are only some of the channels of mediated communication linking membership of the union. Bypassing these are a number of other, potentially more powerful communications – TV programmes, radio programmes, newspapers, magazines – reaching different members of the union and delivering different messages. These different inputs should provide a communications environment which adequately represents the wider context and wider implications of union decisions, and inform the internal debates that determine them.

The divergence of approach between traditional liberal and radical perspectives also gives rise to different normative judgements about the practice of journalism. The dominant strand in liberal thought celebrates the canon of professional objectivity, with its stress on disinterested detachment, the separation of fact from opinion, the balancing of claim and counterclaim. This stems from the value placed by contemporary liberalism on the role of the media as a channel of information between government and governed.[4]

In contrast, the radical approach is more often associated with partisan or investigative styles of journalism. This springs from the emphasis placed within the radical tradition on the adversarial and countervailing role of the media. But it is also justified by a wide-ranging attack on the tradition of 'objective' journalism. Disengagement encourages, it is argued, passive dependence on powerful institutions and groups as 'accredited' sources; it fosters lazy journalism in which journalists fail to ferret independently for information and evaluate truth from falsehood; and, above all, the conventional stress on 'hard news' and factual reporting disguises from journalists their own unconscious reliance on dominant frameworks for selecting and making sense of the news.

This said, there are differences of approach within the radical camp. One school of thought stresses the need to balance alternative statements, perspectives and interpretations. Although this is not very different from the liberal approach, it can be justified within the terms of the radical tradition. The 'balanced' approach assumes that advocacy and group representation is secured through the internal pluralism of each medium; the partisan tradition, assumes that it is secured through the full spectrum of the media.

Thus far, we have discussed the media in conventional political terms. But an important difference between the traditional liberal and radical approaches is that the latter often adopts a broader and more inclusive definition of what is political. In many liberal accounts, the public sphere is equated with the political domain; and the public role of the media is defined in relation to government. In contrast, radical commentators often refuse to accept the conventional distinction between private and public realms that underpins the liberal definition of the public sphere. The mediational role of the press and broadcasting is said to extend to all areas where power is exercised over others, including both the workplace and the home. And the influence exerted by the media is defined not merely in terms of government action but also in terms of effecting adjustments in social norms and interpersonal relationships.

Partly for this reason, the traditional liberal and radical democratic approaches conceive entertainment differently. From a traditional liberal perspective, entertainment is problematic. It does not fit readily within the framework of liberal analysis since it is not an extension of rational-critical debate, and it is not part of the flow of information between government and governed, except in an oblique sense. Liberal commentators have tended to respond to this quandary in one of three ways. Some have criticized the growth of media entertainment as a regrettable diversion from the media's central democratic purpose and function, while others have simply ignored the existence of entertainment and discussed the media as if its political content was its central or defining characteristic.[5] The third response has been to discuss entertainment as if it is a separate category unrelated to the political role of the media; and to define the liberal position as the provision of entertainment in a form that maximizes consumer gratification.[6]

In contrast, media entertainment is accommodated without difficulty within a radical framework of analysis since it is not wedded to a narrow, state-oriented definition of politics. Most media output is, as Raymond Williams once put it, a way of 'talking together about the processes of our common life'.[7] It offers a commentary on the nature of social relations between men and women, parents and children, young and old, the ethnic majority and minorities – on what they are and, by implication, on what they might become. It can also provide a means of obtaining a better understanding of others in a way that fosters empathetic insights between different sections of society and strengthens bonds of social association. Conversely, media entertainment can do the opposite: it can foster misunderstanding and antagonism through the repetition of stereotypes that provide a focus for displaced fears.

This has given rise to the contention that a distinction should be made between different forms of entertainment. While the provision of pleasure through the media is an important public good, entertainment should not be judged solely in terms of consumer gratification. Media fiction should also provide, it is argued, an adequate way for society to commune with itself. This is usually defined as promoting human understanding, mutuality and tolerance, either in classic humanist[8] or feminist[9] terms.

The more inclusive definition of what is political in the radical democratic approach also brings out more fully the latent ideological meanings of all media output. Entertainment can provide a way of exploring, experimenting with and expressing a concept of self in relation to others ('Whom am I like, whom do I identify with, whom do I have a shared interest with?') which can have important political consequences. Media fiction and human interest stories also provide a way of mapping and interpreting society. This can promote a conservative, common-sense view in which social action is explained primarily in terms of individual psychology and elemental human emotion, or it can offer a potentially more radical perspective in which social processes are explained primarily in structural terms. Some seemingly apolitical material also embodies ethical codes or expressive values that lie at the heart of political creeds (egalitarianism, mutuality and a belief in human perfectibility in the case of traditional social democracy, or possessive individualism, self-reliance and social pessimism in the case of neo-liberal conservatism).

This sensitization to the ideological meanings embedded in entertainment also has programmatic implications. If the role of the media is to be conceived in terms of representing adequately different social interests, its entertainment needs to give adequate expression to the full range of cultural-political values in society. Unlike the traditional liberal approach, therefore, which is silent or disapproving of media entertainment or defines it solely in terms of satisfying consumer demand, radical democrats make certain prescriptive demands in relation to entertainment. There is, however, an implicit tension between the demand for the promotion of feminist or humanist values and the demand for the representation of cultural diversity (including anti-feminist and anti-humanist values). This is, in effect, a repeat of the division between those who seek to make the media a representative agency and those who seek to make it a progressive, countervailing one, noted earlier.

The divergence between liberal and radical approaches is even more marked when it comes to a debate about how the media should be organized. This is something that will be discussed more fully later. It is sufficient, here, to signal one important difference. Traditional liberals believe that the media should be based on the free market since this guarantees the media's independence from the state. Radical democrats usually argue, on the other hand, that the free market can never be an adequate basis for organizing the media because it results in a system skewed in favour of dominant class interests.

RADICAL DEMOCRATIC AND TRADITIONAL MARXIST/COMMUNIST PERSPECTIVES

Although the radical democratic approach owes a considerable debt to marxism, it can be differentiated from it both in terms of stalinist practice in the Soviet Union and also in terms of traditional marxist critiques of the media in western liberal democracies.

The radical democratic concept of a public sphere as a public space in which private individuals and organized interests seek to influence the allocation of resources and regulate social relations has no place in a traditional communist conception of society. This assumes that the common ownership of the means of production has removed structural conflicts, and created the conditions in which the common interests of society can be realized through the application of the scientific precepts of marxist-leninist analysis. The Communist Party as the custodian of scientific materialism has 'a leading role' – a euphemism for exclusive political monopoly – in co-ordinating the different elements of society in the realization of its common interests. The role of the media is defined within this framework: it educates people in the tenets of marxist-leninism; it aids the co-ordination and mobilization of the people in the tasks that need to be fulfilled; even media entertainment has an educational role in providing models for emulation and instruction and is expected not to subvert official definitions of Soviet society. Only one element of traditional communist theory of the media – the stress on its function as a safeguard against bureaucratic distortions of the state – allows it a free-wheeling, campaigning role. But the way in which the media was controlled before *glasnost* generally ensured that this remit was interpreted narrowly.[10]

Admittedly, the functioning of the Soviet media before Gorbachev was at times more restricted in theory than in actual practice (thus reversing the pattern of the west where the media has long been more restricted in practice than in theory). When there were tensions and disagreements within the higher echelons of the Communist Party, the Soviet media expressed to some extent a diversity of viewpoint.[11] This was particularly true of the early period of Soviet history, when the Soviet press was also organized and conceptualized in a more pluralistic way than it was to be later.[12] But the communist conception of the media that took hold in the Soviet Union before the Gorbachev regime was deeply authoritarian; and the actual practice of the Soviet media was stunted by the underdevelopment of a civil society independent of the state. Even after negotiating the rapids of cold war scholarship, it is clear that the traditional communist approach is far removed from the radical democratic perspective that has been outlined.

The marxist critique of the media in the west cannot be readily reproduced as a single set of ideas since Marx himself never formulated a fully fledged analysis of the capitalist press, and subsequent marxist interpretations have taken a number of divergent forms. But traditional marxism offers an understanding of the capitalist media that is at odds with the radical democratic approach. According to old-style marxism, the liberal concept of the public sphere is a chimera, disguising the reality of bourgeois domination. The media are agencies of class control since they are owned by the bourgeoisie or are subject to its ideological hegemony. Indeed, the media should be viewed as an ideological apparatus of the state – the ideational counterpart to the repressive apparatus of the police, judiciary and armed forces through which the ruling order is ultimately sustained.[13] The view that the media can be 'reformed' is dismissed as naïve. Significant changes in the media can only be effected through the socialist transformation of society.

This is opposed by a radical democratic view which offers a different understanding of the relationship of the media to power structures in society. Radical democrats usually argue that journalists have sometimes a considerable degree of day-to-day autonomy, particularly in broadcasting corporations which have won a measure of autonomy from government and in commercial media with dispersed shareholdings, where there is no dominant owner. This relative autonomy enables journalists to respond to a variety of influences – a change in the general climate of opinion, a shift in the milieux in which journalists move, the recomposition of accredited sources (due to, for example, a change of government), the emergence of new market trends calling for a competitive response. These responses cannot be automatically dismissed as acts of repressive incorporation in which elements of popular consciousness are selectively assimilated in ways that leave the dominant ideology essentially unchanged. This familiar argument is usually based on a conception of the dominant ideology as a monolithic and faithful rationalization of dominant material interests. This generally overstates the homology between ideas and economic interests, the internal consistency of dominant discourses, the homogeneity of dominant interests and the extent of ideological domination of subordinate classes.

The radical democratic approach is also grounded in a different understanding of the wider environment in which media organizations operate. This is a subject on which it is difficult to generalize since circumstances vary considerably from one country to another, and from one period to another. But in general radical democratic analysis tends to argue that acceptance of the social order in Europe is based on pragmatic rather than ideological consent; that basic antagonisms persist, which generate opposition to the hierarchy of power; and that, as a consequence, dominant interests have been forced to make political concessions, build cross-class alliances and modify their legitimating rhetoric in order to shore up their position.

In many liberal democracies, an equivalent process of coalition building has occurred in 'opposition' to the dominant alliance. Subordinate interests have sought alternative ways of making sense of society; found common ground with other interests in a similar predicament, combined forces and formulated a programme of reform as a basis for seeking wider support; and, very exceptionally, projected a vision of an alternative society that challenged the legitimacy of the social order and provided the basis for mobilizing a broad-based constituency of opposition.

This perspective has the effect of 'repositioning' the place of the media in society. The media are assumed to be caught in an ideological crossfire rather than acting as a fully conscripted servant of the social order. By implication, the media have a greater potential to affect the outcome of social contests since these are no longer viewed as inevitably unequal and one-sided. Underlying this reorientation is the belief that certain reforms such as a progressive tax system and a strong welfare programme, a more egalitarian education system, co-determination at work, legal guarantees of women's and union rights – which are dismissed from one perspective as minor concessions leaving the social system fundamentally unaltered – are important gains in their own right.

This is not to adopt uncritically liberal pluralist arguments. The media systems in most liberal democracies are not representative. On the contrary, most under-represent subordinate interests and are canted more towards the right than their publics. This reflects the prevalence of capitalist media ownership, and consequent influence on personnel recruitment and promotion, market distortions limiting real choice, media dependence on powerful groups and institutions as news sources and the unequal distribution of resources within society for the articulation and generalization of social interests. But the radical democratic approach believes that the media can be reorganized in a way that will make them more representative or progressive. One way in which this can be done is to secure democratic consent for their reform through the state.

HISTORICAL ELUCIDATION: (1) BRITISH PRESS HISTORY

History illuminates the debate about the role of the media in society. Indeed, one of the most influential contributions to this debate – Habermas's celebrated analysis of the media and the transformation of the bourgeois public sphere, first published in Germany in 1962[14] – took the form of an historical analysis. Since the British historical experience loomed large in Habermas's study, it is worth reviewing his thesis in the light of subsequent historical research on the British media.

Habermas's thesis can be briefly stated.[15] In the late eighteenth century, the public sphere was composed of elite, private citizens who were reconstituted as a public body in the form of reason-based, public opinion. An increasingly independent press was central to this process of reconstitution: it provided the main medium through which private opinions were transformed into public opinion, and the principal means by which government was subject to informal supervision.

But in the era of mass politics, the public sphere was transformed by the extension of the state and the collectivization of private interests. Rational public discourse was supplanted by power politics in which large organizations made deals with each other and with the state, while excluding the public. The media were an accessory to this 'refeudalization' of society. They functioned as manipulative agencies controlling mass opinion, in contrast to the early press which had facilitated the formation and expression of organic, public opinion. The only available solution to this crisis of representation, Habermas argues, is to purify the channels of societal communication through the restoration of public reason and open disclosure.

Habermas's characterization of the early British press was derived from the traditional Whig interpretation of British press history (for which there is a well-worn equivalent in French and German historiography). According to this view,[16] an independent press came into being as a result of the evolution of the capitalist market and the dismantlement of state controls on the press. The new generation of free papers became, in the words of the *New Cambridge History*, 'great organs of the public mind'.[17] They empowered the people, acted as a check on government and provided disinterested information enabling an expanding electorate to participate responsibly in Britain's maturing democracy.

This interpretation has come under attack from two opposed directions – liberal revisionist and radical historians. Though Habermas has not been criticized directly (since, though he is a luminous presence in political science and media sociology, Habermas seems to be largely unknown to British historians), his central arguments have been tacitly repudiated in recent historical accounts of the British press.

The radical attack on Whig history has centred on its assumption that the winning of press freedom from state control can be equated with popular control. Instead they offer a more complex narrative in which changes in the press are discussed in terms of how they related to and affected the balance of social forces in society.[18] Thus, in some radical accounts, a sharp contrast is drawn between the first half of the nineteenth century when the popular press reflected a wide spectrum of interests and views, and the second half when it became more closely aligned to the views and interests of the dominant class coalition. This transformation is explained partly in terms of structural changes in the press industry. Before the 1850s, the market system functioned in a way that promoted wide social access to the public domain: newspapers cost little to start and could be profitable without advertising. But in the second half of the nineteenth century, increased dependence on advertising led to the closure of advertising-starved radical papers, while rising publishing costs led to the steady transfer of control of the popular press to capitalist entrepreneurs.[19]

This was followed, in the twentieth century, by the consolidation of newspaper chains, controlled by predominantly right-wing proprietors, and by the death of the Labour press – the bureaucratic voice through which working-class interests came to be represented in the 1920s. These changes reinforced the drift of the press to the right. By 1987, Conservative dailies accounted for 72 per cent of national circulation, even though the Conservative Party won only 43 per cent of the vote in the general election. Even the non-Conservative press was close to the political centre, and joined in the stigmatization of dissidents – left-wing trade unionists, radical councils, militant students, peace and gay rights campaigners.[20]

At first glance, Habermas appears to have anticipated this critique. Thus he was at pains to emphasize the narrow social base of the early independent press rather than to portray it as an institution of the general public. But his analysis never escaped in practice from the terms of reference of Whig history. This is illustrated by the small walk-on part assigned by Habermas to the early radical press. Its rise in the early nineteenth century is briefly hailed by Habermas as part of the process by which the public sphere was expanded: its fall as marking the resumption of a more reasoned public discourse in which 'the press as a forum of rational-critical debate [was] released from the pressure to take sides ideologically'.[21]

This dismissal of the radical press as an ideological pollutant highlights the problematic nature of Habermas's conception of reasoned discourse. The newspapers celebrated by Habermas were engines of propaganda for the bourgeoisie rather than the embodiment of disinterested rationality. Their version of reason was challenged by radical papers which became the circulation leaders in the first half of the nineteenth century. The more militant of these developed a radical and innovatory analysis of society going far beyond the bourgeois critique of the aristocratic constitution (which would have left the reward structure fundamentally unchanged). They challenged the legitimacy of the capitalist order, arguing that poverty was rooted in the economic process and was caused principally by the profits appropriated by capitalists, as well as by a corrupt state controlled by the propertied classes. They also proclaimed a public opinion different from that asserted by the bourgeois press. In effect, the newspapers dismissed by Habermas as deviating from reasoned debate were merely repudiating the premises of this debate, and developing a set of ideas that generalized the interests of a class excluded from the political system.[22]

The conventional categories of liberal history also caused Habermas to analyse changes in the material base of the nineteenth-century press in terms of differential individual rather than class access to the public sphere. In the latter part of the nineteenth century, argues Habermas, the British press became 'an institution of certain participants in the public sphere in their capacity as private individuals'.[23] In other words, the press began to be dominated by chain-owning proprietors.

This fails to comprehend the significance of the changes that took place. In 1837, a great national newspaper like the *Northern Star* was established with less than £1,000.[24] By 1918, another national weekly paper – the *Sunday Express* – needed over £2 million to become established.[25] Whereas in 1837 a modest subscription in radical northern towns had been sufficient to launch a national paper, it required the massive resources of a multinational conglomerate headed by Lord Beaverbrook to do the same thing some eighty years later. The escalation in publishing costs in the meantime did not just affect individual access to the public sphere: it debarred access for large sections of the community.[26]

Thus, radical press history implicitly challenges Habermas's thesis in three ways. It relativizes his conception of reason. It draws attention to the missing dimension of class struggle in his historical portrayal of press representation. And it points to his inadequate understanding of the way in which the market system filtered social access to the public sphere.

But in some ways, liberal revisionist history has generated a still more fundamental assault on Habermas's analysis. A number of liberal revisionists have criticized the mythic idealization of the 'independent' eighteenth-century press. It was caught up, they point out, in an elaborate web of faction fighting, financial corruption and ideological management[27] – a far cry from Habermas's idealized portrayal of the eighteenth-century press as the embodiment of the reasoned discourse of private individuals.

However, the revisionists' more important argument is that a significant part of the press was subject to some form of political control by organized interests from the eighteenth century right through to the twentieth century.[28] This refutes the contrast made by Habermas between the early press as an extension of

rational-critical debate among private citizens, and the later press
as the manipulative agency of collectivized politics. Whatever view
one takes of this historical revisionism, it is clear that Habermas's
arguments need at the very least to be reformulated in the light of
the new historical evidence that has come to light.[29]

HISTORICAL ELUCIDATION: (2) DEVELOPMENT OF BRITISH BROADCASTING

If Habermas's account of the development of the early press is
questionable, his characterization of the modern media is positively
misleading. He claims that electronic mass communications were a
new type of media that induced an uncritical torpor:

> They draw the eyes and ears of the public under their spell but
> at the same time, by taking away its distance, place it under
> 'tutelage', which is to say they deprive it of the opportunity to
> say something and disagree. . . . The world fashioned by the mass
> media is a public sphere in appearance only.[30]

This view of modern media as a stupefying and narcotizing force
is refuted by numerous empirical sociological and psychological
studies.[31] These reveal the variety of filters that limit media
influence – selective audience attention, comprehension, perception and retention of information against the wider context
of the social mediation of communications. Audiences emerge
as recalcitrant, responding to the media primarily in terms of the
discourses that they bring to their media consumption. The mass
public, in short, is neither as malleable nor as passive as Habermas
feared.

Habermas's implicit contrast between the demotic manipulation
of the modern media and the ratiocination of the eighteenth-
century press is also difficult to reconcile with historical reality.
His conception of reasoned discourse is closer, in fact, to the
practice of British public-service broadcasting, with its ideology
of disinterested professionalism, its careful balancing of opposed
points of view and umpired studio discussions than it is to that of
the polemicist and faction-ridden London press of the eighteenth
century, operating in the context of secret service subsidies,
opposition grants and the widespread bribing of journalists. The
structure of the two media systems also differed in a way that
had wider implications. The eighteenth-century London press was

composed of 'conflicting public spheres', which structured reality according to the views of small, highly differentiated audiences. In contrast, British broadcasting was, until the rise of satellite TV, a 'unitary public sphere' in which millions of viewers with divergent views regularly watched the same programmes and were exposed to the same corpus of conflicting evidence and argument. One system fostered ideological reinforcement and factionalism, the other a consensual, anti-partisan, reasoned public discourse upheld by Habermas as a model.

A major challenge to Habermas's pessimistic view of modern media also comes from historical research into the history of British broadcasting. This plays Habermas's own cards against him: it extends his arguments about the rise of the press to the development of broadcasting.

Thus, historians have focused attention on the way in which broadcasting organizations gained an increasing measure of autonomy from government.[32] Key landmarks in this emancipation are said to be the greatly increased independence won by the BBC during the Second World War, the BBC's symbolically important defiance of the Prime Minister during the Suez War, the ending of the fourteen-day rule (prohibiting studio discussion of issues due to be debated in parliament during the next fortnight) in 1956, the first so-called 'TV election' in 1959 and the lifting of the ban on televizing the Commons in 1989. Linked to this development was an enormous increase in the volume of news reporting and analysis. Broadcasting thus became an increasingly independent channel of information and discussion, which facilitated the formation of public opinion and democratic influence on government.

This argument has not gone unchallenged. Some critical studies argue that broadcasters internalized external political pressure by censoring themselves, notably in relation to the conflict in Northern Ireland.[33] Attention has also been drawn to the increasing skill and sophistication with which politicians, and their publicists, manipulated the airwaves.[34] This finds an answering echo in American studies which argue that presidential elections have become manipulated 'TV spectacles' in which meaningful public participation and political choice has been minimized.[35] But in the context of Britain, the fine-tuning of the arts of TV management should be seen as a belated response by politicians to their loss of domination over broadcasting rather than an extension of it. Politicians now have much less control over the agenda and terms of reference of broadcasting coverage than they did in the 1950s.[36]

A second key theme of broadcasting history is that TV and radio helped to democratize the relationship between government and governed.[37] The TV studio, it is argued, eclipsed parliament as a forum of national debate:[38] consequently, politics became a continuous public activity rather than a closed affair between professional politicians followed closely only by a politicized elite between elections. Broadcasting also cultivated from the 1930s onwards a relaxed, 'domesticated' style of discussing politics that made it seem personal and accessible rather than abstract and technical.[39] A more aggressive style of interviewing politicians was also developed in the late 1950s, which symbolically asserted the accountability of political leaders to the electorate. A more egalitarian relationship was also promoted by the development of political satire on TV from the early 1960s onwards.

The rise of broadcasting, like that of the press, is thus portrayed as an emancipatory force that empowered the people. However, some historians have embroidered this thesis by inserting a radical thread into the weave of its whiggish argument. Their central contention is that broadcasting broadened the social and political basis of popular representation in Britain because it was organized along public-service lines.

The policies and views of the Labour Party were more fully represented on the airwaves than in the press because, it is argued, broadcasting was subject to a public-service duty to maintain a political balance. The public-service duty to inform also generated quality news and current affairs programmes at peak times, which won mass audiences. This helped to offset the knowledge gap between elites and the general public, promoted by Britain's class-stratified quality and popular press. Initially, radio was also organized in a way that widened social access to political knowledge, although this policy was first modified and then abandoned in the radio reorganizations of the 1940s and 1960s.

Some historians point more dramatically to the way in which TV and radio have, at times, brought into public prominence the plight of the underclass or facilitated public debate in a form that questioned the status quo. During the 1930s, documentary radio programmes caused a political sensation by enabling the unemployed to speak directly to the nation about their predicament.[40] During the Second World War, the BBC staged debates about peacetime reconstruction which, though carefully policed, called into question the basis of the pre-war political order.[41] During the 1960s, radical plays like *Cathy Come Home* dramatized the problems of homelessness and poverty in a way that stirred the conscience of the nation.

This broadening of political representation also had, it is argued, a cultural dimension. Cultural judgements, which both reflect and legitimate the leadership claims of the political middle class, have long shaped the definition of public-service broadcasting in Britain. But this became a less pronounced feature of public-service broadcasting as it developed over time. The fictional portrayal of working-class heroes and heroines for the first time in radio serials in the 1940s, the projection of ordinary domestic life as an adventure story in 1950s TV soap opera, the breakthrough of young working-class music in the early 1960s and the greatly increased airtime devoted to working-class sports like snooker and darts in the 1980s, were only some of the key moments in the cultural democratization of broadcasting. Implicitly, they validated popular pleasures and affirmed the importance of preferences that did not correspond to 'the social hierarchy of taste'.[42]

But although these historical accounts of public-service broadcasting appear to illustrate the way in which radical and liberal approaches can be interwoven, they in fact privilege a liberal approach at the expense of a radical interpretation. The selective nature of this approach is underlined by a number of sociological studies of TV programmes, some of which are now almost historical documents. Their common theme is that TV coverage has tended to be structured in terms of the assumptions of dominant groups in society, as exemplified by TV reporting of industrial relations, management of the economy, internal conflicts within the Labour Party, the Falklands War, images of east–west relations and of Northern Ireland.[43] Their implication is that broadcasting has functioned not as an open forum of public debate but as an agency privileging dominant discourses and sustaining dominant power groups in Britain. This perspective will doubtless be more fully developed, in due course, in relation to broadcasting history.

There are perhaps two general observations to be derived from this review. The first is that alternative liberal and radical conceptions of the role of media are present, to a lesser or greater extent, in histories of the British media. History thus puts flesh on the skeletal outlines that were sketched earlier.

Second, Habermas's analysis – though stimulating and thought-provoking – is deeply flawed. It is based on contrasting a golden era that never existed with an equally misleading representation of present times as a dystopia. The contrast does not survive empirical historical scrutiny.

THE THIRD ROUTE

The two main approaches to organizing the media – the free-market liberal and collectivist-statist strategies – each have drawbacks. Yet they can be combined in ways that minimize their defects and capitalize on their strengths.

One central deficiency of the market approach is that it produces an unrepresentative media system. The high level of capitalization in most sectors of the modern media restricts market entry to powerful capitalist interests. It also shields them from competition save from other capitalist entrepreneurs and large corporations. In Britain, for example, the establishment costs of a new national daily are at least £20 million; for a local cable TV station around £40 million; for a substantial commercial TV regional franchise up to £50 million; and for a satellite TV service over £500 million. Only in marginal sectors of the media – low-circulation magazines, local free sheets and local community radio stations – are entry costs still relatively modest.

The second, related problem is that most media markets are distorted due to the large economies of scale that are an especially pronounced feature of the communications industries. A small number of 'majors' have long dominated the film and music production industries.[44] Newspaper chains overshadow the press in most liberal democracies.[45] Only in television has state action in some countries restricted the development of private monopoly power, but even in this sector things are changing fast. Government privatization policies and the commercial exploitation of the new TV industries are promoting the development of dominant TV companies.[46]

The character of media oligopoly has also changed. Dominant producer companies in different sectors of the media have merged to produce multi-media conglomerates. These have expanded on a global scale, and in many cases have become linked through cross-ownership to core sectors of finance and industrial capital.[47] Their growth poses a problem for two reasons. It has increased the power of an unrepresentative capitalist elite, symbolized by Murdoch and Berlusconi, to control the distribution of information and ideas on an unprecedented scale. Second, their rise has been accompanied by an erosion of the competitive processes which in a limited but still important way made them publicly accountable.

The third major defect of the market system is that it tends to lead to a narrowing in the ideological and cultural diversity of the media. This is not merely the by-product of market distortions – restricted market entry and global concentration of ownership – but is built into the 'normal' processes of media markets. Intense competition between a limited number of producers encourages common denominator provision for the mass market. This is particularly true of TV due to the peculiarities of the medium. Television can achieve higher sales in terms of larger ratings at minimum extra cost, which reinforces the economic advantages of targeting the middle market. Some TV companies are also funded entirely by advertising, which is less sensitive to intensities of consumer preference than direct consumer payments. This also encourages the production of bland programmes with a universal appeal to an undifferentiated, mass audience.[48]

In short, the free-market approach has three central flaws. It excludes broad social interests from participating in the control of the main media. It leads to concentration of media ownership. And it promotes cultural uniformity, particularly in TV output. These shortcomings should be viewed in terms of what a democratic society should require of its media. At the very least, an adequate media system should enable the full range of political and economic interests to be represented in the public domain, and find expression in popular fiction. A market-based media system, in modern conditions, is incapable of delivering this.

The advantage of the collectivist approach is that it can enable interests with limited financial resource – which are excluded in a market-driven system – to have a share in the control of the media. It can also prevent control of the media from falling into the hands of an unrepresentative, capitalist elite. And through collective arrangements, it can also ensure that media output is pluralistic and diverse.

But the potential promise of collective provision has often been contradicted by its actual practice. This is partly because collective provision through the state can result in state control, as is illustrated notoriously by the stalinist experience. A multi-tiered system of control was evolved in the Soviet Union – based on formal legal censorship, control over the material production and distribution of communications, control over senior appointments, indoctrination in journalism schools and, more indirectly, control over the flow of information – which turned the media into an instrument of the state and the Communist Party.

The collectivist approach proved more successful in European countries with a tradition of liberal democracy. Even so, a number of problems recurred. State pressure was sometimes brought to bear on broadcasters, through control over appointments, public funding and the allocation of franchises.[49] Even when the direct abuse of state power was minimized, effective control over broadcasting was exercised, to a lesser or greater extent, by a professional elite integrated into the hierarchy of power. Their domination was legitimized in some countries by a paternalistic definition of public-service broadcasting which emphasized the leadership role of cultural bureaucrats in educating and informing the masses. This led to insensitivity and lack of responsiveness to the diversity of public taste, particularly in situations where there was no effective competition.[50]

These defects in the functioning of the collectivist approach draw attention to the positive aspects of the market mechanism. A market-based system does not guarantee the autonomy of the media from the state since the same interests that dominate the media can also dominate the state. But it does minimize the exercise of state leverage through control of funding and appointments. Similarly, the processes of the free market do not ensure, as we have seen, that the media mirror the ideological and cultural diversity of the public. But when competition is not deformed by oligopoly and restricted entry, it does result in greater reponsiveness to audience preferences.

The question then becomes how can one combine collectivist and market approaches in a synthesis that incorporates the strengths of both. To judge from the European experience, there are four alternative answers to this question (though each has a number of different variations).

One model is the *centrally controlled market economy*. Its underlying rationale is that the terms of and rules by which competition is conducted should be centrally determined according to the public interest. One example of this approach is provided by the British TV system, in which free-market competition is tempered in a number of ways. The largest organization, the BBC, is publicly owned and is expected to set quality standards since it is run for the public good rather than private gain. The other main players in the system – ranging from a regionally based commercial network (Channel 3), a public trust corporation (Channel 4), local TV stations (cable TV) and a national commercial consortium (B Sky B) – are differentiated in organizational terms in order to promote choice. The principal TV channels are also funded mainly by different sources of revenue (licence fee, advertising and subscriptions) in order to avoid the uniformity induced by direct competition. And all TV channels are subject to content controls, though with varying degrees of stringency and policed in different ways.

The full complexity of the system need not be described here. Built into its design are a number of central objectives: quality defined in terms of a negotiation between elite norms and audience ratings; diversity defined in terms of a mix of different types of programme rather than of values; and political representation defined in terms of Westminster consensus rather than popular dissensus. However, these objectives can be changed and modifications can be made in the system to achieve this. Thus, a number of reforms have been proposed which would strengthen broadcasters' autonomy from politicians, and extend the ideological and cultural range of programme output.[51] Indeed, one of the advantages of the centrally controlled approach is that systemic modifications can be effected relatively easily: the disadvantage is that this facility can be abused.

An alternative approach represented by the Dutch broadcasting system takes the form of a *mandated market economy*. Both airtime and the use of publicly owned production facilities, with technical staff, are allocated in the Netherlands to different groups on the basis of the size of their membership defined by the sale of their programme guides. This results in a plurality of organizations from commercial groups like TROS to VARA (with close links to the Labour Party) and the NCRV (a conservative, protestant organization), each providing a comprehensive package of services. None of these groups, unlike the central news service, is required to adopt a bi-partisan approach. The intention is to produce a broadcasting system that reflects a wide spectrum of political opinion and cultural values. But although the concept behind this system is seductive, it is not without problems.

Broadcasting organizations which lost audiences to TROS began to imitate its commercial entertainment formula, thereby weakening the diversity of the broadcasting system as a whole.[52] The relatively high level of Dutch audiences attracted to cable TV, with a heavy diet of US programmes, also indicates a certain level of consumer dissatisfaction with Dutch broadcasting.[53]

The third approach is the *regulated market economy*, represented by the Swedish press system. The thinking behind this is that the market should be reformed so that it functions in practice in the way it is supposed to in theory. Its most important feature is that it lowers barriers to market entry. The Press Subsidies Board provides cheap loans to under-resourced groups enabling them to launch new papers if they come up with a viable project. The Board has acted as a midwife to seventeen new newspapers between 1976 and 1984, most of which have survived. The second important feature of the system is that it tries to reconstitute the competitive market as a level playing field in which all participants have an equal prospect of success. Since market leaders have the dual advantage of greater economies of scale and, usually, a disproportionately large share of advertising, low-circulation papers receive compensation in the form of selective aid. The introduction of this subsidy scheme has reversed the trend towards local press monopoly.[54]

A number of safeguards are built into the system in order to prevent political favouritism in the allocation of grants. The Press Subsidies Board is composed of representatives from all the political parties. The bulk of its subsidies – over 70 per cent in 1986 – is allocated to low-circulation papers, with less than 50 per cent penetration of households in their area, according to automatically functioning criteria fixed in relation to circulation and volume of newsprint, irrespective of editorial policy. Beneficiaries from the subsidy scheme include publications from the marxist left to the radical right: the paper which has the largest subsidy is the independent Conservative *Svenska Dagbladet*, which has been a consistent critic of successive Social Democratic governments. The subsidy scheme is funded by a tax on media advertising.[55]

The twin precepts on which the Swedish press system is based – the facilitation of market entry and the equalization of competitive relationships – could be extended to broadcasting, even though spectrum scarcity prevents the creation of a full broadcasting market. Indeed, this is already in the wind. In 1989 the European

Commission issued a directive calling for member countries to introduce a system whereby broadcasting organizations are required to commission a proportion of programmes from independent companies. Although the directive set no date, this policy has already been adopted in some countries.[56] Market entry could be further facilitated, it has been argued, by establishing the broadcasting equivalent of the Swedish Press Subsidies Board, which would assist the funding of under-resourced groups, with viable projects, to compete in the radio or TV sectors.

A policy of market equalization is also being considered in a European context. The ability of national agencies to shape the ecology of broadcasting systems so that they are a democratic expression of the societies they serve is threatened, it is maintained, by economies of scale in the global TV market. US programmes are sold for foreign transmission at a fraction of their original cost, and at a price that is much lower than the cost of making original programmes in Europe. The threat posed by cheap US syndication to national broadcast systems has been blocked hitherto by official and unofficial quotas limiting the import of American programmes. But this protectionism is being breached by the emergence of satellite TV enterprises which transmit quota-breaking US programmes across national borders. This has prompted the call for satellite TV to be brought within the ambit of a regulated market economy through the auspices of the Council of Europe and European Commission. So far, both bodies have proposed an undefined limitation on non-European imported programmes to be policed by national agencies at the point of up-link to satellite TV delivery systems.[57] This lack of definition ensures, however, that it will have no practical effect.

The fourth approach arises from the current debate in Poland about how broadcasting should be reorganized, with similar discussions occurring elsewhere within social democratic parties. It takes the form of a proposal for a regulated mixed economy, composed of *public, civic and market sectors*.[58] One version of this proposal entails having a major, publicly owned sector committed to public-service goals, including the provision of mixed, quality programmes and politically balanced reporting. The market sector would be subject to minimum controls, and would be established through the sale of franchises to commercial companies which would also pay an annual spectrum fee. This would help fund, in turn, a civic sector whose role would be to extend the ideological range and cultural diversity of the system. The civic sector would have assigned frequencies and an Enterprise Board which would help fund new and innovatory forms of ownership and control, including employee ownership, subscribers with voting rights, consumer co-ops and stations linked to organized groups. The Enterprise Board would function not as a traditional regulatory body, policing programme content, but as an enabling agency assisting financially the emergence of new voices in the broadcasting system.

These four approaches represent alternative responses to the question of how a media system can be constructed that enables divergent interests to be fully represented in the public domain. They all have one thing in common: they marry a collectivist approach to market processes. They thus represent an attempt to define a third route which is superior to failed market and collectivist policies. Their aim is to recreate the media as a public sphere in a form that is relatively autonomous from both government and the market.

NOTES

1 An alternative term, perhaps more recognizable in a broad European context, would be 'social democratic'. But this has been rejected because in Britain social democratic has a narrowly denominational meaning, ever since a right-wing splinter group from the Labour Party formed the Social Democratic Party.

2 George Boyce, 'The Fourth Estate: the reappraisal of a concept', in George Boyce, James Curran and Pauline Wingate (eds), *Newspaper History: from the 17th Century to the Present Day*, London: Constable, 1978.

3 For a gloomy assessment of the role of trade unions in reality, see Tony Grace, 'The trade-union press in Britain', *Media, Culture and Society*, vol. 7, no. 2 (1985).

4 In nineteenth-century liberalism there was an important strand which celebrated advocacy as a means of arriving at the truth, but this became a much less prominent feature of liberal conceptions of journalism during the twentieth century. See Fred Siebert, 'The libertarian theory' and Theodore Peterson, 'The social responsibility theory', in F. Siebert, T. Peterson and W. Schramm, *Four Theories of the Press*, Urbana and Chicago: University of Illinois Press, 1956, and Michael Schudson, *Discovering the News*, New York: Basic Books, 1978.

5 These two divergent positions are taken respectively by the first *Royal Commission on the Press 1947–9 Report*, London: HMSO, 1949, and the third *Royal Commission on the Press 1974–7 Final Report*, London: HMSO, 1977.

6 Samuel Brittan, 'The case for the consumer market', in Cento Veljanovski (ed.), *Freedom in Broadcasting*, London: Institute of Economic Affairs, 1989.

7 Cited in Richard Sparks and Ian Taylor, 'Mass communications', in Philip Brown and Richard Sparks (eds), *Beyond Thatcherism*, Milton Keynes, Open University Press, 1989, p. 59.

8 Jay Blumler, *Multi-Channel Television in the United States: Policy Lessons for Britain*, Markle Foundation Report (mimeo), 1989.

9 Melissa Benn, 'Campaigning against pornography', in J. Curran, J. Ecclestone, G. Oakley and A. Richardson (eds), *Bending Reality*, London: Pluto Press, 1986.

10 Mark Hopkins, *Mass Media in the Soviet Union*, New York: Pegasus, 1970; Gayle Hollander, *Political Indoctrination in the USSR*, New York: Praeger, 1972.

11 Ellen Mickiewicz, *Media and the Russian Public*, New York: Praeger, 1981; Ellen Mickiewicz, *Split Signals: Television and Politics in the Soviet Union*, New York: Oxford University Press, 1988.

12 Brian McNair, *Glasnost, Perestroika and the Soviet Union*, London: Routledge, 1991.

13 Louis Althusser, *Essays in Ideology*, London: Verso, 1984.

14 Jürgen Habermas, *The Structural Transformation of the Public Sphere*, Cambridge: Polity Press, 1990. This has inspired numerous commentaries, of which two are particularly interesting for our purposes since they focus on the media. Frands Mortensen advances what is in some respects a similar critique to what follows but in the context of Danish history in 'The bourgeois public sphere – a Danish mass communications research project', in M. Berg, P. Hemannus, J. Ekecrantz, F. Mortensen and P. Sepstrup (eds), *Current Theories in Scandinavian Mass Communication Research*, Grenaa, Denmark: GMT, 1977. For an interesting 'alternative' take, which seeks to divest Habermas of his more questionable historical assumptions but rehabilitate his central analysis as a justification for public service broadcasting, see Nicholas Garnham, 'The media and the public sphere', in Peter Golding, Graham Murdock and Philip Schlesinger (eds), *Communicating Politics*, New York: Holmes & Meier; Leicester: Leicester University Press, 1986.

15 There is a basic ambiguity in what Habermas himself calls his 'stylized' historical analysis. It hovers uncertainly between a normative account (what it ought to have been like) and a descriptive account (what it was actually like). Thus, his portrayal of the early press is presented in normative terms; his critique of the modern media in descriptive terms; and, to confuse things further, this critique contains references back to an idealization of the early press as something approximating to descriptive reality.

16 For representative versions of this view, see Arthur Aspinall, *Politics and the Press, c. 1780–1850*, London: Home & Van Thal (Republished Brighton: Harvester, 1973), and Ian Christie, *Myth and Reality in Late Eighteenth Century British Politics*, London: Macmillan, 1970.

17 C. W. Crawley (ed.), *War and Peace in the Age of Upheaval (1793–1830)*, Cambridge: Cambridge University Press.

18 For example, E. P. Thompson, *The Making of the English Working Class*, London: Gollancz, 1963; Patricia Hollis, *The Pauper Press*, London: Oxford University Press, 1970; Dorothy Thompson, *The Chartists*, Temple Smith, 1984.

19 James Curran, 'Capitalism and control of the press, 1800–1975', in James Curran, Michael Gurevitch and Janet Woollacott (eds), *Mass Communication and Society*, London: Edward Arnold, 1977; cf. James Curran and Jean Seaton, *Power Without Responsibility*, 4th edn, London: Routledge, 1991.

20 Stuart Hall, 'Deviancy, politics and the media', in Mary McIntosh and Paul Rock (eds), *Deviance and Social Control*, London: Tavistock, 1973; Mark Hollingsworth, *The Press and Political Dissent*, London: Pluto Press, 1986; *Media Coverage of London Councils*, Goldsmiths' Media Research Group Interim Report, London: Goldsmiths' College, University of London, 1987 (mimeo); Simon Watney, *Policing Desire*, London: Methuen, 1987.

21 Habermas, op. cit., 1989, p. 184. Habermas is not alone in following the trajectory of Whig argument, against his own instincts. Thus, Raymond Williams wrote: 'the period from 1855 is in one sense the development of a new and better journalism, with a much greater emphasis on news than in the faction-ridden first half of the century . . . most newspapers were able to drop their frantic pamphleteering' (Raymond Williams, *The Long Revolution*, London: Penguin Books, 1965, p. 218), though Williams at least later changed his view. See Raymond Williams, 'The press and popular culture: an historical perspective', in Boyce, Curran and Wingate (eds), op. cit., 1978.

22 Curran and Seaton, op. cit., 1991, ch. 2.

23 Habermas, op. cit., 1989, p. 185.

24 Donald Read, *Press and People, 1790–1850*, London: Edward Arnold, 1961.

25 A. J. P. Taylor, *Beaverbrook*, London: Hamish Hamilton, 1972.

26 The rise of the *Daily Herald*, a working-class newspaper established by a small group of radicals in 1912 which became the largest circulation daily in Britain in the early 1930s, appears at first glance to show that there continued to be broad, unqualified access to the public sphere. In fact, its detailed history (currently being researched by my doctoral student, Huw Richards) reveals the opposite. The *Daily Herald*'s early development was blighted by lack of resources, causing it to charge double the price of its rivals for a paper half the size, without offering the inducements like reader insurance then widely deployed to promote sales, and with the further major disadvantage of lacking a northern printing plant. It was saved in 1922 by the TUC but only became a mass-circulation paper when it was given a massive infusion of cash by the Odhams group in 1929. In other words, what its history indicates is that working-class access to the public sphere could be negotiated by drawing upon the collective resources of trade unions and a major publishing group. But this negotiation entailed a heavy

price: acceptance of highly restrictive, right-wing Labourist editorial control.

27 See, especially, L. Werkmeister, *The London Daily Press, 1722–1792*, Lincoln, Nebraska: University of Nebraska, 1963, and Jeremy Black, *The English Press in the Eighteenth Century*, London: Croom Helm, 1987.

28 Boyce, op. cit., 1978; Colin Seymour-Ure, 'The press and the party system between the wars', in Gillian Peele and Colin Cook (eds), *The Politics of Reappraisal*, London: Macmillan, 1976; S. Koss, *The Rise and Fall of the Political Press in Britain*, vols 1 and 2, London: Hamish Hamilton, 1981 and 1984; Lucy Brown, *Victorian News and Newspapers*, Oxford: Clarendon Press, 1985; Black, op. cit., 1987.

29 Habermas's thesis on the press can perhaps be reconstructed in two ways. First, his characterization of the early press most closely corresponds to the provincial press in England before the bourgeoisie became politically organized. (See, in particular, John Brewer, *Party, Ideology and Popular Politics at the Accession of George III*, Cambridge: Cambridge University Press, 1976.) Second, the decline of political control celebrated by liberal revisionists was replaced by conglomerate control, about which they say little.

30 Habermas, op. cit., p. 171.

31 A useful summary of predominantly US research is provided by Alexis Tan, *Mass Communication Theories and Society*, 2nd edn, New York: Wiley, 1985. For a survey of European research, see James Curran, 'The new revisionism in mass communication research: a reappraisal', *European Journal of Communication*, vol. 5, nos 2–3 (1990).

32 Asa Briggs, *The BBC: The First Fifty Years*, Oxford: Oxford University Press, 1985; Asa Briggs, *Governing the BBC*, London: BBC, 1979; Asa Briggs, *The History of Broadcasting in the United Kingdom*, vols 1–4, Oxford: Oxford University Press, 1961–79; Grace Wyndam Goldie, *Facing the Nation: Television and Politics, 1936–76*, London: Bodley Head; Bernard Sendall, *Independent Television in Britain*, vols 1 and 2, London: Macmillan, 1982 and 1983.

33 Philip Schlesinger, Graham Murdock and Philip Elliott, *Televising 'Terrorism'*, London: Pluto Press, 1983.

34 Michael Leapman, *The Last Days of the Beeb*, 2nd edn, London: Coronet, 1987; Michael Cockerell, Peter Hennesy and David Walker, *Sources Close to the Prime Minister*, London: Macmillan, 1984.

35 For example, Joe McGinnis, *The Selling of the President*, New York: Trident, 1969.

36 Michael Cockerell, *Live from Number 10*, 2nd edn, London: Faber & Faber, 1989.

37 For a general statement of this argument, see Paddy Scannell, 'Public service broadcasting and modern public life', *Media, Culture and Society*, vol. 11, no. 2 (1989) to which I am indebted.

38 Colin Seymour-Ure, 'Prime Ministers' reactions to television: Britain, Australia and Canada', *Media, Culture and Society*, vol. 11, no. 2 (1989).

39 David Cardiff, 'The serious and the popular: aspects of the evolution

of style in the radio talk, 1928–1939', *Media, Culture and Society*, vol. 2, no. 1 (1980).

40 Paddy Scannell, 'Broadcasting and the politics of unemployment, 1930–1935', *Media, Culture and Society*, vol. 2, no. 1 (1980).

41 David Cardiff and Paddy Scannell, 'Radio in World War 2', in *The Historical Development of Popular Culture in Britain*, Block 2, Unit 8, U203, Open University Popular Culture Course, Milton Keynes: Open University, 1981.

42 Scannell, op. cit., 1989; cf. Curran and Seaton, op. cit., 1991.

43 David Morley, 'Industrial conflict and the mass media', reprinted in Stan Cohen and Jock Young (eds), *Manufacture of News*, 2nd edn, London: Constable, 1981; Ian Connell, 'Television news and the social contract', in Stuart Hall, Dorothy Hobson, Andrew Lowe and Paul Willis (eds), *Culture, Media and Language*, London: Hutchinson, 1980; Glasgow University Media Group, *Bad News*, London: Routledge & Kegan Paul, 1976; Glasgow University Media Group, *More Bad News*, London: Routledge & Kegan Paul, 1980; Glasgow University Media Group, *Really Bad News*, London: Writers and Readers, 1982; Glasgow University Media Group, *War and Peace News*, Milton Keynes: Open University Press, 1985; Brian McNair, *Images of the Enemy*, London: Routledge, 1988; Schlesinger *et al.*, op. cit., 1983.

44 Nicholas Garnham, *Capitalism and Communication*, London: Sage, 1990; Robert Burnett, 'Economic aspects of the phonogram industry', in Ulla Carlsson (ed.), *Ekonomiska Perspektiv i Forskning Mass-medier*, Goteborg: Nordicom-Sverige, 1988.

45 Svenik Hoyer, Stig Hadenius and Lennart Weibull, *The Politics and Economics of the Press: A Developmental Perspective*, Beverly Hills: Sage, 1975; Ben Bagdikian, *The Media Monopoly*, Boston: Beacon Press, 1983; Keith Windschuttle, *The Media*, Ringwood, Victoria: 1985; J. Farnsworth, 'Social policy and the media in New Zealand', *Report of the Royal Commission on Social Policy*, vol. 4, Wellington: Government Printer, 1989; *Facts in Figures*, London: Press Council, 1989; Ingela Strid and Lennart Weibull, *Mediesverige 1988*, Goteborg: University of Goteborg, 1988.

46 Graham Murdock, 'Redrawing the map of the communications industries: concentration and ownership in the era of privatization', in Marjorie Ferguson (ed.), *Public Communication*, London: Sage, 1990.

47 Graham Murdock, 'Large corporations and the control of the communications industries', in Michael Gurevitch, Tony Bennett, James Curran and Janet Woollacott (eds), *Culture, Society and the Media*, London: Methuen, 1982.

48 In Britain, this arises from the fact that programmes do not generally organize audiences into consumer categories that facilitate advertising targeting. (See James Curran, 'The impact of advertising on the British mass media', in R. Collins *et al.* (eds), *Media, Culture and Society: A Critical Reader*, London: Sage.) But this could change with the proliferation of channels and fragmentation of the TV audience.

49 For a cautionary analysis of French broadcasting during a highly authoritarian phase, see Ruth Thomas, *Broadcasting and Democracy in France*, Crosby Lockwood Staples, 1976.

50 For example, the BBC failed to adapt to the transformation of popular music taste until a large section of its youth audience tuned into illegal radio stations in the 1960s.

51 These are summarized in Curran and Seaton (eds), op.cit., 1991, ch. 19.

52 K. Van Der Haak, *Broadcasting in the Netherlands*, London: Routledge & Kegan Paul, 1977.

53 Richard Collins, 'The language of advantage', *Media, Culture and Society*, vol. 11, no. 3 (1989).

54 *Mass Media in Sweden*, Stockholm: Swedish Institute, 1988.

55 For a description of how the system operates, see Olof Hulten, *Mass Media and State Support in Sweden*, Stockholm: Swedish Institute, 1984. For a more critical account in Swedish (with readily comprehensible statistical tables), see Strid and Weibull, op. cit., 1988.

56 Thus the 1990 Broadcasting Act requires both the BBC and the third TV channel to commission 25 per cent of its programmes (with some exemptions) from independent companies.

57 Council Directive (3 October 1989), *Official Journal of the European Communities*, no. L298/23; *European Convention on Transfrontier Television*, Council of Europe (text adopted 15 March, 1989), Article 7.

58 I am indebted to Karol Jakubowicz, currently advising the Polish government about the reorganization of Polish broadcasting, for information about the broadcasting debate in Poland. The concept of a tripartite broadcasting system closely resembles proposals discussed in a British Labour Party policy committee in 1989.

Chapter 2

Goodbye, Hildy Johnson: the vanishing 'serious press'

Colin Sparks

Scholarly discussion of journalists is dominated by the belief that what they do is terribly important for the functioning of modern society. In this it is joined by journalists' conception of themselves and by both official and popular accounts of their activity. This unusual unanimity is predicated upon the view that journalism is a vital part of political life. In the 'western democratic' version the argument usually runs that a free and independent media, and thus free and independent journalists, are necessary parts of the political structure in that they are the major mechanism by which citizens are informed about the world and the activities of their political representatives, come to form their opinions as to political and social issues and are enabled to exercise a genuine choice between different policies. It is usually recognized that this is not the only function that the media in general, and the press in particular, actually fulfil, but it is by far the most important, and it is with reference to this function that the press is praised or criticized. A representative statement of this view was that given by the last British Royal Commission on the Press, which argued:

> Newspapers and periodicals serve society in diverse ways. They inform their readers about the world and interpret it to them. They act both as watch-dogs for citizens, by scrutinising concentrations of power, and as a means of communication among groups within the community, thus promoting social cohesion and social change. Of course, the press seeks to entertain as well as to instruct and we would not wish to dismiss this aim as trivial, but it is the performance of the serious functions which justifies the high importance which democracies attach to a free press.[1]

No one would wish to deny that at least some parts of the press, and thus some journalists, actually do undertake these 'serious functions'. What I want to argue in this chapter is that it is a mistake to take the 'serious functions' of the press and of journalism as canonical, either from the point of view of understanding the press or its relationship to society.

The serious functions of the journalist are normally attributed to reporting of political and social news. The Royal Commission, and subsequent writers, sustained their position despite the fact that their own content analysis told them that unequivocally serious news took up around 15 per cent of the news content of the two most widely read papers, while sport took up more news space than 'political, social and economic in general' material in every national daily paper they looked at bar the *Financial Times*. In the case of the two most popular papers, there was around six times as much space devoted to sport as this serious material commanded.[2] A great deal of what is in the press is not at all serious, at least in the sense that this has been traditionally defined. This development in the British press is not a new one: it has been going on at least since the 1930s.[3] It is high time that this lack of seriousness was taken more seriously itself. There are important ideological reasons why journalists should stress their serious functions, but there are no good grounds for scholars to follow them.[4]

One of the reasons these evident facts have not been taken at all seriously by academic writers is because of the way in which theories of the press fit into accounts of the nature of bourgeois democracy. The function of the press, and its historical evolution towards its supposed current status, are for many commentators amongst the constitutive elements of the theoretical framework which allows them to speak of Britain, or any other society, as a 'democracy' at all.

This powerful ideological component in thinking about the press is particularly clear if we look at the way in which the development of the press is commonly discussed. In the case of the UK, it is usually argued that press history may be thought of as having a four-stage development which closely parallels the extension of the franchise and the 'maturing' of democracy. In the period up to 1850, the press was essentially suborned to state control via subsidies and legal restriction: those sections which were not were largely the voice of the unenfranchised poor. After the abolition of the 'Taxes on Knowledge', the groundwork was laid for the development of a commercial press, but the full flowering of this was somewhat delayed. For the last half of the nineteenth century the dominant press was 'political' in the sense that it was closely tied into the existing party system, either through ownership or subsidy.[5] The close relation between some journalists and the still very restricted governing classes gave the press a crucial role in debates about political decision-making. This political press, partisan in nature and concerned more with comment than with reporting, was sufficiently powerful to render even the nascent commercial press, which began to develop as a daily press at the turn of the century, politicized. However, the decline of this type of party press was more or less inevitable once a mass circulation and genuinely popular press developed, along with the extension of the franchise to ever-wider groups. After the end of the Second World War the press became decreasingly partisan. Commercial considerations replaced political motivations and these meant that, in order to reach as broad an audience as possible, it was essential to replace the partisan comment which might offend the reader with news reporting of a kind which all could read with equanimity.[6]

A number of observations need to be made about this school of analysis. In the first place, the notion that the 'political press' declined can only be sustained by insisting on the sharp difference between a press that is more or less directly owned and run by a political party or faction in order to serve their immediate ends and one which is owned and run by a commercial operator for profit and only incidentally takes factional political stands of one kind or another.[7] There is indeed an important difference between these two kinds of newspapers, and we shall return to some of its implications below, but it is doubtful whether this is best thought of in terms of the changes of function of the press itself. An obvious alternative account would be that it is the nature of the political function that has changed. The mass-circulation press is no longer concerned primarily to articulate the different opinions of competing sections of a narrow political elite but with the general maintenance of the conditions upon which the continued dominance of that elite rest.[8] This, surely, is best seen not as the decline of the political role of the press but its adaptation to the conditions of bourgeois democracy.[9]

Second, and immediately following from such a reformulation, the perspective of declining partisanship now seems greatly exaggerated if not plain wrong. Its persuasive power was more a product of the relaxed atmosphere of the long post-war boom than of a permanent change in a feature of the British press. As the social and political atmosphere has become more tense, the contours of continuing partisanship have emerged more and more clearly. Certainly there is no evidence that there has been a uniform shift towards more impartial and responsible reporting. It is difficult to see the qualitative difference in practices between the fabrication of the 'Zinoviev Letter' in 1924 and the numerous fabrications recorded by James Curran in his study of the press and the London Labour Councils sixty years later.[10] It may be that the press has ceased to be the mechanism by means of which different factions of the ruling class jockey for position amongst themselves, but it seems that it remains unrelentingly hostile to anyone who proposes to do something, however feeble, about social inequalities. The fact that only the *Independent* of national daily newspapers did not advise its readers how to vote in the 1987 General Election is not conclusive evidence of a general trend towards non-partisanship.[11] The bulk of the press remains extremely and regularly partisan and it is widely thought that it is actually getting more partisan. Before the last election a prominent journalist and Labour supporter was worrying that 'there is not a single national daily newspaper that can be expected to give *full* support to the Labour Party come polling day'. He cited this as evidence of a tendency towards a decrease in Labour's press support, not a decrease in press politicization, since 1945.[12]

The most substantial problem with this account, however, is a theoretical rather than empirical one. This version of press history is 'teleological' in that it assumes that there is an immanent process working itself out which was present all along and which finds its fullest expression in the present state of the press. This history is written around the political and news functions of the daily press as though they were self-evidently the common yardstick by which it should be measured. Other types of press activity than that of the non-partisan, commercial press devoted to giving its audience information about the political and social world, are effectively marginalized by the framework of thought itself. Not only is this actually untrue as a description of the modern British press but it obscures by its very definition of its object the possibility that other types of press activity might be at least as significant.

An alternative account of this history would begin by recognizing that newspapers, like any other cultural artefact, are complex both in their internal structure and in their relationship to their audiences. They are inserted into a matrix of cultural practices which are differentiated along the major lines of division in a society.[13] There is no warrant for claiming that one particular type of content, or one particular type of readership, is the absolute standard by which all and every aspect of the press is to be judged. On the contrary, it is likely that to speak of a single unified category of 'the press', or 'newspapers', or 'journalism' conceals very much more than it reveals. We know that there is a definite sociology of taste in a wide range of cultural practices: music is not the same in content or utility for the Heavy Metal fan and the devotee of Bach. The supposition must surely be that this is true of newspapers, too.

In the case of Britain, the differences are particularly clear from the readership of the papers themselves. If we look at the social profiles of the readership of the most widely read and the least widely read of British papers, we find that they are markedly different. Using the widely available but unfortunately not very scientific measure of 'Social Grade' developed by the advertising industry, we get the figures in Table 2.1. Social Grade is not Social Class in any precise sense, but the figures clearly indicate that the readership of the two kinds of papers is skewed towards different ends of the social scale. One sort of paper is read disproportionately by a group clustering around manual workers, the other by a group clustering around upper white-collar and professional people. We may genuinely claim, I think, that these papers have their homes in different social classes.

Table 2.1 Readership of four national dailies by Social Grade

Newspaper	Readership	A	B	C1	C2	D	E
		(rounded percentages)					
Sun	11,340,000	1	6	18	35	26	15
Daily Mirror	9,062,000	1	6	18	37	26	13
Times	1,213,000	16	41	26	9	5	3
Financial Times	757,000	12	40	33	8	5	1
Adult population		3	15	23	28	18	14

Source: National Readership Survey, 1989

The modern press is produced for different social classes and it has to be understood as part of the differing cultural lives of those classes. The place and content of a newspaper in working-class culture is quite different than in middle-class or ruling-class culture. The press in general is not and never has been a single self-evident and undifferentiated category. The 'press' is a portmanteau term which includes a range of different artefacts produced by different sorts of organizations for different reasons, which are consumed in different ways at different times in history and in biography by different types and numbers of people who derive different things from them. More or less the only elements the varied things which we would want to put in the category have in common is that they are products of a similar technical process of reproduction, and in that they are not at all unique.

We can see this quite clearly if we look at some of the distinctive features of the working-class press. There is a relatively long tradition of a working-class political press, in the narrow sense, at least from Chartism onwards. It does not occupy a single place in working-class life, nor does it have a uniform weight in the consciousness of the class. On the contrary, its importance both in terms of its 'reach' and its efficacy has varied widely over the years, but it is true to say that it has had a marginal influence at least since the defeat of Chartism.[14] It has, intermittently, contained 'unserious' material, too, but this has always been secondary to the political material. On the other hand, there has always also been a 'popular' working-class press, although it has not always taken the form of the newspaper.[15] The popular press has certainly often contained a political content, but the nature of that material and the relative weight it has had compared with other matter has varied considerably over time. It has always been secondary to the 'unserious' elements which have provided the core of the material in these publications and, it seems likely, the prime reason why large numbers of workers purchased them. These are two different kinds of newspaper which have quite a different relationship to their readership, which we may, in Lukácsian terms, describe as the difference between an articulation of the empirical and the maximum potential consciousness of the class to which they are addressed.

It is in the tradition of popular working-class entertainment that we have to see that section of the modern press which is purchased today by working-class people – centrally those mass-circulation tabloids with their readership skewed towards the C2–E Social Grades but also, increasingly, the mass-circulation tabloids with a C1–C2 skew. The primary content of these papers is their entertainment material. The 'serious' parts of this press are secondary to both their construction and appeal. They certainly contain overtly political and social material, although in relatively small proportions compared with the amount of space they devote to other matters. The skew of their content, however, is towards entertainment and away from the 'serious'.

These papers now have a mature history of some fifty years and we can state with confidence that they are established as a central and important part of modern working-class cultural life. Over time they have diverged increasingly in their major news-values from the much more obviously 'serious' quality press and there is really very little ground today for the claim that they are at all the same sort of cultural artefact. Such a perspective allows us to start to make sense of what these papers contain and why they are so popular in ways that an analysis which begins from a comparison with the serious and political middle- and upper-class press does not. We can, at the very least, take these extremely important cultural phenomena as objects of study in their own right rather than as exemplars of the lamentable debasement of popular taste compared with that shown by intellectuals.

An adequate grasp of the different kinds of cultural artefacts which lurk within what looks like a plain simple newspaper illuminates an important feature both of press history and some contemporary newspaper projects. There have long been attempts to construct a mass-circulation popular newspaper based upon the primacy of the political content. The detailed history of the life, as opposed to the death, of the most important British example of this, the *Daily Herald*, remains to be written, but it is clear that the acquisition of the title by Odhams represented a shift away from what had been until then a working-class political paper in the narrow sense we have been discussing above. This early version of the paper had been closely tied first to trade-union struggles and then to the Labour Party, but it remained a relatively small-circulation paper. As a left Labour paper under Lansbury it had a chequered history and even under the much more moderate official leadership of the TUC its circulation remained around 500,000. The development of its circulation in the 1930s does not appear to have been the result of the 'serious' content of the paper: one ex-editor argued that the sharp rise in circulation was the result of 'every sort of circulation stunt'.[16]

What is more, there was even in its high period a perceived conflict between the serious and the popular elements of its content. Another ex-editor, Francis Williams, wrote that:

> To be its editor . . . was, I found, no easy task; particularly if one was, as I was, more interested in serious news and its significance than in bright headlines or display and wanted the paper to be the mirror of intelligent cultural movements into the bargain.[17]

Williams found himself engaged in a continual struggle between the publishers and the party. Odhams were prepared to honour their pledge to keep the *Daily Herald* a Labour Party paper and to devote considerable space to publicizing the views of the Labour and Trade Union leadership, but they were also a commercial concern who had devoted very considerable resources to gaining a mass circulation and they needed a return on their investment. On the other hand there were the members of the Labour Party who regularly moved that the concessions to popularity had gone so far as to render the paper useless to their political aims. The strain became intolerable:

> But as time passed the controversies between myself and the business management of the paper became increasingly acute. I had certain very positive convictions regarding the responsibility of a newspaper to give its readers full reports of, and informed comments on, serious news. These convictions deepened as the war approached and hostilities began. It appeared to me that even more than before it had become the duty of a newspaper to devote its space to a serious and reasoned criticism of the problems social and economic as well as military that were arising, and which seemed to me to require serious thought and concentrated attention on the part of both writers and readers if they were to be solved. I do not imagine there could have been disagreement on principle in this. But in the application of the principle there certainly was.[18]

Williams was forced into an intolerable position and resigned. There had quite clearly been a conflict between the dynamic of producing a popular paper on the one hand and the commitment to a serious political paper on the other.

This problem has not disappeared. The desire to create, or to sustain, large-circulation left-wing papers is pandemic in parts of Europe. In Scandinavia the widespread use of state subsidies seems to be designed to perpetuate the life of left-leaning papers in the face of much more market-oriented rivals. In the UK the very idea of press subsidies is the stuff of the wildest dreams of Labour Party press reformers, and considerable energies and capital have been invested in attempts to produce a left-wing popular press within the confines of the market. One of these ventures even got off the ground and the disaster surrounding the attempt to produce a Sunday paper devoted to this project in 1987, the *News on Sunday* débâcle, demonstrates quite clearly that, other problems apart, the tension persists and is, if anything, greater than it was.[19] For much longer than the popular daily press, the popular Sunday press has been a working-class entertainment organ and the *News on Sunday* was an attempt to short-circuit that history. It proved in practice what theory suggested: that the cultural spaces of working-class entertainment and politics do not, at least at present, coincide and that they cannot be joined by will-power together.

While the problem of the cultural complexity of the newspaper can be seen most clearly in the working-class press, it is not one which is exclusive to that social position. The same distinction occurs in the middle- and upper-class press, although in rather different form and with quite different results. Of the national newspapers in the UK today only the *Financial Times* can be regarded as unequivocally 'serious' in its address: *all* of the other papers devote much more space to sport than to parliament, for example.[20] The peculiar economics of an advertising-financed press system means that at the top end of the market it is still possible to combine the serious and the unserious elements of the press in one newspaper while further down the market it is much more difficult, if not impossible, to produce the same mixing, even with very different proportions.

In arguing this, I would not wish to minimize the serious consequences of unserious material. There can be little doubt that the ideas and attitudes articulated by the popular elements of the press have implications for the serious parts. Nor is it the case that the serious material, in its selection and presentation as much as in its substantive content, is an unimportant element in the popular press. What is crucial, however, is to recognize that a theory and history of the press which begins from the premise of the serious role of the press obscures much that is central to the understanding of the papers read by most people in modern Britain. What is more, the purchase it does give is for the recitation of a long and extremely familiar list of complaints which have been echoing around since at least 1896. On the left it provides a perch from which to denounce the market and all its works, from the right it provides a perch from which to denounce the low intellectual level of the working class. Whatever truth either position may contain is far outweighed by the way in which they both obscure reality.

If we are prepared to accept that our current focus is not really adequate, and to admit the necessity of adjusting our attention to take account of the fact that quite a lot of the press, and thus of journalism, is primarily concerned with producing a product whose function is entertainment, then certain things follow. One is that the term press, and thus the terms journalism and journalist, must give much more weight to the magazine sector. There may once have been an intellectual justification for drawing a sharp line between those people whose function it was to provide social and political information to the population and those whose tasks were more centred around the provision of information about private interests. If that division retains any validity, it no longer corresponds even approximately to the conventional division between newspapers and magazines. From every point of view it seems sensible to adopt a more catholic definition of journalism and of the scope of the press. This is not simply a question of tidying our mental universe by altering the margins of our definitions but more importantly of recognizing one of the fundamental contemporary realities of the press and the actual dynamic of its development.

The number of newspapers in the UK has been falling over the century: while there has recently been a small reversal in the number of national papers, the development of the entirely advertising-financed 'free sheet' has meant either the end of a large number of local papers or their transformation into products virtually identical with the free sheet. The 1977 Royal Commission on the Press estimated there were just over 1,000 local weekly newspapers and some 150 free sheets.[21] In 1986, the Newspaper Society (a trade organization representing the publishers of local newspapers), estimated there were 850 local weeklies and 850 free sheets, of which 350 belonged to their own members.[22] Overall, the rate of growth is very quick indeed.

The consequence of these shifts, other things being equal, should be a decline in the number of journalists, since even if the total number of titles were to remain the same or to rise, the free sheet tends to employ fewer journalists than the traditional local newspaper. In fact, the evidence is that the reverse is true: there are more and more people thinking of themselves as journalists. This would be more or less inexplicable except for the fact that the number of magazines is certainly increasing rather rapidly and has been doing so for a very long time. The balance within journalism is clearly away from newspaper employment and towards the magazine sector.

At least some of the magazine journalists are, of course, engaged in news reporting every bit as much as someone working for a newspaper, but this is often not directed at a general public but a closed and specialized group of people who get information about matters very remote from the concerns of public life which the press is claimed to address. Within the total output of the press, including both newspapers and magazines, the historical trend is towards an erosion of those products concerned primarily with issues of the public sphere. The two areas of growth, as Table 2.2 shows, are publications aimed at particular occupational niches and those aimed at particular leisure niches. The 'address' of the press is less and less to the general public in its role as citizen and more and more to the individual defined as a particular specialized occupational or interest group. While there may be an epistemological identity between a report of parliament in a newspaper and a report of a fashion show in a clothes magazine,

Table 2.2 UK publications categorized by focus of main content

Year	Public	General	Work	Leisure	Total
1900					
No.	214	1,252	1,050	342	2,858
%	7.5	43.8	36.7	12.00	100
1989					
No.	144	1,201	5,112	1,002	7,459
%	1.9	16.2	68.5	13.4	100

Notes: Public = publications addressing wholly or mainly issues of the public sphere.
General = publications addressing a variety of questions.
Work = publications addressing a particular occupation.
Leisure = publications addressing a particular leisure activity.
Source: Willing's Press Directory

it is extremely hard to see them as activities having a similar social import for their readers, and more journalists, then, are directly concerned with entertainment or specialized information provision rather than the general political and social functions which have traditionally been ascribed to them.

The developments we have identified have been present for a considerable period of time. The development of an entertainment-based working-class newspaper press is more than a century and a half old. The decline of the newspaper press relative to the magazine press is at least fifty years old. The shift in the balance of journalism away from the production of serious material towards entertainment is certainly not a new phenomenon. There is little evidence of a sharp qualitative break between two distinct epochs in press history. To the extent that ideas about a 'new media age' give us any special purchase on these developments in the media today it seems to me that we can identify three trends which are usually taken as characteristic of the period and which impact upon our subject.

The first and most obvious is the internationalization of economic life and the concomitant internationalization of news production. The old claims made for the 'serious' press were, I have argued, closely bound up with the claims of bourgeois democracy and thus of the nation-state as the arena in which it operated. To a very considerable extent the serious press was and still is addressed to, and in Britain read by, the national ruling class and their elite servants and hangers-on. The development of a global economy has meant that the site of at least some of the key decisions about the economic and political life of even the largest capitalist countries is now outside of the immediate control of the appropriate state. Of course, the realities of imperialism have meant that for most of the world's population this has been the case, either formally or informally, for at least the last century, and much of the debate about the NWICO (New World Information and Communication Order) has been concerned with the consequences of these realities for national media systems. What is new about the latest phase is that this process has reached into the heartlands of imperialism themselves.

The last few years have seen an internationalization of the production of a number of newspapers, most obviously the *Financial Times* and the *Wall Street Journal*. Both in content and in global form these newspapers correspond to the evident globalization of the world financial markets. They provide information and commentary to what we might call the 'international ruling class' and they are, pre-eminently, newspapers of the serious type of legend. The *Financial Times* is by far that newspaper in Britain which is most concerned with matters of the 'public sphere'.

The second important trend located by theories of a 'new media age', and in particular by theories of the postmodern, concerns the development of self-reflexivity as a conscious strategy of media artefacts. Again, this is most often thought of as an aspect of television, but it clearly also relates both to the relationship between television and the popular press and to the content and form of the popular press itself. The full implications of this trend are not apparent if we confine our attention to television. In broadcasting, as we have noted above, there is an organized separation between news and current affairs on the one hand and entertainment on the other which is not reproduced in the organization of the popular press. This is reinforced in that the priorities of TV news continue to reflect very clearly the priorities of the serious rather than the popular press. Thus the debate about TV news tends to be one about the possible limitations of the form in which it is presented rather than its substantive content. If we look at the press, on the other hand, it is clear that this sharp division between self-reflexive entertainment and serious news cannot be sustained and that what has in fact happened in the popular press is that the boundary between the two has become eroded. In the popular press the 'news' is the same thing as 'entertainment': one provides the substance for the other and the form of presentation of even that news which is not, substantially, entertainment, is that of entertainment itself.

We should beware of overstating the newness of this tendency since the interpenetration of news and entertainment has been an observable feature of the press since at least the 1930s.[23] However, in terms of the content of newspapers themselves, in terms of the relative weight of different tasks within the classical newspaper and in terms of the relative weight of newspaper journalism with regard to the occupation as a whole, the tendency is clearly towards the dominance of entertainment both in and over news. This would seem to imply a shift in emphasis within journalism as a whole towards a concentration upon the presentation of material, the rewriting, design and layout of the paper or magazine, rather than the traditional reportorial functions of news generation and writing. This, of course, has long been the reality of the popular newspaper press and it is likely to become correspondingly more a central aspect of other branches, too.

The third feature we may observe is the tendency towards the fragmentation of the audience. This is often taken as a counter-tendency to the trend toward internationalization noted above but in fact it is complementary. Because much of the current debate focuses on television, this double-sided development is often obscured. If on the one hand the internationalization of news is creating a new supranational forum of debate and decision-making, this is going hand in hand with the destruction of the limited public sphere of bourgeois democracy. The international order, lacking any semblance of a 'constitution', does not have a public sphere of any kind and the destruction of the national broadcasting systems tends to erode even those limited forms of national public spheres which did exist. The same process is true, even more strongly, for the press, since the high price and complex language of the international press renders it difficult of access to the mass of the population, even when they are relatively prosperous native speakers. On the other hand, this destruction, or at least erosion, of the constitutive public life of society throws the private sphere into ever-greater prominence. The disparate pursuits of the individual come to occupy the space once filled by the citizen. The growing number and importance of the fragmentary and specialized media of leisure pursuits are the concomitant of this objective process. In this field, the press and radio, with their radically different economic logics, are the central media since television is such a relatively expensive medium that it cannot, at least for the moment, adapt to this aspect of reality. As the public sphere disappears, its characteristic organs atrophy or transform themselves. Those that survive, and the newly created replacements for the casualties, are more and more concerned with the narrow private world defined within a pre-given framework of politics, economy and society.

Hildy Johnson, you will recall, was a reporter. He worked for a big city daily newspaper. His reporting assignments included all of the classic situations of hard news. His great triumph was to expose a corrupt city administration and save the life of a deranged murderer, at the expense of his personal future. His day is passing.

Already in 1940, Howard Hawks had given him a sex-change and today statistics are catching up with the cinema. Hildy Johnson is no longer a reporter. She is a sub-editor and she works for a magazine. Her work involves processing copy and designing pages and what matters is not whether it is hard or soft news, news or feature, politics or sport, but how to make it entertaining. She no longer dreams of bringing down the mayor or the government in the wake of a great scandal. That only happens in the movies.

NOTES

1 *Royal Commission on the Press: Final Report*, London: HMSO, Cmnd. 6810, 1977, p. 8.
2 D. McQuail, *Analysis of Newspaper Content*, London: HMSO, Cmnd. 6810–4, p. 24.
3 James Curran first drew attention to this long-term shift in J. Curran *et al.*, 'The political economy of the human interest story', in A. Smith (ed.), *Newspapers and Democracy*, Cambridge, Mass.: MIT, 1980).
4 For critical accounts of the journalistic uses of the serious definition, see G. Boyce, 'The Fourth Estate: the reappraisal of a concept' and P. Elliott, 'Professional ideology and organizational change: journalism since 1800', both in G. Boyce, J. Curran and P. Wingate (eds), *Newspaper History: From the 17th Century to the Present Day*, London: Constable, 1978.
5 It is important to keep in mind that by 'political press' we mean something rather different in the British case than the role of the press in the construction of the mass social democratic parties of the European continent, most notably in Germany before 1933. Only the *Daily Herald* of British papers plays any similar role, and then only to a limited extent.
6 The classic statement about the 'political press' is S. Koss's two-volume *The Rise and Fall of the Political Press in Britain*, London: Hamish Hamilton, 1981 and 1984. The most influential statement of the 'decline of partisanship' thesis is by Colin Seymour-Ure in Chapter 8 of his *The Political Impact of the Mass Media*, London: Constable, 1974.
7 That is Koss's key distinction, for example at op. cit., vol. i., pp. 16–17.
8 This is most vividly illustrated in the case of external threats to the national elite. The case of Northern Ireland is very well known but it is not unique. Fred Halliday concluded a study of the British media coverage of a colonial war in Dhofar in the 1970s by arguing that 'The Oman story is therefore a particularly striking case of press collusion over many years in a case where strategic interest, commercial advantage and publishing timidity interlocked' ('New management and counter-insurgency', in J. Seaton and B. Pimlott (eds), *The Media in British Politics*, Avebury-Gower, 1987, p. 199).

9 Koss, op. cit, vol ii, pp. 657–8, quotes, and dismisses much too readily, a version of this explanation advanced by Richard Crossman in 1952.

10 See L. Chester, S. Fay and H. Young, *The Zinoviev Letter: A Political Intrigue*, London: Heinemann, 1967. The authors, journalists, write: 'This (high) degree of political commitment was the single most significant feature of the newspapers in the 'twenties. Political prejudice, and sometimes political ambition, was the motivation underlying the opinions of most proprietors, and expression of prejudice was almost the *raison d'être* of their papers. Reporting an approximation of the truth was subordinated recklessly to a determination to get some message across' (pp. 128–9). This might stand as a fair comment on the material recorded by James Curran in *Media Coverage of London Councils: Interim Report*, London: Goldsmiths' College Media Research Group, 1987, and which claimed: 'Our conclusion is that not one of these stories is accurate. A few appeared to have been conjured out of thin air; the rest, although loosely connected with some basis of fact, have got important details wrong and are misleading' (p. 1).

11 This stance by the *Independent* was certainly important and I will return to its implications below.

12 Geoffrey Goodman, 'Not one national paper backs Labour', *New Statesman*, 9 January 1987, p. 14. In the event there were two equivocating supporters. The Alliance did even worse with only one. Readers were, in general, fairly well aware of the political views of their chosen papers, although those papers with large working-class readerships and Tory politics recorded low percentages of awareness (Bob Worcester, 'Trying the food on the dog', *New Statesman*, 24 July 1987, p. 13).

13 Raymond Williams's work, and in particular his essay 'The press and popular culture', in Boyce *et al.*, op. cit., is the classic development of this idea. Williams, and the present writer, tend to argue the case in terms of social class but the point is most easily grasped in the instance of a society in which there are substantive linguistic divisions.

14 It is this press which can be compared in social role with the party press of the classic European Social Democracy.

15 The mid-nineteenth-century popular Sunday press, for example, can be considered in the context of the whole range of 'street literature' and other printed ephemera at least as usefully as it can be compared to *The Times*.

16 Hamilton Fyfe, *Press Parade*, London: Watts, 1936, p. 109.

17 Francis Williams, *Press, Parliament and People*, London: Heinemann, 1946, p. 156.

18 ibid., p. 158.

19 The fact that Williams and the staff of the *Daily Herald* in the 1930s were all, or almost all, highly experienced and successful mainstream journalists who did succeed in building a mass-circulation paper is important, since one of the major schools of thought about the failure of *News on Sunday* is that it foundered on the lack of journalistic sense

of its political controllers. See P. Chippendale and C. Horrie, *Disaster! The Rise and Fall of News on Sunday*, London: Sphere, 1988, for a particularly crude and unthinking version of this thesis. This school of thought avoids the painful conclusion that the problem is structural rather than personal.

20 On this aspect of the 'quality press', see C. Sparks and M. Campbell, 'The inscribed reader of the British quality press', *European Journal of Communication*, 2, 4, December 1987. Preliminary results of a follow-up study suggest that the changes in this sector of the UK press market since then have acted to accentuate the gap between the *Financial Times* and the other papers.

21 op. cit., pp. 14–15.

22 Newspaper Society, *Annual Report 1986*, London: Newspaper Society, p. 6.

23 See, for example, Leo Lowenthal, 'The triumph of the mass idols', in his *Literature, Popular Culture and Society*, New York: Spectrum, 1961.

Chapter 3

Selling consent: the public sphere as a televisual market-place

John M. Phelan

PUBLIC SPHERES: JOURNALISM AND THE MARKET-PLACE

The broadcast system of the United States, of which television is a principal part, is commercial; it is fundamentally an advertising medium. Although there are small or seeming exceptions to this systematic characteristic, they are inconsequential.[1] Television news is considered the primary source of public information about 'world and national events' for the overwhelming majority of Americans.[2] Current events in the American system are packaged in a variety of ways: in straight newscasts, in talk and discussion shows featuring officials and experts who discuss pressing issues of the day and in many localized discussion formats which deal with matters of public concern, such as the alleged AIDS epidemic, or the mounting death and damage toll from drunken drivers, or the widespread illegal use of debilitating narcotics and addictive substances.[3]

Although actual policy decisions that form as well as merely affect the public sphere may be made behind the closed doors of government agencies and commissions, the board rooms of major corporations, and the conferences of establishment 'think tanks' like the American Enterprise Institute or the Heritage Foundation, the publication of these policies and the persuasion, or what Ellul has called the integrative propaganda, that ensures their legitimacy – all this takes place in the public sphere created by news media and particularly the dominant television forms of news and issue coverage.[4]

As a result, the public sphere in the United States is over-whelmingly dominated by the cultural forms of television and those cultural forms are in turn shaped by the political economy of mass-production-advertising-consumption; in short, by the commercial system of advanced capitalistic communications. News and views, to use the cliché, are commodities, to use another cliché.[5]

The *agora*, the Greek market-place, where the few free like Plato and Socrates met to discuss the politics of their *polis*, was at the narrow beginning of the western tradition of democracy. Bacon called the received public wisdom of his time, 'the idols of the market-place'. John Stuart Mill conceived of the free discussion of ideas in an enlightened public realm as 'the market-place of ideas'.

In this chapter I propose to follow this tradition by examining how:

- new technologies of communication affect the market-place of television;
- news and 'journalism' play a central role in the market strategies of American television entities;
- a special cultural form of packaging news and views in a consciously integrative propaganda form, the public service/ community campaign, shapes the public consciousness and the public agenda: the public sphere.

Finally, I will indicate *why* these campaigns, which usher in an era of unabashed 'activist television', are an inevitable result of the political economy of the advertising market-place, the cultural diction of mass media and the determining conditions of advanced industrial technology.

TECHNOLOGY AND THE PUBLIC MARKET-PLACE

Technology has radically altered the roles of major players in the television world. Networks are steadily feeling the pressures brought about by cable and satellite access, with a number of alternative paths being opened for national distribution of programming, their former oligopoly.[6] At the same time, the replacement of film with videotape and ever smaller instruments for live on-the-spot coverage have made the production of local news much more attractive for affiliate stations and independents, lowering the need for 'clearance' of network offerings further.

These same technologies of accessible and affordable production have added new encouragement to local stations to produce shows of such caliber that they can be sold to or otherwise shared with other outlets.[7]

However, just as the networks are less necessary to local stations, so too are local stations less necessary to the local television market. The technology that has helped local broadcast stations has also enabled out-of-market 'superstations' to beam in on many lucrative markets all over the country. Low-power television stations and other methods of expanding the available spectrum have been added to the multiple channels available through cable, whose share of market has catapulted in recent years.[8] San Francisco, for instance, has gone from five to twenty-two television outlets in the eighties.[9] All of these factors are added to the burgeoning home use of VCRs, not only for rented videocassettes but for time-shifted viewing and commercial zapping of broadcast fare.

The net result of all this technological innovation is to radically reduce the market share of each outlet and to even more seriously undercut the revenue base of advertiser-supported television media, whose rates are not only based on raw numbers but increasingly on demographically targeted market segments.

A further pressure on broadcast stations, at a time when revenue is being squeezed, is a demand from ownership for ever higher return on investment. This obsession for maximum profits in the immediate term is a broader disease of the entire corporate American economy, fueled by crushing debt service created by leveraged buy outs. Although the effect on networks, all three of whom are now part of far larger corporate conglomerates with a great demand for cash flow, has been widely noted, the effect on individual stations, whether independent, affiliated with networks, or part of chains, is enormous.[10]

Despite increasing deregulation, stations remain the most highly regulated node in the many-stranded television web. They not only are the primary responsible agents for programming liability, they also are under pressure to serve the local community by both the terms of the license and the public interest tradition from the original Communications Act – an obligation not shared by other program producers and distributors.

Enlightened management has over the years seen the obligation of local service as the advantage of local identification, the characteristic which a station can use as a classic 'unique selling point' against all those other competitors (except for other local stations, of course). This is achieved in practice by building on traditional avenues of community involvement, adapted to broadcasting realities.

It should be noted that 'identity' for any medium that exists in time, rather than space, takes the form of 'continuity'. Although the local station obviously has an address on a real street in a real town, it is presented to its market on screens everywhere, along with other entities from New York, London, Tokyo, even outer space. Thus the repetitive display over time of the station logo, the network mark, the series 'billboard', is the fundamental tool of establishing identity, just as scheduling is the fundamental programming tool for reaching specific audiences.

Since the enormous appetite of a 168-hour broadcast week requires that most production be imported from the tape factories that have replaced the film factory of Hollywood, the only window the local station has to establish its continuity is the local news window. Its news presenters are the electronic equivalent of a magazine cover or a newspaper masthead and its coverage of local news is the way the station is 'present' locally.

As a result, most stations have early evening news programs that are often at least two hours long and late news from thirty minutes to one hour.[11] More stations are inaugurating hour-length audience participation shows in early morning and late afternoon, to which some even provide van or bus service.[12] In addition, regularly scheduled or 'special' programs, usually on weekends or in fringe times, are focused on specific local issues.[13]

What sort of content characterizes these local programs, whatever the format? In 1983, the Television Information Office, as research arm of the television wing of the National Association of Broadcasters, conducted a survey on precisely this and allied questions. The sample was large and representative, 257 stations from every region, including Alaska and Hawaii, 111 of them from 47 of the top fifty markets and 60 from 37 of the second fifty.[14]

Local news can be divided into three parts: hard, soft and feature. Hard news concentrates on spontaneous events, like floods and fires and as such cannot be part of a planning process. Most news is, in fact, soft: planned occasions of interest to the community.

The TIO Survey found sports was at the top of the list, followed by ethnic festivals, local government affairs, neighborhood and church activities, awards, Chamber of Commerce meetings, school matters and cleanup drives. The performing arts and any occasion that raises funds for charity, like the Special Olympics, form the second tier. Minority activities such as local celebrations of Martin Luther King Day came last. About 10 per cent of such coverage was in the form of specials, in addition to regular local news programming.[15]

Feature news treatment consisted of discussions, specialist-interviews and often exhortation, about crime, drug abuse, good health practices, family conflict, education, sexual problems, employment, the environment and consumer complaints. Since these topics are perennial, they are recycled regularly, sometimes in the form of a short series, or a monthly 'drive' that orchestrates various formats, from specials to short announcements to news segments. Although many of these topics raise heated controversy, such as abortion or nuclear hazards, the overwhelming tendency is to preserve an atmosphere of upbeat optimism. If hard news is bad news, then local public affairs features tend to be good news, or at least comforting information.

Controversy can be addressed in editorials, which are usually one- or two-minute talking heads, the head often that of the station manager or the public affairs director, if there is one. Another NAB survey, with a sample of 422 stations, found that less than one-third bother to editorialize and that of these less than 3 per cent will actually endorse a candidate in a contested election.[16] So, although the occasional station, like KPIX-TV in San Francisco, may occasionally take an unpopular position it believes in, most stations play it safe for fear of alienating viewers or of triggering equal-time rebuttals from sources that will surely alienate viewers, for whose loyalty all this localism is expended.

Boosting the status quo cannot be left to on-air activities. General managers, like executives of any business that depends on public acceptance, spend a great deal of time attending civic affairs, visiting schools, speaking at ceremonies. The better stations make sure that their on-air talent, which is the key to news and public affairs ratings, is visible in the flesh for public affairs and local charities. Stations themselves sponsor dinners for the elderly, music concerts, park and zoo days for families, fund-raising ball games with their own employees participating. Weather reporters are increasingly fitting a central casting type of the all-purpose warm community person, visiting schools and hospitals with some sort of science or health presentation.[17]

Since all of these strategies, on- and off-air, are often common within the same market, the competition for ratings among local stations revolves around two intangibles: the personalities of the talent and the perception of the station as 'the' local station. Hiring charismatic talent is still much of a mystical operation, with successful producers referring to ineffable visceral cues as the determining factor. Scarcely open to rational discussion, the star factor is thus underemphasized in studies of programming strategy. The other factor – competitive edge in local identification of the station as a whole – admits to some logical planning.

The key to this planning is a special form of one of the oldest methods of organizing a variety of forces against a variety of obstacles in order to focus on one objective: the campaign.

Flowing from a creative transformation of an alleged weakness into a strength, the public or community service campaign manages to mobilize all the strategies local stations have mustered to meet their obligations to owners, advertisers, viewers, government and, of course, the local community in one policy gesture. It seems almost too good to be true.

PERSUASIVE NEWS: THE CAMPAIGN

For the last fifty years, a significant part of the study of communications has been the study of campaigns.[18] Communication campaigns have been employed in three principal areas: (1) politics, (2) public health, safety and welfare and (3) product promotion and corporate image enhancement.

An overwhelming amount of specific case study has been commissioned by the customers for product promotion and corporate image enhancement and is in fact the bulk of what is known as market research. Media advisers and political pollsters are performing an increasing amount of research on elections and referenda.

Although government and varied public-service agencies, from the New York Public Library to the United States Army, have commissioned research into effects as well as other research called 'formative' (= analysis of the needs and vulnerabilities of the target before designing the campaign), for the most part research into American public or community service campaigns has not been nearly as abundant.[19] It is nowhere near as thorough, for instance, as the research commissioned by India into the effectiveness of its population control campaigns.[20] The reason for this may be that in many instances the campaign involves a so-called 'preventive innovation' such as not taking drugs or not starting to smoke. How does one count the number of dogs who do not bark in the night?

Total campaigns are indeed an outgrowth of the long-established practice of using broadcast facilities to get the public to do things in general. For instance, it has been the mandated and voluntary practice of stations to provide free airtime for a given number of public-service announcements, most of them produced by the interested parties (like the Post Office urging use of zip codes) or the National Association of Broadcasters, as an aid to member stations. Currently, both taxpayer and freely contributed dollars have provided a large number of such announcements (PSAs) directed against drug abuse, which broadcasters show without charge as their contribution to the Reagan Administration's 'Just Say No [to Drugs]' campaign. But this is a government campaign that uses broadcasting among other means. Broadcasting is on board, but not in the driver's seat. If the PSAs are orchestrated by station management into a larger plan that uses other formats of on-air programming, *plus* off-air activities, then it is a communications community *campaign*. Stations often do this: the latest NAB survey indicates that when it comes, for instance, to AIDS issues, local stations not only show PSAs (85 per cent), use local news stories on the issue (57 per cent), feature it on their own public affairs programs (27.7 per cent) and locally produce their own PSAs (17.7 per cent), they also participate in community outreach activities off-air (22.1 per cent). It should also be noted that 23.1 per cent of all such programming focuses on strictly local matters that often include fund-raising for charities.[21]

Just as the NAB does, network and group owners often provide packages of PSAs on a given theme, the current favorites being drug abuse, drunken driving and AIDS.[22] Some local stations might not have the facilities to produce acceptably slick spots nor access to national celebrities who often donate their time to nationally distributed PSAs. But another important reason is to protect the local station from being deluged with requests for free time by plugging the holes with unimpeachably 'safe' spots for 'safe' causes. Saving the saved, of course, is the essence of integrative propaganda.

Local stations also often contribute time for fund-raising announcements from area charities. These activities are often called campaigns, but they are not usually tied to any organized station effort beyond themselves.

The focused orchestration of a variety of marketing tools toward a particular goal, and one that could gain underwriting from commercial sponsors, is one that naturally arises in a commercial system. But nothing happens without leadership. One of the chief American executives responsible for creating the commercial campaign is Mr Lawrence Fraiberg, now President of MCA Broadcasting and formerly head of television for Group W or Westinghouse Broadcasting Company, which today is the only syndicator (packager for other broadcasters) of public-service campaigns. In an interview he recounts how the idea developed while he was at Group W:

[When I was] at GW I felt we should consolidate all the dollars we were spending here and there into one focused program so that we had more dollars to do better programming and do it more effectively; to promote those [public service] programs, to do it over at least a year and finally to find some way to measure our impact. The worst thing you can do is dissipate time, energy, money, anything.

We try to pick a specific issue or problem peculiar to a given market and make our station the champion in that area. If we do something, I think we should own it, if you see what I mean. We started in Boston with YOU GOTTA HAVE ARTS right after Reagan came in and chopped the National Endowment for Arts, then the Mass. legislature also reduced subsidy to arts. Boston being a cultural hub had a strong identity with arts. We started by having the company make a contribution to the arts of 75 thousand dollars, as a basis for the campaign so that in the end we would have a foundation of sorts for continuing support for the arts. We owned it. Any other station who later wanted to get involved with the arts would be confused with [W] BZ [TV]!

My role was inspiration. The station people focused in on it and did a fabulous job. Then they started the Anti-Crime Team (ACT) and used the station to focus on community activities – using car decals. Lots of off-air meetings we handled and a lot of collateral [= non-broadcast material such as posters, stationery, outlines for local strategies, etc.]. We owned them and continued to live with these projects and programs. The Police Chief said the crime rate went down about 8%. Well, if it only went down 2%, we were still doing a lot. These programs were devices for converting members of the station staff into evangelistic enthusiasts. Management at KDKA [in Pittsburgh] were quick to pick up on what was going on in Boston and they got the idea. It started from the chance event of a letter being read with a check on the news from someone who wanted to help create food for the poor. As a result, a flood of checks hit the station – this led to the creation of KD's Army [= the groups of volunteers who pitch in for station-supported programs] sending barges up and down the river collecting food; station folk worked joyfully seven days a week, lots of volunteers.

Earlier on we had market research study which placed KDKA behind the competition, with a perception of a cold operation. KD's Army changed all that.

The most focused campaign to date and the one most directly tied to news is 'AIDS Lifeline'. AIDS is a topic that inhabits a vital place in the public sphere of both small communities and global politics. How has the 'mass media treatment' affected the way people think and act about AIDS?

GOING PUBLIC WITH AIDS

On 26 August 1987 the National Academy of Television Arts and Sciences granted KPIX-TV its 1986 Community Services Award, from a field of two hundred entrants and fifteen finalists. For the same year, 1986, KPIX also won the Peabody Award. Both occasions of professional kudos were in recognition of KPIX's extraordinary local campaign effort, 'AIDS Lifeline', which started with one spectacularly successful documentary in 1983. By 1986 it had blossomed into a massive campaign of ten Eyewitness News special segments, sixty-two PSAs using forty-five celebrities and a number of sixty- and thirty-minute specials. Eight months after the period judged KPIX was still at it, having aired *Heterosexuals and AIDS*', a live studio call-in discussion, two weeks before the announcement of the award.

'AIDS Lifeline' is a true community campaign focused narrowly on a special subject but reaching and holding the attention of the widest possible audience. It is a terrifying, unpleasant subject that in many of its particulars impinges on controversial political questions which raise tempers to a boil. Not the ideal selling environment. Yet KPIX began this campaign because it wished to be *the* San Francisco station[23] and San Francisco has in relative terms the largest gay population in the country and without doubt, irrespective of size, the most organized and politically active gay population in the world, in terms of its impact on community awareness, civil services, electioneering and municipal hiring practices. KPIX anticipated the AIDS 'story' as worthy of major coverage by at least a year in the broadcast news media.

Sceptical critics can point out that although AIDS is hardly upbeat, it wields a powerful fascination for a mass audience, mixing the perennial dramatic themes of sex, death, forbidden fruit and apocalyptic plague. It is thus a topic easily open to exploitation, like that of serial murder or pornography, on the one hand, and like that of miracle cancer cures and 'Florence Nightingale' tear-jerkers on the other. Both facets, the terror and the triumph, are proven box-office hits.

Whatever the courage required to begin coverage of AIDS, the orchestrating of a campaign, one might argue, can be totally explained in terms of sheer good business. That first one-hour special in 1983, *Our Worst Fears: the AIDS Epidemic*, turned out to be the highest-rated public affairs show in the history of KPIX, sparking the most hotline calls to the San Francisco AIDS Foundation since it began. After the program was repeated, more than one million people viewed it locally, an enormous number for public affairs in the fifth-ranked US broadcast market. This program was broadcast by all the Group W stations and was successfully syndicated from New York to Honolulu. Requests for videotapes came from as far as Australia and it was ultimately shown all over the world and domestically by over one hundred companies, schools, local governments and service associations.[24]

From this beginning KPIX went into an all-out effort by 1985 called 'AIDS Lifeline': over a four-year period (up to the announcement of the Emmy) the station presented over 1,000 news reports, not only from California, but from their own crews filing stories from Australia, Brussels, Geneva, as well as domestically from coast to coast. The different celebrity PSAs were expanded to a roster of over sixty. All this time talk shows, call-ins, additional documentaries were produced as part of the campaign.

These on-air elements were complemented by an unusual number of off-air activities. Not just a flyer, but a hefty booklet about

AIDS with lists of helping agencies was published in co-operation with the San Francisco AIDS Foundation and went into over one half-million copies in several languages. A further co-operative effort with the Foundation and a new twist on off-air collateral was the production of an educational videotape about AIDS made available at local video rental stores (the Captain Video chain).[25]

Off the air, KPIX was a senior partner or instigator of many local events, from huge walkathons to school 'safe sex' programs. KPIX made sure that its own employment practices did not discriminate against AIDS patients in terms of workplace, insurance or work-mates.[26]

By 1985 WBZ-TV in Boston hooked into this campaign and began doing its own version of the blanket coverage and community outreach that it had applied so well to other subjects. The national interest led KPIX to head a national co-op of ultimately over one hundred stations, who shared AIDS-related news stories by satellite feed.[27]

Authoritative testimony to the campaign's local effectiveness is offered by Ron De Luca, the Development Director of the San Francisco AIDS Foundation, who readily declares that KPIX is easily the single most important outreach tool that local AIDS helping agencies have. He points out that in San Francisco the annual care per AIDS patient costs $75,000 less than the national average. Although this cannot be attributed to one cause, he believes the greater community of San Francisco, which has responded magnificently to the special needs of the gay community, is the major factor – volunteers have replaced paid professionals. De Luca credits KPIX's outreach programs and awareness campaign as indispensable in raising volunteers of various kinds to help AIDS patients.[28]

On 28 July 1988 the AIDS Foundation, Herth Realty Company, radio station KGO and KPIX sponsored 'AIDS WALK San Francisco', which raised in the neighborhood of one million dollars for the following local agencies: AIDS Emergency Fund, AIDS Health Project, Asian AIDS Task Force, Black Coalition on AIDS, Instituto Familiar de la Raza-Latino AIDS Project, Mobilization Against AIDS, San Francisco AIDS Foundation, STOP AIDS Resource Center, Visiting Nurses and Hospice of San Francisco. The catalogue of sponsors and beneficiaries is a testimony to the broadness of KPIX's community base and the integrated local nature of the campaign.

As with all such events, KPIX featured the walk prominently on its news programs before the event and with follow-up, and of course covered it live with the same style of celebrity and people-on-the-street interviews, with cutaways to prepared 'up-close-and-personal' related features. The night before the walk, the station broadcast *Talking with Teens*, a half-hour guideline for parents on the subject of talking about AIDS, hosted by Jane Curtin, an actress starring in a popular CBS melodrama (KPIX is a CBS affiliate). (This particular program as aforementioned was also distributed as a rental videotape.)[29]

The style, attitude and level of discourse in this slick video is typical of this entire campaign, and of TV campaign 'texts' in general.

In this half-hour program which is intended as a serious guideline for parents who wish to protect their children from AIDS, the word homosexual is not mentioned once. The word 'gay' is mentioned once, in a joking manner, by an actor portraying a straight male teenager: 'Gee, Dad, I'm not gay or anything.' To which the father replies, 'Fine, son, but the AIDS virus doesn't know that.'

The film begins with Curtin in an empty classroom, thinking about her days as a teenager, when her generation didn't have to worry about AIDS. We cut to a matronly Hispanic school counselor who sympathizes with Curtin about the difficulty parents have accepting that their child is a sexual being, who may well be in the intimate hands of some stranger (to the parents).

Curtin then voices over a series of billboarded simple statistics: that seven girls and eight boys of every ten are sexually active as teens, that one in ten teenage girls becomes pregnant and that one out of seven of either sex get some sexually transmitted disease. There is also the figure of 200,000 intravenous drug users among all American teenagers, cited as a low estimate. No AIDS statistics are introduced at all. But after these general statistics there is a cut to Dr Robert Scott, a black internist who practices internal medicine in Oakland and specializes in AIDS cases. He states flatly, on the heels of these statistics, that 'The potential for getting the disease [AIDS] in that population is going to be explosive.'

We then cut to a group of teenagers having a discussion in school about sexual activity in general with random references to AIDS. The discussion leader, Ms Kim Cox, 'health educator', then says to Curtin and us, 'Sex is a natural way of living. Unfortunately, it is becoming a common way of dying.'

After this *mélange* of statistics and random comments, about teen sex in general and pointed dire predictions and statements from authority figures about AIDS, Curtin states: 'Accurate information is the best defense.' There follows a short graphic depiction of virus invasion of the body's immune system cells with a voice-over stating that the AIDS virus is 'very hard to catch. It is a fragile' – and here the face behind the voice, that of Dr Mervyn Silverman, Director of the American Foundation for AIDS Research, fills the screen – 'virus; it can be destroyed by soap and water. . . . Study after study shows that you don't easily get AIDS.'

The good doctor is interrupted so that Curtin can voice-over large billboard statements to the effect that AIDS cannot be contracted from casual contact, which is defined as sharing a glass of water, hugging, handshakes, even kissing, if it is not deep open mouth kissing. Dr Scott reappears to indicate that one can care for a person with AIDS and even have skin contact with urine, feces and vomit without being in danger, provided one is careful.

Curtin then asks the rhetorical question, how *do* you get it? Graphics return in the shape of male and female having genital-to-genital heterosexual intercourse while Curtin intones 'Any unprotected sexual contact, sharing of semen and vaginal fluids with someone who has AIDS, male or female.' There is a brief mention of sharing of needles. Dr Silverman returns to point out that abstinence is a sure way to protect yourself, but short of that, a condom and a spermicide should be used during sex, 'from beginning to end'. He points out that one should not take drugs, but if one does, at least do not share a needle.

This part of the video constitutes the accurate information part. There follows the advisory examples of how to talk to your teenage child about the problem.

First we are shown the Stone family, a white professional middle-class couple who have lost their only son, Michael, to AIDS. Stills of Michael reveal a strikingly handsome young man. The parents say they knew he was sexually active, but wish they had talked more. The Stones are an attractive and brave couple, who are unusually articulate and frank about their experience. We cannot help but admire and feel for them.

From this we are exposed to three little dramas that illustrate situations in which parents may inject their values about sexual activity and the dangers of AIDS into conversations with their children.

The first situation takes place in a kitchen, an affluent middle-class kitchen similar to those used for commercials featuring kitchen products, in which a very young black girl (who talks like a 'valley girl') has a friendly and very quick chat with her substantial, earth-mother mom. With some embarrassment, the girl reels off rote instructions from school on how to have safe sex. The mom does not reveal any technical knowledge, but rather urges her daughter to be careful and wait for someone who has respect for her ('I am not telling you what to do, I am telling you how I feel').

The second situation takes place in a parked car where a divorced Dad is meeting his son. He urges the son to be careful because of AIDS and because he should have respect for the girls he goes with. This is the context for the remark about being gay and its seeming irrelevance to the AIDS question. The final scene is in the living-room, again white and middle-class, where a young teenage girl is about to go off 'with friends' until midnight. There is an embarrassed series of little jokes that show the unease of all three with the topic, but it frankly deals with the concern of the parents that their little girl not have sex with anyone nor take drugs nor drink and drive. In the course of the conversation, the threat of AIDS and the need for precautions are emphasized.

Although there is not one untruth in *Talking with Teens* the film editing and comparative weight given to different facets of the topic by graphics, authority figures and the settings for parent–teenager interchange, are misleading.

Is the subject AIDS and how to guard against it or how to deal with your child's first steps into sexuality? The video never made up its mind.

Furthermore, two juxtapositions seem to be deliberately mis-leading. After giving prominence to the statistic that one in seven sexually active teenagers will contract a sexually transmitted disease, there is a cut to a doctor who claims (we do not know the context of the interview from which this snippet was taken) that there is a potential for an 'explosion' of AIDS in that population. When another authority figure is pointing out how difficult it is to get AIDS, the sound is fighting graphics of the AIDS virus vividly succeeding in infecting an immune system. Immediately after the correct information of how weak the virus is, the script jumps to the conclusion that it is casual contact (not the virus) that is 'weak', that is, hardly likely to spread the disease. This distortion is followed by a description of how one does get the disease, with graphics displaying normal heterosexual intercourse. The true parts add up to the false, and seriously false, impression that there is a serious risk of contracting AIDS from normal heterosexual intercourse.

As for the tone of the parent–teenager interchanges and the sad story of Michael Stone, the clear implication is that middle-class heterosexual non-drug users with caring affluent parents are at serious risk of AIDS. Although we can all use sex education and although drug abuse in the non-intravenous forms of crack, speed and marijuana, unwanted teen pregnancy and sexually transmitted diseases like herpes and clamydia (which are not laughing matters) are certainly not unknown among the affluent, mostly white middle classes, AIDS is rare in this group. It was rare two years ago, when the film was shown, and it remains rare today, two years into the epidemic 'explosion'. AIDS *is* on a rampage, however, among those who practice the risky behavior of anal and oral sex promiscuously and among intravenous drug abusers who share needles. This risky behavior is particularly prevalent among the risk groups of homosexuals, who are the overwhelming majority of victims of the disease, and drug abusers, who are beginning to catch up with the homosexuals (as are the children of women, mostly drug abusers, with AIDS). Although both groups can come from all walks of life, intravenous drug abuse accompanied by sharing of needles is overwhelmingly a practice in racial and economic ghettoes; put another way, such self-destructive behavior is most often the consequence of poverty and racial discrimination. Any kind of unprotected sex with someone who has AIDS does put one at risk, but the question is among what populations does one have a significant risk of meeting someone who has AIDS. With this in mind, it would seem the choice of Jane Curtin and the atmosphere of the safe suburban school is aiming at the wrong target.

Furthermore, if the threat were as serious as one is led by innuendo to believe, the facile and fleeting encounters in kitchen, car and living-room that are shown as models would hardly suffice, nor would a string of such superficial verbal joustings between embarrassed teenagers and unconfident, unknowledgeable and tentative parents. Given the real statistics, parents should want to know if their children are homosexual and/or intravenous drug users, which would put them at serious risk. Yet these questions are not addressed at all.

This video does not reach those at risk but does reach those who can misread the message as not for them (about AIDS) so they can ignore the rest (about parent–child communication and sexual responsibility in general).

Like any aid to family communication and any video that deals frankly with sex, especially in a general population scared out of its wits by stories about AIDS, *Talking with Teens* was enormously popular.

Metropolitan Life has underwritten 'AIDS Lifeline' for Group W to the tune of one million dollars. As a result, Mr John Creedon, the CEO of Metropolitan Life, presents the Group specials through a brief tape made in his office, in which he declares how important Met Life feels proper information and public education about AIDS is. In this context he then states: 'We believe the AIDS epidemic may be the most serious health issue facing our nation and the world in this century.' Not malnutrition, not toxic and radioactive pollution, not even smoking and alcoholism, all of which either actually do, or seriously threaten to, kill far more humans? No one can make light of the seriousness of a fatal and loathsome disease for those who have it and those likely to get it. A large variety of cancers are such diseases. But hyperbole and fear are not helpful. To paraphrase Jane Curtin, accurate information is the best defense.

AIDS is a complex disease involved with all the psychological twists and turns we associate with sex and with sexual deviance. Its major victims are a controversial group who have a huge political stake in distancing themselves from a disease which might be labeled 'the gay disease', and thus add to the motives for discrimination they already suffer. The heart-breaking slow course of the disease and its pandora box of secondary infections and other diseases makes AIDS a treatment nightmare which severely taxes health resources at every level, a factor that attracts significant interest from hospitals, insurance companies and caring agencies in any campaign effort that might alleviate a strain on their resources.

It pays to be aware that AIDS is among the top three topics for all national public-service announcements on television, in or out of Group W's 'AIDS Lifeline', a further testimony to its mainstream relevance, if not to its marketability. But precisely because of this relevance, as Edward Brecher and John Langone have pointed out conclusively, the mainstream media have seriously misreported the AIDS problem, as they did with radon and as they often do with science and health stories.[30]

MOBILIZING MARKETS

At this point, the research community and evaluators of campaigns in general are still stuck with the effectiveness model that dominated all communications research until recently.[31] Concrete measurable effects, on the model of billiard-ball causality – how many boxes of cereal? how many people recognize a name? – was seen as the 'real' measure of what media do. In the same vein, the number of volunteers or checks or generous partners resulting from a campaign are seen as the 'real' significance of a campaign. From a management point of view, this can hardly change because the bottom line is the last ball on the billiard table (to mix metaphors). From a research point of view, however, the contemporary television public-service/community campaign raises questions of politics and culture and thus fundamental questions of values.

Local campaigns adapt causes to the mass culture milieu of mainstream television programming. Syndicated public-service/community campaigns, since they are reaching for a much wider market, adapt causes more radically and thus must deal very carefully with problems of adaptation. If areas like AIDS that require some scientific understanding can cause trouble, it is even more true in the realms of politics and religion.

Television campaigns are above all messages of their medium, and they have more in common, in form, with commercials and sports coverage than with church meetings or lecture halls, to say nothing of inspiring texts read in solitude. Different as they are, televangelists like Jerry Falwell and Pat Robertson have far more in common with entertainers like Johnny Carson and Phil Donahue than they do with Martin Luther King or Mother Theresa.

Broadcasting in effect is the American Ministry of Culture. Whatever the particular form, radio and particularly television programming are the premier vehicles for American mass culture. Increasingly, this mass culture is not just a matrix for sports and entertainment; it has become the arena for much of politics and religion. Whereas there are legitimate concerns for people becoming passive couch potatoes who no longer go to church or vote, there can also be concern for people who all too eagerly follow calls to action and advice on how to care for their health from those who may not be qualified to lead or advise.

NOTES

1 The Public Broadcasting System and National Public Radio, for instance, together account for less than 5 per cent of the national audience. And, in so far as they depend on corporate underwriting for many programs (the respected McNeil–Lehrer News Hour is underwritten by the American natural gas industry, for instance), they are subject to much the same constraints.
2 This trend is gloatingly, but accurately, reported year after year in the annual Roper surveys, *Public Attitudes Toward Television*, commissioned by the Television Information Office, the public relations and research arm of the commercial television industry in America.
3 National Association of Broadcasters, *Broadcasters Public Service Activities*, Washington, DC: NAB Research and Planning, 1988.
4 John M. Phelan, 'Communing in isolation', *Critical Studies in Mass Communication*, vol. 5 (September 1988), pp. 347–51.
5 Edward S. Herman and Noam Chomsky, *Manufacturing Consent: The Political Economy of the Mass Media*, New York: Pantheon, 1988.
6 Sydney W. Head and Christopher H. Sterling, *Broadcasting in America*, 4th edn, Boston: Houghton Mifflin, 1982, pp. 192ff. and *passim*. Cf. also Harry F. Waters, 'The future of television', *Newsweek*, 17 October 1988, pp. 84ff.
7 All the networks and Public Broadcasting, for instance, use programming segments produced by local affiliates or member stations. Over 70 per cent of Group W Community Campaigns, which are sold in dozens of markets outside the group, are produced by stations. Its earlier *PM Magazine* uses features of a co-op arrangement, sharing station-produced segments (among other components).
8 Waters, op. cit.
9 Interview with Mr Kennen Williams, General Sales Manager, and Ms Carol Tweedle, Marketing Development Manager, at KPIX offices and studios, 855 Battery Street, San Francisco, 18 July 1988.
10 Neal Rosenau, 'After the cutbacks: what's the damage to local TV news?', *Columbia Journalism Review*, Sept.–Oct. 1988, pp. 46–50. For a specific example, cf. 'Buying in prime time has George Gillett in a bind', *Business Week*, 31 October 1988, pp. 32–3.
11 J. Max Robins and John Flinn, 'Local television under fire', *Channels '89 Field Guide to the Electronic Environment*, December 1988, pp. 10ff.
12 Interview with Mr Ron Lorentzen, Executive Producer, Programming, at KPIX offices and studios, 855 Battery Street, San Francisco, 19 July 1988.

13 Cf. The Television Information Office 1984 report on local television community programming, *Voices and Values: Television Stations in the Community*, p. 6.
14 ibid.
15 ibid., pp. 5–7.
16 ibid., pp. 8–9.
17 ibid., pp. 22–4.
18 Everett M. Rogers and J. Douglas Storey, 'Communication campaigns', in Charles R. Berger and Steven H. Chaffee (eds), *Handbook of Communication Science*, Beverly Hills: Sage, 1987, pp. 817–46.
19 R. E. Rice and W. J. Paisley (eds), *Public Communication Campaigns*, Newbury Park, Calif.: Sage, 1981.
20 E. G. McAnany (ed.), *Communication in the Rural Third World: The Role of Information in Development*, New York: Praeger, 1980. Mukhopadhyay, Rajatsubhra, 'Political communication and political behaviour in a Bengal village', *Journal of the Indian Anthropological Society*, vol. 18, no. 2 (July 1983), pp. 97–110.
21 National Association of Broadcasters, *Broadcasters Public Service Activities*, Washington, DC: NAB Research and Planning, 1988, p. 7. Percentages are of a base sample of 249 television stations, of which 27.6 per cent were from the top fifty markets, 18 per cent among the second fifty markets. 69.1 per cent were network affiliated.
22 ibid., p. 11.
23 Interview with Ms Carolyn Wean, General Manager, at KPIX offices and studios, 855 Battery Street, San Francisco, 19 July 1988.
24 Interview with Mr Rick Bacigalupi, Production Assistant, at KPIX offices and studios, 855 Battery Street, San Francisco, 19 July 1988.
25 Interview with Ms Candy Meyers, then National 'AIDS Lifeline' Co-ordinator, at KPIX offices and studios, 855 Battery Street, San Francisco, 19 July 1988. Ms Meyers provided me with a number of releases from her office which covered the essential facts of 'AIDS Lifeline' hereinafter reported.
26 Interview with Brenda Lowe, Human Resources Manager, at KPIX offices and studios, 855 Battery Street, San Francisco, 20 July 1988.
27 Interview with Mr Peter Maroney, News Director, at KPIX offices and studios, 855 Battery Street, San Francisco, 18 July 1988.
28 Interview with Mr Ron De Luca, Development Director, San Francisco AIDS Foundation, 25 Van Ness, San Francisco, 19 July 1988.
29 ibid.
30 Edward Brecher in 'Street sex, age and the mixed-up press', *Columbia Journalism Review*, March–April 1988, pp. 46–50, and John Langone, *AIDS: The Facts*, Little, Brown & Co., Boston, 1988.
31 John M. Phelan, 'Humanists and hardheads', in *Disenchantment: Meaning and Morality in the Media*, New York: Hastings House, 1980, pp. 19–27.

Chapter 4

Beyond balanced pluralism: broadcasting in Germany*

Vincent Porter and Suzanne Hasselbach

By the end of the 1970s, the established duopoly of public broadcasters in the Federal Republic of Germany[1] was under attack by the political parties of the right. The trouble flared up in the CDU-governed *Länder* of Lower Saxony and Schleswig-Holstein, where their respective *Ministerpräsidenten*, Ernst Albrecht and Gerhard Stoltenberg, found themselves unable to control the current affairs output of the Hamburg-based ARD station, NDR, which was set up by an inter-*Land* treaty signed between Hamburg and their two *Länder*. In 1977, under a CDU majority, the NDR administrative council used its extremely wide-ranging powers to rule that NDR's report on the proposed nuclear power station at Brokdorf was contrary to its constitution. So too was its transmission on its third programme, together with RB, SFB and WDR, of the thirteen-part series *Der Betriebsrat* (the Works Council), which the West German Employers Association considered too leftist. Incensed by this decision, the NDR director-general, Martin Neuffer, appealed to the Hamburg Administrative Court that the broadcasting council's ruling was *ultra vires*. He won his case. Stoltenberg's and Albrecht's next move was to announce their *Länder*'s withdrawal from the NDR Treaty, to come into effect in 1980. Both *Ministerpräsidenten* not only objected to the supposedly leftist reporting, but also wanted more regionalization and, importantly, saw a chance to set up private, fully commercial stations. But the courts prevented the break-up of NDR. This time it was the Federal Administrative Court in West Berlin which put a stop to the politicians' interference.[2]

THE LURE OF NEW TECHNOLOGY

Initially, the SPD/FDP federal government introduced cable and satellite in response to the economic crises that had begun in 1967 and which led to inflation and marked unemployment in the early 1970s. But for conservative politicians, it also offered an opportunity to restructure the public sphere in broadcasting.

When the new CDU/CSU and FDP coalition came to power in October 1982, it curbed public spending and endeavoured to create favourable investment conditions for private enterprise. One weapon in its strategy was to use the monopoly position of the *Deutsche Bundespost* (DBP), the federal telecommunications authority, to expand the broadcasting infrastructure. The SPD/FDP coalition had already set up two federal commissions, the *Kommission für den Ausbau des technisches Kommunikationssystems* (KtK) in 1974, and the *Enquete-Kommission 'Neue Informations- und Kommunikationstechniken'* in 1981, to look at these questions. Their aim was to analyse new information and telecommunication developments, and to assess not only their economic potential, but also their legal framework and their likely political and social impacts. The central argument of the *Enquete-Kommission* was that the German telecommunications market was economically decisive, since 70 to 80 per cent of telecommunications equipment was sold at home and it was important as a testing ground for exports; and it emphasized the DBP's strategic role as the largest purchaser. Satellites would be most effective in conjunction with the small cable networks or existing MATV systems, but reception was not expected to be individual. But because of ideological differences between its members, the *Enquete-Kommission* did not produce any recommendations and the change of government in 1982 cut short its deliberations.[3]

The conservatives on the *Enquete-Kommission* were motivated by an industrial-political rationale. German telecommunications cable manufacturers, and the brown goods sector of the electronics industry in particular, were suffering from stagnation and severe export problems which, it was hoped, could be ameliorated by the short-term expansion of copper cable systems for television distribution. They therefore stressed that the *Länder* had to create the regulatory framework for new programme channels so as to make the desired expansion of cabling cost-effective.[4] But by 1983, when the new CDU Minister for Posts and Telecommunications, Christian Schwarz-Schilling, launched his nationwide cable distribution policy, the future for big business lay in optical fibre rather than copper cable. Although the commercial benefits of developing cable broadcasting had become marginal for the large companies, coaxial cabling was expected to create new market opportunities for small and medium-sized enterprises, especially those involved in connecting the cable and in servicing MATV; the promotion of small and medium-sized enterprises being a traditional aim of the FRG's industrial strategy.[5] Finally, cabling was expected to stimulate the German media economy by creating employment opportunities in the telecommunications sector, opening the market to new entrants from the private sector and boosting the broadcast advertising market.

The cautious social and political arguments for cable television, based on the expansion of local communications and citizen participation in the communication process, which had informed the debates under the SPD/FDP coalition, were quickly replaced by a mixture of economic and ideological rationales. Apart from the industrial benefits, the advertisers welcomed the increased opportunities for advertising and competition between the public broadcasters and the new networks in selling airtime. The conservative politicians also looked to the new channels to be more sympathetic to their point of view than the public broadcasters, whom they considered 'red'.

Although Christian Schwarz-Schilling insisted that the new cable grid only created a technical infrastructure and did not therefore influence broadcasting policy, he was clear how it should be used. According to him, the investment of the huge sums necessary was justified because public-service broadcasting was occupied by radicals and the left so that it could no longer work towards social integration. Economic and ideological arguments were yoked together. As the federal government noted in 1985,

In the interests of *diversity of opinion*, [the federal government] considers it not only desirable, but also necessary, that the population will, on demand, be provided with the infrastructure to distribute television and radio programmes via broadband cable networks. Equally, it is the opinion of the federal government that the new information and communication technologies, in particular broadband cable technology, are important from an economic point of view.[6]

But what would be shown on these new cable channels? The federal government saw satellite programmes as one way to increase the number of services that could help sell the new cable networks. Only by relaying an increasing number of German and European channels could cable be marketed cost-effectively.[7] The *Länder*, who were legally responsible for broadcasting policy, were virtually forced into allowing new programmes, if they did not want to stand accused of putting a major public investment at risk.

PRIVATE BROADCASTING AND THE FEDERAL CONSTITUTION

Although some SPD-governed *Länder* saw little future in the new channels, many conservative *Länder* welcomed them. Not surprisingly Lower Saxony, led by Ernst Abrecht, was one of the first to enact a law permitting private broadcasting. If NDR could not be brought to heel by administrative arrangements, then the CDU would establish a new private rival to compete with it. The SPD doubted whether Lower Saxony's new broadcasting legislation was constitutional, however. Accordingly, the SPD members of the *Bundestag* referred the new law to the Federal Constitutional Court. The Court ruled that it was only prepared to accept the Lower Saxony law if eight provisions were removed, and a further twenty-nine were given the specific interpretation to them laid down by the Court.

In its first broadcasting decision in 1961, the Court had confirmed, and thereby institutionalized, the Allies' view of democratic pluralism and its implications for the formation of public opinion which were enshrined in the FRG's Basic Law. Article 5 guarantees the free formation of opinion.

> Everyone shall have the right freely to express and disseminate his opinion by speech, writing and pictures and freely to inform himself from generally accessible sources. Freedom of the press and freedom of reporting by means of broadcasts and films are guaranteed. There shall be no censorship.[8]

The Court noted that

> Article 5 of the Basic Law demands the enactment of statutes that organise the providers of broadcasts so as to provide for an effective participation of all relevant forces in their organs,

giving them the opportunity to air their views within the overall programme schedule. [These statutes must] contain obligatory content guidelines to guarantee a minimum of balance, objectivity and mutual respect.[9]

Using the public broadcasting structure as a model, the Court had already established in 1961 the three interlinked aspects of pluralism which, it ruled in all later decisions, would also have to be enshrined in private broadcasting. These were pluralism in control, in organization and in programme content. The formation of individual and public opinion was not merely activated by

> news broadcasts, political commentaries or series on past, present and future political problems, but also by radio or television plays, musical presentations or entertainment broadcasts.[10]

In a decision in 1981,[11] the Court accepted the principle of private commercial broadcasting as long as the legislators also enforced these standards in the private sector. It was on this basis that the conservative *Länder* started to introduce private broadcasting legislation in 1984. But even conservative broadcasting policy was not aiming for pure 'deregulation'; the 1981 decision was felt to have opened the barriers without dropping them altogether.[12]

The Court's decision in 1986[13] was fundamental for the restructuring of German broadcasting into a dual system, which combines public-service and private commercial structures. It was necessary to continue to regulate for pluralism for three reasons. First, the technologies of cable, satellite and low-power terrestrial broadcasting, all of which provided the technical basis for private broadcasting, did not yet guarantee universal reception. Second, the economics of the market were only likely to permit the development of a very limited number of new stations, especially in television where entry costs were still high; and the press sector, which was used as a model, had not proved a good example for a liberal broadcasting system, as it had serious concentration problems. And third, pending EC legislation made it likely that foreign satellite signals would tend to depress quality. The Court therefore set the following guidelines for the regulators to respect, and elaborated them in its 1987 decision.[14]

● The public-service system, but not individual corporations, was to be the 'cornerstone' of German broadcasting. Because of its specific organizational set-up and programme remit, it represented the pluralist forces of West German society. It was therefore assigned the task of providing 'the functions of broadcasting that are essential for the democratic order and cultural life in the Federal Republic'. Its duty was 'the provision of basic services' (*Grundversorgung*), i.e. to supply comprehensive programme services. These included not just political and informative elements, but also entertainment, music, sport and education, as well as universal geographical coverage.[15]

- The private system, in contrast, only had to meet a 'minimum' standard of pluralism (*Grundstandard*) in respect to its organization and programme offerings. This was clearly a concession by the Court to the precarious economic position of the emerging market. The minimum standard was not defined precisely, although the Court did demand 'the highest possible degree of pluralism' in the private sector as a whole, which meant that all views, including those of minorities must be given a 'chance' to find an airing in private broadcasting. Although the Court implied that it did not expect private broadcasters to offer a full range of high-quality programmes, if they did offer information programmes, they would be obliged to inform objectively, comprehensively and truthfully. Imbalances in the presentation of information would only be acceptable if they were 'of minor importance', or 'not aggravating'. Furthermore, the minimum standard had to include a right of reply and a respect for human dignity.[16]

- Importantly, the Court specified that the *Land* legislatures had to prevent powerful media players from gaining 'a dominant influence upon the formation of opinion'. This was to be ensured over and above the rules of the federal anti-cartel law. The rules were not only to restrict multi-channel ownership but also press/broadcasting cross-ownership. Moreover, the fewer channels there were, the more pluralistically organized the individual broadcaster had to be. Significantly, the Court ruled that '[o]pportunities in the market place may relate to economic freedom, but they do not relate to freedom of opinion'.[17]

- The statutory control of the private-sector pluralism requirements, through licensing and programme monitoring, was to be the duty of a panel of experts, external to the broadcasters. Not only should those experts be recruited from all socially relevant groups, but they should be independent of the state. The Court thus affirmed that the system of controlling West German private broadcasting should be closely modelled on that of the public sector. It conceded, however, that the external control bodies for private broadcasting would have less power than the internal control bodies of the public sector. The latter were responsible for the development of the overall programme output, while the former were only supervisory and reactive, since once a private broadcaster had been licensed, the regulatory body could only intervene if a contravention took place.[18]

Thus private broadcasting legislation passed in all *Länder* has been essentially constrained by the Federal Constitutional Court since it rejected unfettered deregulation for both the public and private broadcasting systems. Moreover, because of a traditionally strong reliance on constitutional norms, and in order to reduce the legal insecurity which characterized the private broadcasting debate in the Federal Republic, the *Land* legislators repeated, almost word by word, the Court's basic formulations on pluralism and tended to take over those rules from the broadcasting acts of Lower Saxony and Baden-Württemberg, that were specifically sanctioned by the Court. However, the different geographic, economic and political situations within individual *Länder* gave rise to broadcasting legislation which meets the criteria of the Federal Constitutional Court in a number of different ways.

THE 1987 INTER-*LAND* TREATY

One of the main outcomes of the 1986 judgement of the Constitutional Court was the signing in 1987 of a new Inter-*Land* Treaty. It is now a major plank in the regulatory framework for broadcasting in the FRG. Its underlying objective is to create a constitution for the 'co-habitation' of public-service and commercially funded private broadcasting.

Between 1984 and 1987, all eleven *Länder* had introduced legislation for private commercial broadcasting which differed widely in their licensing conditions, advertising rules, and their requirements for youth protection and programme diversity. The private broadcasters, both German and foreign, therefore lobbied strongly for a common framework of national regulations.[19] Thus the *Länder* had to agree, not only how to allocate the new cable and satellite distribution channels, but also how to harmonize the conditions under which public and private broadcasters could operate.[20]

Article 8 of the Inter-*Land* Treaty embodies the essence of the German pluralism requirements when licensing private broadcasters.

> The content of private broadcasts has to express essentially the pluralism of opinions. General interest channels have to grant means of expression to the significant political, ideological (*weltanschaulich*) and societal forces and groups; minority views have to be taken into consideration. Thematic or special interests channels may be offered in addition.

As long as there are less than three private nationwide radio or television channels, pluralism can only be guaranteed by general interest channels. To this end, the regulators in each *Land* have to ensure that diverse interests are represented within the broadcasting organization itself. They may, for example, require the broadcaster to establish a pluralist internal programming council 'with an effective influence upon programming'. No such provision need be made if the broadcaster is a joint enterprise of several interests none of which has more than half the capital and voting rights. The regulatory authority should also attempt to have programme providers with an explicitly cultural remit included in any joint enterprise, although this clause is not legally enforceable.

Thus the provisions of the Treaty permeate the ideology of pluralism in private broadcasting which is intended for the whole of the FRG. Its application is limited, however. The Treaty only lays down minimum requirements, which may be increased by the *Land* granting the original licence or franchise on the basis of which the broadcasts can be redistributed, by cable or satellite, over the whole country. Even a German DBS broadcaster needs a licence from at least one *Land*, and since cable penetration is very slow, the present privately owned national television broadcasters rely heavily on low-power terrestrial television channels to reach their audiences. Terrestrial frequencies are considered to be a means of *Land*-wide distribution and are therefore exclusively covered by *Land* rules. Once the Inter-*Land* Treaty had been signed, however, most of the relevant parts of the *Länder* legislation were homogenized to avoid private national broadcasters flocking to the *Land* with the lowest requirements. The Treaty therefore established a common base from which to analyse any significantly different regulations in individual *Länder*.

THE PUBLIC BROADCASTING CORPORATIONS

Control structure

The legislation establishing the ARD corporations and ZDF specifies that they are to be non-profit institutions incorporated under public law. They are to be self-governing and autonomous, especially in programme matters. Although subject to formal legal supervision by the *Länder*, their autonomy is guaranteed by the representative nature of their broadcasting councils.

The public-service system has a three-tier structure which consists of a supervisory board or broadcasting council,[21] an administrative board, and a director-general, the *Intendant*. The broadcasting councils come mainly from social groups and associations, with wide differences in the degree and extent of political and government participation. The earlier model of NDR and WDR, where party politicians appointed even the representatives of the social groups, has now been modified by redrafting the relevant legislation.

The administrative councils are smaller with between seven and nine members. They do not have to be pluralistically composed and often include management experts. They control financial management. The *Intendant* is solely responsible for the structure and content of programmes and for preparing the budget.

The broadcasting councils explicitly represent the 'interests of the general public'.[22] They take the final decisions on all policy matters and watch over the interpretation of the corporations' programme remit. They have the right to issue guidelines, define long-term programming strategy, appoint the *Intendant*, and sometimes his deputy, and deal with public complaints.

The public-service control system has been attacked on two main grounds. First, the meaning of social relevance is open to a wide variety of interpretations. It is almost impossible to represent a dynamically changing society with councils whose constitution is, by law, largely static. It may be possible where a *Land* parliament has the right to elect members of newly emerging social groups, but even here, a group has to be large and powerful enough to attract political attention. It is therefore established associations and organizations, which are also important players in other parts of the political process, which dominate the broadcasting councils. Their constitution can exclude, or at best marginalize, from access to public radio, minorities and poorly organized interest groups, such as citizen initiatives.

Decision-making on the broadcasting councils is therefore strongly influenced by the political sympathies of its members, even those that represent social groups. The independent members, who often come from the churches, have to struggle against the so-called 'circles of friendship' of the political parties which help to determine the voting behaviour of other social representatives on the councils. Fortunately, however, some members of the broadcasting councils have also developed a degree of institutional independence which makes them wary of simply following the party line. Even so, many representatives are also criticized for lacking the necessary professionalism to reach independent and informed conclusions.[23]

The political majorities on the boards determine the choice of *Intendant* and his departmental directors, which frequently results in political manoeuvring at senior levels.[24] Appointments are often made by trade-offs between the CDU and SPD, while smaller parties, such as the Greens and the FDP, tend to be excluded. Editorially, politicization means that party politicians can exert an indirect influence upon programmes. This is done either retrospectively by reprimand, or in advance through contacts on the councils and in the organization. Internal self-censorship plays a critical role. As a correspondent of the German weekly, *Die Zeit*, has noted,

> The system of party-political membership in public-service television has been refined for many years. This is one of the reasons why television journalists think of themselves, wrongly, as 'microphone stands'.[25]

This potential for direct transmission of political power to programming is inherent to the public-service system, whereas the private sector is far less open to influence from the regulatory authorities. It is not surprising, therefore, that even those politicians who were recently railing against the public-service system and its weaknesses are now trying to increase their influence on the public sector.

The best barrier against political influence is a strong *Intendant*. This is probably why the two ARD corporations where this is the case, HR in Hessen and SDR in Baden-Württemberg, have recently found their statutes under attack. In Hessen, the CDU tried, unsuccessfully, to cut back the wide-ranging powers of appointment of the HR *Intendant* and chairman of the ARD, who, although elected by the council because of his alleged CDU bias, displayed a surprising independence. Similarly the CDU *Ministerpräsident* of Baden-Württemberg tried hard to merge the SDR into SWF, the other corporation which covers part of Baden-Württemberg. Unlike SWF, there are no government representatives on the SDR broadcasting council, and the SDR's *Intendant*, a former chairman of the ARD, is very independent.

Programming pluralism in the public corporations

The *quid pro quo* of the independence of the public broadcasters from the state, which is written into the relevant broadcasting acts and statutes, is a firm commitment to the German concept of pluralism. Both the ARD and ZDF are required to assist in the realization of a free democratic order. The 1987 Inter-*Land* Treaty forbids the misuse of violent material, the glorification of war, incitement to racial hatred and pornography.[26] This provision, and the specific youth protection rules, apply to all broadcasters, whether public or private, national or local. This represents a change from the previous practice when the public-service broadcasters made their own rules.

The programming responsibilities of the public sector broadcasters are set out in the various programme guidelines of the ARD corporations and the ZDF. Apart from the formal requirements for balanced pluralism, obedience to the general law, objective reporting and granting airtime to the political parties and the churches, programme offerings must be as comprehensive and varied as possible. Not only is the audience to be informed, educated and entertained, but it must be given

> an objective and comprehensive overview of international, national and *Land*-wide events in all essential realms of life. The demand for pluralism is to be especially respected in information

broadcasts and those that serve to form opinion. Significant political statements and analyses, as well as information on so far unknown facts and [their] contexts are essential parts of the programme. The duty to inform also requires reports on unconstitutional opinions, events or states of affairs.[27]

Apart from following similar general principles, ZDF's programme guidelines are more overtly political than those of the ARD. They specify that its programmes are 'to promote the reunification of Germany in peace and freedom, help to preserve freedom for Berlin and foster efforts aimed at European unification'.[28] This is a slightly different emphasis from the political remit of NDR, the North German ARD corporation, where 'NDR programmes are to . . . support peace and German unity as well as to extol [the principle of] *social justice.*'[29]

THE PRIVATE BROADCASTING SECTOR

The extent to which the statutes regulating the public corporations have influenced the pluralism requirements for the emerging private sector has depended on the local political situation. In some SPD-controlled *Länder* the same pluralism principles apply to both sectors. According to the letter of the law, a pluralist output would then also seem to be guaranteed throughout the private sector. However, the legislation seems difficult to implement. Instead of pluralism being an end in itself, as it is in the public sector, these principles are the price which the private sector has to pay in order to have a licence to make a profit by selling airtime. But the need to spell out the requirements for elements of local and regional diversity in nearly all the private broadcasting Acts also indicates the significance to the private sector of concepts which have not yet been adequately realized by the public-service corporations, especially in radio.

Control structure

All eleven *Länder* have set up regulatory authorities, as autonomous corporate bodies under public law, to license and supervise the private broadcasters. Thus they are not government agencies and not therefore directly open to changes of basic policy. The authorities normally have a three-tier structure, not unlike the control structure of German public limited companies. At the top is a pluralist supervisory board of between eleven and fifty members (the average is around thirty) which represents the public interest. The board licenses the private broadcasters, monitors their programming, implements the cable redistribution rules as laid down in the legislation and, if not specified in the relevant Act, decides how to allocate the money which is available for its various duties.

An executive body, which can either be internal or external to the pluralist board, prepares and implements the board's decisions. It develops administrative and budgetary policies and can issue emergency orders. The director heads the administrative office of the authority and represents it in court. Programme monitoring, advice to broadcasters and technical co-ordination are also his major responsibilities. The director, who is frequently a lawyer and tends to come from the *Land* administration, possesses the necessary legal and technical expertise. His powers of decision vary from *Land* to *Land*. In Bavaria, where there is a separate administrative board but an executive president at the top of the office, they are very strong. They were weakest in CDU/FDP governed Lower Saxony where orders for broadcasters were implemented by the *Land* government and the director's function was purely administrative.

Although the constitutions differ for the various pluralist regulatory bodies, party-political and government interests are generally less than those in the public-service broadcasting councils. Membership overall is also less for widely represented groups, such as churches, trade unions, culture, municipalities and even journalists; and significantly less in science and education. Less well represented groups, such as professional bodies, consumers, charities and environmentalists, have gained somewhat, although the overall weighting towards the traditional social organizations has hardly changed. The so-called minority interests, such as the anti-nuclear and animal rights movements, are hardly represented at all; and environmentalists or old age pensioners and women, who can hardly be regarded as minorities, are still clearly under-represented. As for the lower socio-economic groups, virtually nobody represents them.

Despite its slight decline, political representation is still substantial. This political influence is often reinforced by permitting parliamentary factions to select additional social groups according to their strength; for example, the Hamburg parliament appoints all the representatives of the social groups. Direct political representation is in some *Länder* also increased by the non-voting attendance of a member of the cabinet office during the meetings of the boards, be it in CDU/FDP Lower-Saxony or SPD Northrhine-Westfalia. This is officially justified by the governments' formal legal supervision over the regulatory authorities.[30]

Pluralism in organization

But since the regulatory authorities are institutionally separated from the private broadcasters, they can only have limited control over editorial content. Unlike the public sector where supervisory control goes hand in hand with administrative responsibility, in the private sector the two functions are carried out by different organizations. If genuine pluralism is to be achieved, the regulation of the constitution of each broadcasting organization licensed is of particular importance.

Three different basic models have been developed to achieve pluralism. The main system is the mixed model as laid down in the Inter-*Land* Treaty. It was written into the Treaty because most *Länder* had adopted it. Until three private channels are available nationwide, each channel has to be a fully comprehensive general interest channel. This means it must contain a balanced mixture of the various opinion-forming elements.

If the required number is reached, the so called externally pluralist model applies. In this case, no specific rules for the internal balance of each channel are written into the legislation. It is assumed, as for the press, that the available range of all channels will automatically represent pluralism.

The third model is one of internal pluralism. For this, each channel must be provided either by an organization composed of many different social and economic interests, or else contain an internal programme supervisory council. Each channel must then be a general interest channel and follow programme-content rules that approximate to those of the public-service channels.

At the present time, despite the provisions of the Inter-*Land* Treaty, there is insufficient advertising to support the anticipated broadcasting revolution of the 'new media'. The CDU is already discussing directions for future change. In particular, it is proposing to review the public-service concepts underpinning public broadcasting and motivating the regulatory authorities for private broadcasting. Changes to the licence fee system and a single federal regulatory authority are on its agenda.[31]

A NEW PROGRAMME ORDER?

As yet, the size and quality of the editorial output from private broadcasting is almost as unclear as the pattern of regulation. Although only a few content studies of private programme services have been carried out,[32] some general tendencies may be worth noting.

As in other countries, the hopes of some politicians of being able to influence the editorial policies of private commercial broadcasters more easily than those of the public-service corporations, have not been borne out. In radio in particular, political information programmes have shown their independence and a preference for investigative journalism which has not spared party-political allegiances, especially when a political scandal can capture audiences. Topical reports, if they are broadcast at all, are frequently more subjective and stimulating than those on the public stations, where reticence and balance can often create audience indifference.

Unorthodox leftist views, which are often denied access to public-service radio, now have at least the theoretical, if not necessarily economic, chance to get their own, possibly non-profit-making, stations. But only two of these have been licensed, in West Berlin and Freiburg. Neither has a large market share and they have both had their problems. On both stations, women are given plenty of airtime; and there are also programmes produced by women for women audiences.

The fears of political bias on the part of private broadcasting critics have not been substantiated. The national television and large commercial radio stations cannot afford to alienate half their audience by adopting a particular political stance; and in radio, the regulators have made sure, so far, that local stations with a political message are limited in number.

The two private *Land*-wide radio stations in Lower Saxony and Schleswig-Holstein have tended to imitate the formats of public-service news broadcasts. Whether they will be able to retain a certain quality in their information output when, as planned, two new commercial *Land* radio stations start broadcasting, remains to be seen. Since the news programmes are one of the strong points of the public-service channels and are highly appreciated by the audiences, the private television channels too have been trying to improve the journalistic quality of their news output, but they have run into cost problems. Light entertainment has been their big audience-puller instead.

Most radio and television stations provide hardly any socio-political background information. News programmes, which are normally very short, are mainly 'rip and read' programmes, relying on news agency feeds. Outside broadcasts and foreign correspondents are expensive to maintain, especially for television. On radio, telephone interviews predominate; and on television, talking heads and innumerable self-styled experts have replaced well-researched in-house background material. Topical information programmes emphasize the human interest touch; and the verbal style is deliberately casual and easy-going, optimistic, non-confrontational and apolitical. According to a former SAT 1 news editor:

> We want to produce a programme service which clearly shows the people that everyday life is worth living, and that it is worthwhile to be active. We want to present the world as it is. [That is] primarily positive, that is not to say that we keep problems under cover . . . but we do not want to send people to bed . . . with the feeling that the next day they'll have to face a vale of tears [sic].[33]

It is appropriate here to recall that, among other things, the Constitutional Court saw the public responsibility of all broadcasting as vital to the democratic process. But ironically, in order to compete with the private sector for the same audience, the popular radio channels on the public stations, which sell the most airtime, have restyled their news output and relegated background information and serious reporting to specialist channels.

The real innovation of private broadcasting is local radio, although its economic viability is far from secure. Local news and information clearly meet a need. Although radio competes with local newspapers, it is faster. Different teams of radio and newspaper journalists often compete with one another, although frequently employed by the same publisher. But there have also been reports of local radio stations simply reproducing newspaper items without even mentioning the source; and much local news is often little more than announcements of forthcoming events.

But it is mainstream pop and rock that is the staple fare of the commercial radio stations. In addition there are a few specialist services, such as jazz stations. But in general, expansion has produced more of the same and little diversity in available programming.

The changes in private television have been similar. Apart from a few business programmes and music videos, the huge increase in programme hours has given audiences more light entertainment and talk shows; and more of the same old films and series. In line with its young modern image, RTL plus pulls its audiences with light-hearted sexual advice programmes and soft porn shows, while SAT 1 cherishes its image of a dignified family channel.

Meanwhile, the public-service corporations are increasingly strapped for cash. So far, they have only managed to get a limited increase in the licence fee. They are facing competition in the sale of airtime, especially in radio. And there is a huge increase in the costs of television programme material and programme rights. All this can be felt in their programming policies. Instead of increasing pluralism, economic competition is eating away at the edges of the constitutional cornerstone of the German broadcasting system.

The ARD radio channels have been streamlined, thus jettisoning the traditional public-service ideal of mixed channels. The aim of the exercise is to build listener loyalty to one radio channel, by creating a predictable and firm programme structure and establishing channels with identifiably distinct outputs of music and news, like those in BBC radio. Less money is available for cultural specials, such as experimental music programmes or radio plays. Money spent on sponsoring cultural events will also be cut back unless legislation, as in Hessen, earmarks additional funds for this purpose. Radio drama does not feature on private stations.

For different political motives, politicians of both main parties are increasingly critical of public broadcasting's practice of cutting back in cultural programming and competing in the commercial market-place. In television, there will be more repeats of expensive films and series; more co-productions and less material produced by the smaller independent German producers. Minority interest programmes and political magazines have already been pushed from prime-time to late evening viewing to make way for entertainment programmes. The third programme channels, which are not allowed to take advertising, and which were a traditional outlet for education and advisory programmes, in-depth discussion and special movies, have gradually been popularized.[34]

Are the media politicians satisfied with the structure they have created? Ironically, many conservative politicians, especially those who fought to introduce private commercial broadcasting and to defeat the alleged socialist bias in the public-service corporations, are disappointed with the poor quality of the commercial radio and television stations. They are particularly dismayed by the virtual disappearance of the cultural, folkloric and educational components in their programming. CSU voices are quoted as calling the new programming 'boring drabness'.[35] And the newly popularized public radio channels, which have been designed for mass appeal, have also occasioned numerous complaints.[36]

Conservative media politicians have started to appreciate afresh the value of the public-service corporations, not only as upholders of traditional conservative values, but also as a platform for their policies; and SPD politicians have always valued public broadcasting as part of their social ideology. It is doubtful however, whether political interference in programme content will continue to be so easy in future. The need to face up to commercial competition could well force the public corporations to assert their political independence.

At first glance, it seems that the re-regulation of West German broadcasting has effectively secured the constitutionally required, minimum standards of pluralism in private broadcasting and has kept market forces at bay.[37] The decisions by the regulatory authorities on the organization of the new private broadcasting market have created a complex, but precarious, federal structure which has restrained the broadcasters.

But already, neo-liberal economists are criticizing this regulatory framework for being bureaucratic and offering only 'loopholes', but not a truly liberalized broadcasting market. In particular, it is argued that the broadcasting market is distorted because of the remaining public-service obligations of the private broadcasters and the licence-fee-supported broadcasting sector.[38] The licensing decisions of the authorities have narrowed organizational diversity as they have restricted market entry, especially as at the end of a long licence period the same broadcaster will probably have its licence renewed. Market choice is being narrowed beyond the desired level by strong concentration tendencies; and the ideal of a pluralist federal broadcasting landscape, which had inspired so much of the original broadcasting legislation, is crumbling in the face of increasingly pragmatic regulation.

On the other hand, many of the attempts by the legislators and regulatory authorities to create positive, enabling regulation, in order to allow a diversity of programme output as demanded by the Constitutional Court, have failed because editorial pluralism cannot simply be created through a structure based on external pluralism. The root of the problem is the conceptual incompatibility between the constitutional principle of pluralism, which aims at the socio-political effects of broadcast content, and the economics of market-led forces. Not only has external pluralism been scaled down in organizational terms, but broadcasting in general and television in particular, whose resource demands only allow marginal organizational diversity, is increasingly restricted to providing entertainment.[39] With a few exceptions, private broadcasting is essentially non-political, and follows a middle-of-the-road programming philosophy designed to appeal to as many viewers and listeners as possible. At the same time, the public broadcasters have narrowed the range of their programmes under the competitive pressures for ratings, the increased costs of rights to films and sports events and the politically conditioned financial restraints on the size of the licence fee.

This process is taking place, despite the caution of the Federal Constitutional Court and the intentions of the politicians and the regulatory authorities to create a series of positive, enabling regimes. To audiences, the German broadcasting system begins to look increasingly like those in the USA, Italy and France. Although these countries all have different regulatory approaches, the differences are only superficial compared with the developing structure of the international market place to which all broadcasters, both public and private, are increasingly exposed.[40] Yet paradoxically, as regulatory policies fail to live up to expectations, the more appreciation there has been of the role played by the public broadcasters in providing culture and political information.

Hans Bausch, the former head of the ARD network, who resigned over the issue of state control over broadcasting, summed up the condition of broadcasting regulation in the Federal Republic with some bitterness. He said:

It would be presumptuous to discover in this labyrinthine confusion a concept that befitted the idea of a liberal and pluralist political culture in the Federal Republic.[41]

The authors would like to acknowledge the financial support of the Economic and Social Research Council, as part of its Programme on Information and Communication Technology (PICT). All translations are by the authors unless otherwise stated.

NOTES

* The changes discussed in this contribution took place in West Germany prior to unification. Broadcasting in the Eastern *Länder* is now being organized according to the same regulatory principles.

1 Since 1961, there had been two public television channels in West Germany. The ARD network is a consortium of nine separate stations which were established by individual *Länder* or by inter-*Land* treaties. (The *Länder* are the eleven individual states of the Federal Republic, with separate jurisdiction for broadcasting.) The nine stations are *Westdeutscher Rundfunk* (WDR) in Northrhine Westfalia, *Bayerischer Rundfunk* (BR) in Bavaria, *Hessischer Rundfunk* (HR) in Hessen, *Süddeutscher Rundfunk* (SDR) in Baden-Württemberg, *Radio Bremen* (RB) in Bremen, *Saarländischer Rundfunk* (SR) in the Saarland, *Sender Freies Berlin* (SFB) in West Berlin; and *Norddeutscher Rundfunk* (NDR) established by an Inter-*Land* Treaty between Lower Saxony, Schleswig-Holstein and Hamburg, and *Südwestfunk* (SWF) established by an Inter-*Land* Treaty between Baden-Württemberg and Rhineland-Palatinate. The second channel is provided by *Zweites Deutsches Fernsehen* (ZDF) which was established in 1961 by an Inter-*Land* Treaty signed between all *Länder*.

2 For a more extended discussion, see R. Collins and V. Porter, 'West German television: the crisis of public service broadcasting', *Sight and Sound*, vol. 49, no. 3 (Summer 1980), pp. 172–7.

3 Germany, Bundestag, *Drucksachen* 9/2442, 28 Mar. 1983, pp. 37ff.

4 ibid., pp. 190f., 233.

5 See Federal Government, *Jahresbericht der Bundesregierung*, Bonn, 1988, p. 217; Deutsche Bundespost, *Geschäftsbericht*, Bonn, 1987, p. 24.

6 See Federal Government, 'Vorstellungen des Bundes für eine Medienordnung der Zukunft, 13 March 1985', printed in *Medienpolitik*, ed. Press and Information Office of the Federal Government, Bonn: 1985, pp. 12ff (all translations by the authors).

7 Germany, Bundestag, 'Antwort der Bundesregierung', *Drucksachen* 10/499, 19 Oct. 1983.

8 *The Basic Law for the Federal Republic of Germany*, ed. Press and Information Office of the Federal Government, Bonn: 1986 (official translation).

9 Decision of 28 Feb. 1961, excepts in *Medienpolitik*, loc. cit., p. 77.

10 Decision of 4 Nov. 1986 printed in *Media Perspektiven*, Dok. IV, 1986, p. 227.

11 Decision of 16 Mar. 1981, printed in *Media Perspektiven*, no. 6, 1981, pp. 421ff.

12 See H. W. Klein and W. Lauff, 'Neue Medientechnik – neues Rundfunkrecht', *Aus Politik und Zeitgeschichte* (supplement to *Das Parlament*), 19 Dec. 1981, p. 12.

13 Decision of 4 Nov. 1986, op. cit.

14 Decision of 24 Mar. 1987, printed in *Media Perspektiven*, Dok. III, 1987, pp. 145ff.

15 ibid.

16 Decision of 4 Nov. 1986, op. cit.

17 ibid., pp. 234ff.; decision of 24 Mar. 1987, op. cit., p. 160.

18 Decision of 4 Nov. 1986, op. cit.

19 See 'Bundesverband Kabel und Satellit', *Presseerklärung*, Bonn: 5 Mar. 1986.

20 For a more extensive discussion of the 1987 Inter-*Land* Treaty, see S. Hasselbach and V. Porter, 'The 1987 Inter-*Land* Treaty: West German broadcasting re-regulation between politics and the marketplace', in *Politics and Society in Germany, Austria and Switzerland*, vol. 3 (2), 1991, pp. 29–46.

21 ZDF, which does not broadcast radio programmes, has a television council.

22 See for example §16, WDR Act 1985, printed in *Media Perspektiven*, Dok. II, 1985, pp. 92ff.

23 See E. Etzioni-Halevy, *National Broadcasting under Siege*, London: Macmillan, 1987.

24 ibid.

25 Cf. N. Grunenberg, 'Kopfnicken und Katzbuckeln', *Die Zeit*, 11 Dec. 1987.

26 Art. 10

27 *Grundsätze für die Zusammenarbeit im ARD-Gemeinschaftsprogramm 'Deutsches Fernsehen'*, ARD, 1 Dec. 1982.

28 See *German Television*, ed. Information und Presse/ Offentlichkeitsarbeit des, Mainz: ZDF 1985, p. 12.

29 Printed in *ARD Jahrbuch 1988*, Frankfurt a.M.: ARD, 1988, p. 216 (emphasis added).

30 The same practice applies to most public-service broadcasting councils.

31 Excerpts from a federal CDU discussion paper on strategies for the media market of the 1990s, printed in 'Finden sich ARD/ZDF und private Sender unter einem Dach wieder?', *Frankfurter Rundschau*, 1 July 1988, p. 10.

32 See U. M. Krüger, 'Infos-Infotainment-Entertainment', *Media Perspektiven*, no. 10, 1988, pp. 637ff., and 'Konvergenz im dualen Fernsehsystem. Programmanalyse 1989', *Media Perspektiven*, no. 12, 1989, pp. 776ff.; the Hans-Bredow-Institut, Hamburg and the Institute for Communication Science at the University of Göttingen both analysed the Northern German radio output, 1989; see also J. Schmitz, 'Privatradios: Beispiel München', 3 parts, *epd Kirche und Rundfunk*, no. 17, 4 Mar. 1989; no. 18, 8 Mar. 1989.

33 Quoted in an interview on NDR 3, 28 Dec. 1988, printed in M. W. Thomas (ed.), *NDR 3, Medienreport (12)*, 1989, Hamburg: NDR Offentlichkeitsarbeit, 1989, p. 52.

34 See 'Unter der Planierraupe des Konkurrenzkampfes', *Frankfurter Rundschau*, 16 Sept. 1988, p. 18.
35 See 'Neues Mediengesetz in Baden-Württemberg', *Frankfurter Allgemeine Zeitung*, 12 Dec. 1987; 'Stabhochsprung mit der Salzstange', *Der Spiegel*, no. 13, 1989, p. 243.
36 See 'Gegen die Durchhörbarkeit', *Süddeutsche Zeitung*, 16 Feb. 1989, p. 47.
37 See J. Engler, 'Das Rundfunksystem der Bundesrepublik Deutschland', in *Internationales Handbuch für Rundfunk und Fernsehen 1988/89*, ed. Hans-Bredow-Institut, Baden-Baden: Nomos, 1988, p. B113.
38 See 'Wirtschaftsexperten: Mehr Markt im Rundfunk', *Frankfurter Rundschau*, 12 Dec. 1989, p. 16.
39 See W. Hoffmann-Riem, *The Philosophy of Broadcasting Re-regulation: The West German Approach*, paper delivered at the CCIS/Goethe-Institut Conference, 'Whither Pluralism', Goethe-Institut, London, Nov. 1989.
40 ibid.
41 'Zur Entwicklung des Rundfunks seit 1945', in P. Glotz and R. Kopp (eds), *Das Ringen um den Medienstaatsvertrag der Länder*, Berlin: Spiess, 1987, p. 31.

Part II

Politics and journalism

Chapter 5

Bites and blips: chunk news, savvy talk and the bifurcation of American politics

Todd Gitlin

In the pilot film for ABC's 1987 TV series *Max Headroom*, an investigative reporter discovers that an advertiser is compressing TV commercials into almost instantaneous 'blipverts', units so high-powered they can cause some viewers to explode. American television has been for some time compressing politics into chunks, ten-second 'bites' and images that seem to freeze into icons as they repeat across millions of screens and newspapers. The politics of the American 1980s is saturated with these memorably memorialized moments. As a symbolic display, the decade begins with the image of the blindfolded hostages in Teheran, emblems of American victimization and helplessness, fairly begging to be released by (to take up succeeding images) Ronald Reagan at the Korean demilitarized zone, wearing a flak jacket, holding field-glasses, keeping an eye on the North Korean communists; or in a Normandy bunker, simulating the wartime performance he had spared himself during the actual Second World War. The decade proceeds with the image of the American medical student kissing American soil after troops have evacuated him from Grenada. The aura of invulnerability bears traces of Star Wars cartoon simulations, depicting hypothetical streaks cleanly knocking off Soviet blips far off in the fastness of electronic space. Not a moment too soon, the fading years of the 1980s are marked by the image of Oliver North saluting and Mikhail Gorbachev pressing the flesh of Washington crowds.

But the sense of history as a collage reaches some sort of fever pitch in the 1988 presidential election campaign. There it is hard to recall anything *but* blips and bites – George Bush conspicuously reciting the Pledge of Allegiance; Bush in a paid thirty-second spot touring what is supposed to be the garbage of

Boston Harbor (leaving aside that some of the spot was shot in Rhode Island); the menacing face of Willie Horton, the black murderer from Massachusetts who, freed on a routine prison furlough, committed a brutal rape and was widely advertised by the Republicans as a definitive product of Democratic policies (despite the fact that, as Democratic ads belatedly pointed out, Federal furloughs issued routinely under Reagan's administration had freed still more murderers to murder again); the ill-at-ease face of Michael Dukakis in an oversized helmet as he drove a tank on a campaign stop designed to make him look like the kind of guy who would be comfortable driving a tank, and which succeeded in making him look like precisely the kind of guy who had never before set foot in a tank and who really thought the exercise ridiculous. The question I want to raise is whether these sorts of ads and news stories have caused democratic politics to explode.

Although I pose the question in an extreme form, it is hardly alien to 1988's endless campaign journalism. Indeed, the journalists were obsessed with the question whether media images had become the campaign, and if so, whose fault that was. That obsession is itself worth scrutiny. But consider first the coverage itself. According to the most relentless of studies as well as the evidence of the senses, the main mode of campaign journalism is the horse-race story. Here is that preoccupation – indeed, enchantment – with means characteristic of a society which is competitive, bureaucratic, professional and technological all at once. The big questions of the campaign, in poll and story, are *Who's ahead? Who's falling behind? Who's gaining?*

This is an observation only a fool would deny. I recall a conversation with a network correspondent in 1980. I criticized the horse-race coverage of the primaries. 'I know,' he said. 'We've been trying to figure out what we can do differently. We haven't been able to figure it out.' To a great though not universal extent, the media still haven't. They can't. The popularity of unexamined military and sports metaphors like 'campaign' and 'race' shows how deep the addiction runs. This is a success culture bedazzled by sports statistics and empty of criteria for value other than numbers to answer the question, 'How am I doing?' Journalists compete, news organizations compete – the channeled aggression of the race is what makes their blood run. In the absence of a vital polis, they take polls.

By 1988, the obsession had reached new heights, or depths: one night, ABC News devoted fourteen minutes, almost two-thirds of the news section of the newscast, to a poll – a bigger bloc by far than any issue. In a perverse way, the journalists' fancy for polls is a stratagem directed toward mastery. Here at least is something they know how to do, something they can be good at without defying their starting premise, which is, after all, deference. Their stance is an insouciant subservience. They have imposed upon themselves a code that they call objectivity but that is more properly understood as a mixture of obsequiousness and fatalism – it is not 'their business' in general to affront the authorities, not 'their place' to declare who is lying, who is more right than whom, and how all the candidates fall short. Starting from the premise that they haven't the right to raise issues the candidates don't raise, or explore records the candidates don't explore, they can at least ask a question they feel entitled to answer: 'Who's ahead?' How can racing addicts be chased away from the track?

By 1988, the fact that the horse-race had become the principal 'story' was itself 'old news'. Many in the news media had finally figured out one thing they could do differently. They could take the audience backstage, behind the horse-race, into the paddocks, the stables, the clubhouse and the bookie joints. Not that the horse-race vanished: when the numbers are crunched, they will probably show quite a lot of horse-racing, probably as much as ever. But this time horse-race coverage was joined by handicapping coverage – stories about campaign tactics, what the handlers were up to, how the reporters felt about being handled: in short, *how are the candidates trying to do it to us, and how are they doing at it?* Anxiety lay behind this new style – anxiety that Reagan really had pulled the Teflon over their eyes, that they had been suckered by the smoothly whirring machinery of his stagecraft. So handicapping coverage was a defensive maneuver, and a self-flattering one: the media could in this way show that they were immune from the ministrations of campaign professionals.

The result is what many people call a postmodern move, in two senses: enchantment with the means toward the means, and ingratiation via a pass at deconstruction. There is a lot of this in American culture nowadays: the postmodern high culture of the 1960s (paintings calling attention to their paintedness, novels exposing their novelistic machinery) has swept into popular culture. An aspirin commercial dizzyingly toys with itself ('I'm not a doctor, though I play one on TV,' says a soap opera actor); an Isuzu commercial bids for trust by using subtitles to expose the lies of the over-enthusiastic pitchman; actors face the audience and speak 'out of character' about the program in which they are acting, *Moonlighting*. Campaign coverage in 1988 reveled in this mode. Viewers were invited to be *cognoscenti* of their own bamboozlement.

This was the campaign that made 'sound bite', 'spin control', 'spin doctor', 'handler' and 'photo op' (for 'opportunity') into household phrases. Dukakis handlers even made a commercial about Bush handlers wringing their hands about how to handle Dan Quayle, a commercial that went over far better with hip connoisseurs than with the unhip rest of the audience who had trouble tracing the commercial to Dukakis. What I will call campaign metacoverage, coverage of the coverage, partakes of the postmodern fascination with surfaces and the machinery that cranks them out, a fascination indistinguishable from surrender – as if once we understand that all images are concocted, we are enlightened. (This is the famous Brechtian 'alienation effect' but with a difference: Brecht thought that actors, by standing outside and 'presenting' their characters, could lay bare social relations and show that life could be changed; paradoxically, campaign metacoverage, by laying bare the campaign's tactics and inside doings, demonstrates only that the campaign is a juggernaut that cannot be diverted.) Thus, voice-overs explained knowingly that the candidate was going to a flag factory, driving a tank, etc., *in order to score public relations points*. Here, for example, is ABC correspondent Brit Hume narrating the appearance of George Bush at a flag factory on 20 September 1988: 'Bush aides deny he came here to wrap himself in the flag, but if that wasn't the point of this visit, what was it?'

In the same vein was the new post-debate ritual: the networks featuring campaign consultants ('spin doctors'), on camera, telling reporters why their respective candidates had done splendidly, while network correspondents affected an arch superiority and print reporters insisted that the spin doctors couldn't spin *them*. Meanwhile, presumably unswayable pundits rattled on about how the candidates performed, whether they had given good sound bite – issuing reviews, in other words, along with behind-the-scenes assessments of the handlers' skill in setting expectations for the performance, so that, for example, if Dan Quayle succeeded in speaking whole sentences he was to be decreed a success in 'doing what he set out to do'.

These rituals exhibited the insouciant side of insouciant sub-servience – reporters dancing attendance at the campaign ball while insisting that they were actually following their own beat. Evaluating the candidates' claims and records was considered highbrow and boring – and potentially worse. For to probe too much or too far into issues, to show too much initiative in stating the public problems, would be seen by the news business as hubris – a violation of their unwritten agreement to let the candidates set the public agenda. Curiously, the morning shows, despite their razzmatazz, may have dwelt on issues more than the nightly news – largely because the morning interviewers were not so dependent on Washington insiders, not so tightly bound to the source-cultivating and glad-handing that guide reportage in Washington. And it was a morning show that discovered that the Bush and Dukakis campaigns had hired the same Hollywood lighting professionals to illuminate their rallies. (Possibly the Dukakis handlers had learned from Walter Mondale's blunder in turning a 1984 debate lighting decision over to Reagan's more skilled people, leaving Mondale showing rings under his eyes.)[1]

As befit the new and sometimes dizzying self-consciousness, reporters sometimes displayed, even in public, a certain awareness that they were players in a game not of their own scripting; that they could be had, and were actively being had, by savvy handlers; and that they were tired of being had. The problem first acquired currency with a tale told about a 1984 campaign piece broadcast by the CBS correspondent Lesley Stahl.[2] Here is Stahl's own version of the story, as she told it on election night on ABC's *Viewpoint*:

This was a five-minute piece on the evening news . . . at the end of President Reagan's '84 campaign, and the point of the piece was to really criticize him for – I didn't use this language in the piece – but the point was, he was trying to create amnesia over the budget cuts. For instance . . . I showed him at the Handicapped Olympics, and I said, you wouldn't know by these pictures that this man tried to cut the budget for the handicapped. And the piece went on and on like that. It was very tough, and I was very nervous about going back to the White House the next day, Sam [she is talking to fellow panelist and prime competitor Sam Donaldson of ABC], because I thought they'd never return my phone calls and they'd keep returning yours. [Thus does competition within the journalistic pack cultivate subservience. – T.G.] But my phone rang, and it was a White House official [according to a good source, this was Richard Darman, now President Bush's director of the Office of Management and Budget – T.G.], and he said, 'Great piece, Lesley.' And I said, 'Come on, that was a tough – what do you mean, "great piece"?' And he said, 'We loved it, we loved it, we loved it. Thank you very much. It was a five-minute commercial, you know, unpaid commercial for our campaign.' I said, 'Didn't you hear what I said? I was tough!' And he said, 'Nobody heard what you said. They just saw the five minutes of beautiful pictures of Ronald Reagan. They saw the balloons, they saw the flags, they saw the red, white and blue. Haven't you people figured out yet that the picture always overrides what you say?'[3]

The 1988 answer was: apparently not. For the networks and the candidates (successful candidates, anyway) share an interest in what they consider 'great pictures', a fluid concept one of whose standard meanings is readily decodable, myth-evoking images. Curiously, the famous cynicism of journalists does not keep them from being gullible. Indeed, in this setting, cynicism and gullibility are two sides of the same con. The handlers count on the gullible side when they produce pictures for television. Not for nothing were the Reagan staffers proud of their public relations triumphs; their business was to produce what one of them called 'our little playlets'[4] – far-flung photo opportunities with real-life backdrops. Print reporters, meanwhile, were unable or unwilling to proceed differently. Although the pressure for 'great pictures' doesn't apply, at least in the non-tabloid press, print gatekeepers are unwilling to cede the 'playlets' to television; they compete on television's terms, leaving the handlers free to set their agendas.

What is not altogether clear, of course, is whether the Reagan staffers were justified to be so proud of their public relations triumphs. We don't know, in fact, that 'the picture always overrides what you say'. Possibly that is true for some audiences, at some times, in some places, and not for others. What is clear, though, is that when the picture is stark enough, or the bite bites hard enough, journalists, especially on television, are unwilling to forgo drama. To be boring is the cardinal sin. Embarrassed by their role as relay stations for orchestrated blips and bites, even amply-rewarded journalists purport to resent the way Reagan's staff made megaphones of them; at the least they have become acutely self-conscious about their manipulability. The White House and the TV-led press have been scrambling for relative advantage for decades; metacoverage was, in part, the press's attempt to recoup some losses.

TOO HIP FOR WORDS

But to make sense of metacoverage I want to look at the dominant form of political consciousness in a formally open but fundamentally depoliticized society – which is savviness.

Already in 1950, David Riesman's *The Lonely Crowd* described what he called the inside dopester – a consumer of politics who

> may be one who has concluded (with good reason) that since he can do nothing to change politics, he can only understand it. Or he may see all political issues in terms of being able to get some insider on the telephone. [In any case] he is politically cosmopolitan . . . . He will go to great lengths to keep from looking and feeling like the uninformed outsider.

The goal is 'never to be taken in by any person, cause, or event'.[5]

Over the past forty years, Riesman's inside dopester has evolved into another type: a harsher, more brittle and cynical type still more knowledgeable in the ways in which things really work, still more purposefully disengaged. The premium attitude is a sort of knowing appraisal. Speaking up is less important – certainly less fun – than sizing up. Politics, real politics, is for 'players' – fascinating term, for it implies that everyone else is a spectator. To be 'interested in politics' is to know how to rate the players – do they have good hands? how do they do in the clutch? how are they positioning themselves for the next play?

Savviness flatters spectators that they really do understand; that people like them are in charge; that even if they stand outside the policy elites, they remain sovereign. Keeping up with the maneuvers of Washington insiders, defining the issues as Washington defines them, savviness appeals to a spirit both managerial and voyeuristic. It transmutes the desire to participate into spectacle – one is already participating, in effect, by watching.

'I like to watch TV' (in the immortal words of Chance the gardener in Jerzy Kozinski's novel and screenplay *Being There*) is *the* premium attitude. If you have a scorecard, you can tell the players. The ultimate inside dopesters are the political journalists.

Today, both advertising and political coverage flourish on, and suffer from, what Mark Crispin Miller has called 'the hipness unto death'.[6] Miller argues[7] that TV advertising has learned to profess its power by apparently mocking it, standing aside from vulgar claims, assuring the viewer that all of us knowing types are too smart to be taken in by advertising – or gaucherie or passion of any kind. In the same way, the postmodern savviness of political coverage – whether glib and smirky, as in the preferred voice of network political experts, or sedate and professorial, as in public television or the Sunday morning talk shows – binds its audience closer to an eerie politics of half-truth, deceit and evasion. If the players are adept enough to evade an issue, the savvy spectator knows enough to lose interest in it as well.

Coverage of the horse-race and metacoverage of the handicappers both suit the discourse of savviness. They invite and cultivate an inside dopester's attitude toward politics – vicarious fascination coupled with knowing indifference.

It might well be, then, that Lesley Stahl's 1984 piece was really three pieces at once. A critical audience got her intended point – Reagan was a hypocrite. An image-minded audience got the White House's point – Reagan personified national will and caring, even as the nice-guy martyr to wise-ass Eastern commentators. And inside dopesters got still another point – Reagan, master performer, was impervious to quarrelsome voice-overs.

Perhaps, too, there was a fourth piece – the backstage piece in which the White House made a point of showing Lesley Stahl her place. This must have been humiliating for any reporter so old-fashioned as to want to take the measure of theatrical images against social realities. The fact that Stahl is a woman may not be incidental – the White House may have felt more comfortable humiliating her. Stahl's story points to a radical moral: the only alternative to complicity would be the damn-it-all spirit of an outsider indifferent to whether the handlers will favor her with scoop-worthy tidbits of information the next time. While telling Stahl that she's been had, the White House knows that, given the conventional understanding of the job of a political reporter, she's going to be coming back for more stories. White House handlers know that the surest way to make a reporter complicit is to feed her with stories. As long as the agenda is set by the White House or the campaign, the watchdog is defanged.

AN AUDIENCE FOR THE SPECTACLE

More must be said about what I just called the image-minded audience. For 1988 was not only the year of metacoverage; it was the year of the negative commercial, the bite, the image-blip. In statewide elections too, subsequent metacoverage has quivered with both righteous and ironic indignation about the prevalence of commercials casting aspersions on the rival candidate's one-time drug tastes, dubious votes, unsavory connections, etc. In theory, both positive and negative associations are television's distinct forte: emotionally charged images in which an entire narrative is instantly present. The image of Willie Horton or the flag is what makes a lasting impression. Research done by Ronald Lembo of Amherst College shows that some TV viewers are inclined to follow narrative while others, disproportionately the young, pay more attention to distinct, out-of-context images.[8]

What professional handlers and TV journalists alike do is find images which condense their 'little playlets' – images which satisfy both lovers of story and lovers of image. Then blip-centered television floods the audience with images that compress and evoke an entire narrative. The American 1980s begin with one of these: the blindfolded American featured in the logo that identified the first late-night news program in the history of American television, the long-running melodrama called *America Held Hostage*, sixty-three weeks of it during 1979–81, running on ABC at 11.30 p.m. five nights a week, propounding an image of America as 'pitiful helpless giant' (in Nixon's phrase). Those were the months when Walter Cronkite signed off at CBS night after night by ticking off 'the umpty-umpth day of captivity for the American hostages in Iran'. In this ceremony of innocence violated, the moment arose to efface the national brooding over Vietnam. Now it could be seen that the Vietnam trauma had eclipsed the larger truth: it was the anti-Americans who were ugly. The blindfolded American, disfigured by anti-Americans, was the contemporary equivalent of the paleface captive of redskins, that American victim-hero whose tradition runs back to the seventeenth century.[9] The image cried out for a man to ride out of the sagebrush on a white horse into the White House. The script for the Teheran playlet was not written by the Reagan handlers (although it is possible that they promised weapons to Iran's Revolutionary Guards in exchange for their keeping the hostages until election day), but they certainly knew how it would end.

We know how adept Reagan was at performing his playlets – he'd been doing them all his life.[10] For eight years we heard endlessly about the mysterious personal qualities of the Great Communicator-in-Chief, from reporters rushing about bearing spray-cans of Teflon and marveling at his peculiar capacity to resist criticism. Reporters routinely declared that Reagan was more popular than the polls themselves revealed.[11] But the mighty Wurlitzer of the media was not devised either by or for Reagan. It was primed for any of a number of possible figures who knew how to play upon it. The adaptability of the apparatus is exhibited by the media success of even as maladroit a figure as George Bush during the 1988 election. Having declared that Bush's central problem was to lick the wimp image (*Newsweek* devoted its 19 October 1987 cover story to what it headlined 'Fighting the "Wimp Factor"'), the media permitted him to impress them that, when he started talking tough, he had turned out 'stronger than expected'. In their own fashion, Bush and his handlers – some of them fresh from Reagan's team – followed. Their masterwork was a Bush commercial which opened with a still photo taken on the White House lawn: Reagan to the right, at the side of the frame; Gorbachev at the center, shaking hands with the stern-faced Bush. The camera moved in on the Vice-President and Gorbachev; Reagan was left behind – having presided, he yielded gracefully to his successor, the new man of the hour. As the camera moved closer, the stern face and the handshake took over, while the voice-over spoke the incantation: 'strong . . . continue the arms control process . . . a president ready to go to work on day one.' The entire saga was present in a single image: Bush the heir, the reliable man of strength who was also savvy enough to tame the adversary by dealing with him.

ON THE PREHISTORY OF BITES AND SPECTACLES

How new is the reduction of political discourse to the horse-race, the handicapping, the tailoring of campaigns to the concoction of imagery? What is particular to television? How good were the good old days?

Tempting as it is to assume that television has corrupted a previously virginal politics, the beginning of wisdom is history. As the campaigns invite us to read their blips, alarm is amply justified – but not because American politics has fallen from a pastoral of lucid debate and hushed, enlightened discourse to a hellish era of mud-slinging and degraded sloganeering. Television is very far from having invented the superficiality, triviality and treachery of American politics. American politics has been raucous, deceptive, giddy, shallow, sloganeering and demagogic for most of its history. 'Infotainment' is in the American grain. So is reduction and spectacle – and high-minded revulsion against both.

Is negative campaigning new? In 1828, supporters of Andrew Jackson charged that John Quincy Adams had slept with his wife before marrying her, and that, while minister to Russia, he had supplied the Czar with a young American mistress. In turn, pro-Adams newspapers accused Jackson of adultery, gambling, cock-fighting, bigamy, slave-trading, drunkenness, theft, lying and murder. Jackson was said to be the offspring of a prostitute's marriage to a mulatto. Papers accused Jackson's previously divorced wife of having moved in with him while still married to her first husband.[12] Not that all mud sticks. Some mud boomerangs. In 1884 a Protestant minister called the Democrats the party of 'Rum, Romanism, and Rebellion' as the Republican James G. Blaine stood by without demurral – which may well have cost Blaine the election.[13]

Is the preference for personality over issues new? Once elected president, Andrew Jackson set to wiping out Indian tribes – but this was not an issue in the campaign that elected him, any more than the New Deal was an issue in the campaign that elected Franklin Roosevelt in 1932. (Indeed, Roosevelt campaigned for a balanced budget.)

Are the blip and the bite new? 'Tippecanoe and Tyler Too', the leading slogan of 1840, does not exactly constitute a Lincoln–Douglas debate. That year, followers of William Henry 'Tippecanoe' Harrison carried log cabins in parades, circulated log cabin bandanas and banners, gave away log cabin pins and sang log cabin songs, all meant to evoke the humble origins of their candidate – although Harrison had been born to prosperity and had lived only briefly in an actual log cabin.[14] A half century later, in 1896, Mark Hanna, McKinley's chief handler, was the first campaign manager to be celebrated in his own right. Hanna acquired the reputation of a 'phrasemaker' for giving the world such bites as 'The Advance Agent of Prosperity', 'Full Dinner Pail' and 'Poverty or Prosperity', which were circulated on posters, cartoons and envelope stickers, the mass media of the time. Hanna 'has advertised McKinley as if he were a patent medicine!' – so marveled that earnest student of modern techniques, Theodore Roosevelt. In that watershed year, professional management made its appearance, and both candidates threw themselves into a whirl of public activity.[15]

The historian Michael E. McGerr has mustered considerable evidence that between 1840 (the 'Tippecanoe' campaign) through 1896, vast numbers of people participated in the pageantry of American presidential campaigns. Especially during the three decades after the Civil War, mass rallies in the north commonly lasted for many hours; there were torchlight parades; there were campaign clubs and marching groups. 'More than one-fifth of Northern voters probably played an active part in the campaign organizations of each presidential contest during the '70s and '80s,' McGerr writes.[16] And with popular mobilization came high voter turnout. National turnout between 1824 and 1836 averaged 48 per cent of eligible voters; but between 1876 and 1900, it averaged 77 per cent. In the north, it was up to 84 per cent of the eligible (all-male) electorate in 1896 and 1900 before it slid to 75 per cent during the years 1900–16 and 58 per cent in 1920–4.[17] (It rose again in the 1930s, with the Great Depression and the New Deal, and then started sliding again.) Arguably, the mass mobilization and hoopla turned out the vote; the act of voting was the consolidation of a collective ritual, not a private act through which the isolated citizen expressed his piety.[18]

In the age of professionalization, reformers recoiled. What developed in the 1870s and 1880s, with a push from so-called 'educated men', was a didactic politics, what McGerr calls an 'elitist' politics. High-minded reformers insisted on a secret ballot; they approved of social science; they wanted enlightened leaders to guide the unwashed. They worked toward a new-style campaign: a campaign of education. Independent journalism helped – newspapers no longer under party management. Alongside the waning partisan press, there emerged a bifurcated press: the high-minded independent papers with their educated tone, cultivating political discernment; and the low-minded sensational papers with their lurid tone, cultivating apolitical passion.[19] The way is already open to our contemporary bifurcation: the *New York Times* and the *New York Post*; public television's daily MacNeil/Lehrer *NewsHour*, with its protracted, detailed round-table discussions of issues current in Washington, and the syndicated Geraldo Rivera with his televised exposés of Satanism and teenage prostitution. This split corresponds to the highbrow/lowbrow cultural split that developed during the latter decades of the nineteenth century, as traced by Lawrence W. Levine in his recent book.[20] Serious politics became, like high culture, 'sacralized', while the political discourse of the working-class press degraded into yellow journalism.

Such sharply bifurcated media reinforce political division: to oversimplify, a progressive middle class takes politics seriously while a diverted working class is for the most part (except for the Great Depression) disabused. Although it takes decades for this process to develop, and there are exceptional periods of working-class mobilization along the way, the lineaments of the modern campaign are already in place at the turn of the century: emphasis on the personality of the candidate, not the party; emphasis on the national campaign, not local events; a campaign of packaging, posed pictures and slogans. Politics as a discretionary, episodic, defensive activity for the majority alongside moral politics for the few. The politics of the consumer society, in short.

The radio hookups of the 1920s made presidential campaigns still more national. Candidates and presidents could reach over the heads of the party apparatus directly to the electorate. Party structures grew steadily more redundant. Some of these changes were welcomed by reformers, and properly so: gradually, candidates found it more difficult to utter racist slogans to white southern voters in the belief that northern voters would not notice. Above all else, though, the powers of the new media created a pressure toward professional management. Intermittently, 'negative campaigning' sought out the media of the moment. Professionally concocted newsreels, in which actors portrayed irate citizens, played an important part in the defeat of the socialist Upton Sinclair's 1934 'End Poverty in California' campaign for governor.[21] A documentary newsreel spliced together at the last minute to counter the Republican Thomas Dewey probably helped the Democrat Harry S. Truman squeak through in 1948.[22]

These precursors are important – television is not the original sin. But only with television and the proliferation of primary campaigns did media management become central and routine to political campaigns. What had been intermittent became routine. In 1952, Dwight D. Eisenhower – whose campaign was the first to buy TV spots – was at first reluctant to advertise. In 1956, the Democrat Adlai E. Stevenson summoned his television consultant one night during the Democratic Convention – to ask him to fix his receiver.[23] After 1960, when John F. Kennedy was credited with having defeated a sweating, five-o'clock-shadowed Richard Nixon in televised debate, the handwriting was on the screen. It didn't matter whether the televised debate had been decisive in Kennedy's victory – in fact, Kennedy's margin was so narrow that any one of a number of factors was arguably decisive. What mattered was that the management of television was one factor that candidates believed they could control. The time of the professional media consultant had arrived. By the time his hour came round again in 1968, the new Nixon had learned to use – and submit to – professional image managers. Nixon was the first president to move advertising and public relations personnel into his high command. And not just for the campaign. The president in office could use the same skills he used for nomination and election. Nixon's right-hand men, Bob Haldeman and John Ehrlichman, the public relations professionals with their enemies lists and *provocateur* tactics, were the founding fathers of what Sidney Blumenthal later called 'the permanent campaign' – a combination of polling, image-making and popularity-building strategy which Reagan's handlers developed to the highest of low arts.[24]

The pattern seems set for the 1980s: metacoverage for the *cognoscenti*; concocted pageantry for the *hoi polloi*. But pageantry only mobilizes the population under two conditions – they must believe there is something at stake, and they must be drawn into some form of participation. As the spectacle becomes more scripted and routine – the parties' nominating conventions are the obvious example – more people turn off. Thus television inspired political withdrawal along with pseudo-sophistication. As campaign coverage proliferates, and the pundits and correspondents pontificate in their savvy way, they take part in what is increasingly a circular conversation – while an attuned audience, wishing to be taken behind the scenes, is invited to inspect the strategies of the insiders. Savviness is the tribute a spectacular culture pays to the pleasures of democracy – middle-class outsiders want to be in the know, while the poor withdraw and fail to vote (partly because legal obstacles are thrown up in the way of their registration, and neither party finds it in its interest to change the law). Politics, by these lights, remains a business for insiders and professionals. While the political class jockeys, the rest of us become voyeurs of our political fate – or *enragés*. Can it be simple coincidence that as voting and newspaper reading plummeted in the 1980s, Morton Downey, Jr arrived with his syndicated right-wing television yellfest, resembling nothing so much as an electronic bar-room brawl?[25] And that at the same time radio talk shows were able to mobilize the indignant against congressional salary raises? Probably not. The vacuum of public discourse is filled on the cheap. Moral panics thrive, disconnected from radical or even liberal politics. The only issue on which radio talk show hosts nationwide could agree was a symbolic crusade in behalf of Congressional ethics; they do not mobilize their listeners against a tax 'reform'that lines the pockets of the corporate rich, or against military-industrial profligacy.

INTIMATIONS OF THE HOLLOWING PUBLIC SPHERE

And what of the future? As the artist Folon says, 'I work at forgetting I'm a pessimist.' Ronald Lembo's research, which I've alluded to above, suggests that younger viewers are more likely, when they watch television, to pay attention to disconnected images; to switch channels, 'watching' more than one program at once; and to spin off into fantasies about images. Of all age-groups, the young are also the least likely to read newspapers and to vote. Do we detect a chain of causation? Does a fascination with speed, quick cuts, ten-second bites, one-second 'scenes' and out-of-context images suggest less tolerance for the rigors of serious argument and the tedium of organized political life? Has the attention span been shrinking; and if so, is television the cause; and what would this prophesy for our politics? Is there, in a word, a music video generation? Future apparatchiks of the media–politics nexus are assuming it – the politicians, the handlers, the publishers of *USA Today* and its legions of imitators. David Shaw of the *Los Angeles Times* writes (15 March 1989):

In 1967, according to the National Opinion Research Center at the University of Chicago, 73% of the people polled said they read a newspaper every day; by last year, the number of everyday readers had fallen by almost one-third, to 50.6%. During that same period, in the 18 to 29 age group, the number of 'everyday readers' dropped by more than half, from 60% to 29%.

While 26.6 per cent of *Los Angeles Times* readers are aged 18 to 29, 36.2 per cent of *USA Today* readers are that age. And whereas young people used to acquire the habit of newspaper reading as they aged, this is apparently no longer happening. To recoup their losses, newspapers are trying to woo the young by filling up with celebrity profiles, fitness features, household tips.

In 1988, the Department of Education published a report – a summary of research hither and yon – on television's influence on cognitive development. The widespread publicity placed the emphasis on TV's harmlessness. The Associated Press story that ran in the *New York Times* among other papers, for example, was headlined: 'Yes, You Too Can Get A's While Watching "Family Ties".'[26] But the report itself, by Daniel R. Anderson and Patricia A. Collins of the Department of Psychology at the University of Massachusetts, is inconclusive on the question of whether television-watching affects the capacity to pay attention. 'The possibility that rapid pacing may produce effects over longer exposure has not been examined,' reads one typical hedge. 'There does . . . appear to be some effect of TV on attention, yet the importance, generality, and nature of the effect is unknown': that is the summary sentence.[27] Some day the grants may flow for the research obligatorily called for. But pending research, one still feels entitled to the pessimism which one must then work to forget. Television may not have eroded all possibilities for democratic political life, but it has certainly not thrown open the doors to broad-based enlightenment. Just as certainly, it has erected obstacles.

I have tried to show that there is ample precedent for a shriveled politics of slogans, deceit and mystifying pageantry. But precedent is nothing to be complacent about when systematic ignorance is the product. And the problem, ultimately, is not simply that Americans are ignorant (such, after all, is the claim of every generation besieged by immigrants). On this score, the statistics are bad enough. According to a 1979 poll, only 30 per cent of Americans responding could identify the two countries involved in the SALT II talks then in progress; in 1982, only 30 per cent knew that Ronald Reagan opposed the peace movement's nuclear freeze proposal; in 1985, 36 per cent thought that either China, India or Monaco was part of the Soviet Union.[28] But ignorance is sometimes – not always – a defense against powerlessness. Why bother knowing if there's nothing you know how to do about what you know? Why get worked up? Again, the promotion of ignorance coincides with the emptying out of the public sphere – the paucity of forms through which political energies could be mobilized. In the end, what is most disturbing is not ignorance in its own right, but, rather, the coupling of ignorance and power. When the nation-state has the power to reach out and blow up cities on the other side of the world, the spirit of diversion seems, to say the least, inadequate to the approaching millennium. Neither know-it-alls nor know-nothings are likely to rise to the occasion.

I wish to thank Jon D. Cruz, John Jacobs, David Riesman, Jay Rosen, Ruth Rosen, Cynthia Samuels and Michael Schudson for their comments on earlier drafts.

NOTES

1 Mark Hertsgaard, *On Bended Knee: The Press and the Reagan Presidency*, New York: Farrar Straus Giroux, 1988, pp. 268–9.
2 Hedrick Smith, *The Power Game: How Washington Works*, New York: Random House, 1988, pp. 412–14.
3 Transcript, ABC *Viewpoint*, Nov. 8, 1988.
4 Smith, op. cit., p. 418.
5 David Riesman with Nathan Glazer and Reuel Denney, *The Lonely Crowd: A Study of the Changing American Character*, abridged edn, New Haven, Conn.: Yale University Press, 1961, pp. 181–2.
6 Mark Crispin Miller, *Boxed In: The Culture of TV*, Evanston, Ill: Northwestern University Press, 1988, p. 3.
7 Mark Crispin Miller, 'Deride and conquer', in Todd Gitlin (ed.), *Watching Television*, New York: Pantheon, 1987, pp. 187–8.
8 Ronald Lembo, 'The symbolic uses of television: social power and the culture of reception', PhD dissertation, University of California, Berkeley, Department of Sociology, 1989, pp. 226–30.
9 Richard Slotkin, *Regeneration Through Violence: The Mythology of the American Frontier, 1600–1860*, Middletown, Conn: Wesleyan University Press, 1973, pp. 94–145. Slotkin writes (p. 95): 'The captivity narratives constitute the first coherent myth-literature developed in America for American audiences.'

10 Garry Wills, *Reagan's America: Innocents at Home*, New York: Doubleday, 1987.
11 Elliot King and Michael Schudson, 'The myth of the Great Communicator', *Columbia Journalism Review*, Nov./Dec. 1987, pp. 37–9.
12 Paul F. Boller, Jr, *Presidential Campaigns*, New York: Oxford University Press, 1984, pp. 44–6.
13 ibid., pp. 149–50.
14 Kathleen Hall Jamieson, *Packaging the Presidency: A History and Criticism of Presidential Campaign Advertising*, New York: Oxford University Press, 1984, pp. 9–11.
15 ibid., pp. 144–5.
16 Michael E. McGerr, *The Decline of Popular Politics: The American North, 1865–1928*, New York: Oxford University Press, 1986, p. 26.
17 ibid., pp. 5, 7.
18 ibid., pp. 22ff.
19 ibid., pp. 107–37.
20 Lawrence W. Levine, *Highbrow/Lowbrow: The Emergence of Cultural Hierarchy in America*, Cambridge, Mass.: Harvard University Press, 1988.
21 Jamieson, op. cit., p. 30.
22 Jamieson, op. cit., pp. 32–4.
23 Jamieson, op. cit., p. 43.
24 Sidney Blumenthal, *The Permanent Campaign: Inside the World of Elite Political Operatives*, Boston: Beacon, 1980.
25 After two years, Downey squandered his populist capital. The controversy he generated kept his show out of certain metropolitan areas. Moreover, questions were raised about his veracity. The show's ratings declined, stations decided not to renew, and the Downey program sank into media oblivion in 1989.
26 *New York Times*, national edition, 8 Dec. 1988, p. B3.
27 Daniel R. Anderson and Patricia A. Collins, *The Impact on Children's Education: Television's Influence on Cognitive Development*, Washington, DC: US Department of Education, Office of Educational Research and Improvement, 1988, pp. 53–4.
28 Jay Rosen, *Democracy Overwhelmed*, Occasional Paper of the Center for War, Peace, and the News Media, New York University, 1989, pp. 36ff.

Chapter 6

The public sphere and the use of news in a 'coalition' system of government

Paolo Mancini

SOME DEFINITIONS AND CONTEXTUAL DATA

In recent years some important changes have taken place in the Italian public sphere and, in particular, in political communication. I refer especially to the personalization and dramatization of politics and news, the use of advertising techniques in political communication, the progressive erosion of the 'protected'[1] circuits of communication and the functions of socialization which, up to now, have been the functions of the political party. These changes are mainly linked to the birth of commercial television and yet they have occurred in an overall picture which has remained essentially unchanged, where many aspects have even been considered reinforced. At this point I therefore felt it appropriate to deal with the problem from a different angle, one that could explain not so much the changes but rather the persistencies. And this essay is aimed at being the first step in that direction.

The sacred texts of journalism, I refer especially to the works by Lippman (1965) and the theories of Siebert, Peterson and Schramm (1963), have taken as models several specific public spheres (above all, the Anglo-Saxon countries) and mainly have defined the functions of journalistic information in relation and in opposition to the political systems in force in those countries. It is possible to define these political systems as 'majoritarian', in which a clear boundary line exists between the majority and the opposition and there is more than just the theoretical possibility that different political forces will alternate in the government. They are systems which may be called, for the sake of brevity, 'simple', based on bipartisanism with the presence, at the most, of an alliance between two political forces. Such models, and the resulting systems of relationship with journalistic information, have been, so to say, universalized; other public spheres have been forgotten or described using these as point of reference and also of judgement.

Indeed, when a public sphere of a different system is referred to, such as, for example, Italy, it is judged in terms of backwardness, blaming delays and malfunctions on the lack of journalistic professionalism, on the overall degeneration of the parties as a whole, on the historical distortions of the relations between the party system and the media in which the latter have always been considered greatly dependent on the former. Certainly all these are the ingredients of a partial and, in many ways, contingent interpretation which can only partly explain the peculiarities of this situation and the similarities and differences compared to the situation of other western-style democracies. The aim of this study is to describe the workings of the public sphere in Italy, with special reference to political communication, and place them in a theoretical frame of reference which defines the right parameters of comparison with other national situations.

More exactly, this study examines the workings of a public sphere in relation to a political system we shall call 'coalitional complex'. Let's begin with several definitions, first of all of the public sphere. With this term we refer to communicative exchanges and relations which focus on subjects of public interest, in which the institutions of political power and the institutions of mass media mainly, but not solely, interact[2] with each other.

In particular, in this chapter we shall examine political communication which is a predominant ambit of communication in the public sphere and defined on the basis of content (messages having politics as their subject matter) or the persons involved (when those issuing or receiving the messages are active mainly in the political system).[3]

Our analysis brings together the results of a rather vast body of empirical investigation carried out in Italy (Grossi 1984; Agostini, Fenati and Krol 1987) with theoretical methods of comparative investigation (Blumler and Gurevitch 1975, 1981, 1986). It seems necessary to begin with a description of several characteristics of the Italian political system that are assumed as *constants*, that is as parameters, which are relatively stable in time, for illustrating the workings of the public sphere in relation to them and for comparing different national situations. We shall also assume as constants the structures of the relationships between the political system and the mass media, according to the explanatory model suggested by Blumler and Gurevitch (1975), in order to have the first comparative instrument.

As for the method proposed by these authors, we note very briefly that in Italy, first of all, *strong state control of mass media exists* and is expressed, on one hand, in the state-owned television[4] and, on the other, in various forms of state-owned or economically supported press, even though in theory the press operates in a commercially competitive situation. The coexistence of public-service broadcasting and a commercial press is a characteristic of many European countries (Garnham 1986). *The degree of mass media partisanship is also strong*: the political parties, also in relation to the various forms of ownership and control exercised, have always been involved in editorial choices and the structure of mass media, thereby assuring their loyalty. *Equally strong is the degree of media–political elites integration*: actors in the two systems share values and a single symbolical universe; there is strong professional interchange and professionals in the political world have often come from the world of journalism, and those in politics, in many cases, have successfully established themselves in journalism. Several Italian authors, following Seymour-Ure, have spoken of 'political parallelism' between the mass media system and the political system: 'the substantial support that the mass media gives to the political system is expressed at different levels: organizational, economic, professional, thematic and ideologic' (Grossi and Mazzoleni 1984: 139). Last, *the absence of a consolidated and shared independent professional ethic* capable of assuring recognition and legitimation as a profession is the final characteristic of a system of relationships between media institutions and political institutions, a system which is complex and differentiated with regard to different mass media and also characterizes, in a special way, Italian society.

As to the extension of these last three comparative dimensions to other countries, analyses and specific data for the different situations are required. Nevertheless Renate Kocher has offered important insights into the various perceptions of the role of journalists in West Germany and England. In Germany they are characterized by a strongly social and political involvement and are referred to as 'missionaries', while in England they interpret a role defined exclusively in terms of news hunters and are labelled 'bloodhounds' (Kocher 1986).

Let's review now the constants of the political system. It should be stated that only a few of the variables in the system have been isolated here and they are the ones which most greatly influence the institutions of the media, at least according to the analytical perspective proposed here. The Italian political system can be defined as '*coalitional*'; this term refers both to the processes of forming government majorities as well as to the type of debate and exchange established between the majority and opposition.[5] Since the end of the Second World War, even though according to different formulas, the Italian political system has produced coalition governments formed and supported by several political parties. During the 1950s and early 1960s there were centre and centre-right governments and, later, centre-left governments, according to different formulas and compositions.[6] In all these years no party ever achieved a majority in Parliament which would have allowed it to govern alone. Even most of the local administrations were supported by coalition governments formed, in many cases, by parties opposed to each other in the central government.[7] Incidentally, it should be noted that the coalition formula is the main cause of the many government crises and therefore frequent changes in the make-up of the executive as a result of the undeniably difficult, forced coexistence of parties (five in the current formula) that compete with each other for the same electorate.[8] As for extending this description to other countries, we note that Israel, even though in a profoundly different political context, has now been governed for several years by a coalition of parties that are in strong, direct electoral competition; Germany too is governed by a coalition, albeit of only two parties. Many other cases (e.g. Greece, Norway, etc.) could also be mentioned.

But the term 'coalition' can also be applied to relationships between the majority and the opposition. As Marletti states: 'Political life in our country is not dominated by a clash and continuing contrast between the two major parties, the Christian Democrats and the Communists, but by a constant search for various points of encounter, mediation, and compromise' (Marletti 1987: 31). In most of the daily, routine legislative activities, the majority tries to involve also the vote of the Communist Party, at least to avoid a head-on confrontation which would make such activities more difficult, subject to continuous voting and the consequent risk of defeat and fall of the coalition formula.[9]

From what has been stated above, it is easy to understand that *the Italian political system is highly complex* because of the coalition formula used in forming its governments and especially because of the large number of political parties, currently eleven, represented in Parliament. In addition, within each party there are various and different factions competing with each other for the control of the party organization. To these can be added a generous array of other institutions legitimized to act within the public sphere, making the debate between the groups described above even more complicated. We refer in particular to trade unions, economic organizations, cultural organizations, etc. Among these numerous political groupings relations, alliances, overlapping representation and/or situations of preconceived and historical hostility exist which render the political system even more complex. Other countries, France, Spain, Greece and Portugal, to keep within the European sphere, have similar, highly complex political systems.

Another of the variables from which to begin analysing the role of political communication is the widely spread so-called *'affiliation' vote*. For those who cast it,

> it entails a relative departure from taking an objective position on a series of policy alternatives and instead casting their vote as a statement of subjective identification with a political force they believe to be integrally, and not just representively, identified with their own social group.
>
> (Parisi and Pasquino 1977: 224)

This affiliation is expressed not only during elections; it continuously characterizes relationships between most Italian citizens and the parties, and consequently determines the symbolical context within which political communication is developed in Italy. The messages issued by the political players within this context must take into account the importance of identification and therefore the need for confirming or invalidating, a need associated with the predominance of the affiliation vote. Some recent studies (Parisi 1980, Mancini 1984, Mannheimer and Sani 1987) have hypothesized a slow spreading of the opinion vote, but it is not yet capable of significantly affecting the predominance of the affiliation vote, and hence the electoral picture remains substantially static. The affiliation vote and its shift towards the opinion vote is a characteristic which is common to most Western European countries (France, Great Britain, etc.).

THE NEGOTIAL USE OF POLITICAL COMMUNICATION

In this situation, *political communication becomes the instrument for interaction among the players in the political system: by using it they can mediate their respective positions and reach or break agreements*. This use appears perfectly congenial to the complex coalition system which seems to require, as an indispensable ingredient for it to function, a place and the instruments through which to settle the differences of the various groups and reach the minimum threshold necessary for making policy decisions. This use also appears perfectly congenial to the relationships which are traditionally established between the political system and the media and which, as we have already said in part, place the latter in a position which may be defined as non-conflictual in relation to the political system.

We can now attempt to specify better what is meant by the negotial use of political communication and how such use is distributed. First of all, we can speak of two spheres of negotiation: in the first, political communication performs a function of intermediation between the majority and the opposition and, in the second, a function of intermediation between the factions of government coalitions. As regards the first sphere, Marletti speaks of informal formations of 'superparties' (also between the majority and the opposition), defined as

> transversal organizations of political interests . . . systems of alliances in which segments or groups of a party fight against other segments and groups in the same party and, in order to carry on this struggle effectively, they become associated in various ways, openly or covertly, with segments and groups in parties other than their own.
>
> (Marletti 1987: 40)

Again, more simply, as some studies have shown (Parisi and Pasquino 1984), much of the legislation in Italy is the fruit of a continuous process of intermediation between the majority and the opposition which almost always succeeds in avoiding the open opposition of the factions at vote taking. The process of negotiation, which leads to 'non-opposition', is carried out in institutional seats (Parliament, Parliamentary Committees, etc.) according to the formal and informal rules adopted by them. More often than not, the institutional seat involves 'non-publicity': this does not mean secrecy or non-access by the media, but rather the fact that this negotiation is based on personal or group exchanges and starts therefore from a framework consolidated by practices which are, because of their habitualness, either of little public importance, or must, in order to succeed, be non-official. However, the non-opposition, and therefore the process of non-public negotiation, is quite often the result of an initial public exchange of communications, such as statements, suggestions, etc., published in the newspapers or broadcast on television.

The public nature of the mediation among factions of the governing coalition is certainly more important. The mediation is first carried out outside the administrative seats, among the parties which must reach an agreement before negotiating later in the institutional seat of Parliament, with factions in the opposition. The traditional closeness with the media system assures this phase with publicity, in the 'Habermasian' sense of the term. This function also applies to the dynamics between the various components of the same party, each producing in different forms (statements, press releases, interviews, meetings, etc.) information picked up, commented on and amplified by the journalistic system. Thus a political communication is generated and initially promoted by the political parties and then circulated, amplified and publicly legitimized by the institutions of the media, because they, by privileging a communication produced by the parties, decree its *public relevance*. We shall return later to the concept of public relevance.

But what does the function of intermediation and therefore the negotial use of political communication mean? We can distinguish some of its aspects: first of all, it means *setting up channels of communication of public relevance* between the majority and the opposition, among the parties in government coalitions and among factions within the same party. The messages of political communication permit setting up circuits of communication endowed with public importance and therefore a certain 'officialness' between groups which in some cases, and particularly at certain times, may not have any. The type of public communication reported in newspapers and on television becomes a fact which cannot be ignored, one which cannot be denied without taking responsibility for the action. It is easy to give examples: all too often meetings, debates, events and statements are occasions for political forces to open or reopen dialogues which have never been held or had been interrupted. Through the channels of political communication political actors send messages and receive essential information from other political forces.

A second function performed by political communication is the *definition of issues* on which agreements must be reached: the speeches and statements by individual politicians or parties may often have as their main, and sometimes only, objective that of calling the attention of the public and other interlocutors in the political system to the subjects on which negotiations among political forces should be based. This manner of presenting the issues is typical of coalition governments, and the communication of proposals by one of the government's members creates the setting for constructing or destroying alliances. An example is given by the interview granted in February 1987 by the President of the Cabinet and Secretary of the Socialist Party, Bettino Craxi, during the television current affairs programme *Mixer*. In the interview the President refused to accept the principle of the so-called 'staffetta' (relay) which had constituted, even though informally, the basis for the agreement to the formation of his own government, and which provided that the Socialists after having the presidency of the Cabinet for three years would pass it to Christian Democrats. The interview set off a long and bitter fight with the Christian Democrat leader Ciriaco De Mita, who accused the Socialist Secretary of not respecting agreements, and ended with the fall of the Craxi government and early elections.[10]

Political communication also serves to publicize, specify and stress the phases and state of progress of a negotiation. There exists, as also occurs in the field of international relations, an informal ciphered code, generated by the politicians and used by the journalists, which serves to give an account of the phases of the negotiation and report them to those concerned. Public institutionalization of this process serves to define and redefine the party's position in relation to its adversaries and allies, to indicate what room is still open for manoeuvre and warn against rash steps. Every political decision, from the initial formation of the governing majority to important legislative proposals, is subject to publicity in which those involved play their cards under the public eye. A significant case is offered by the recent Convention of the

Christian Democrat Party in February 1989. The main problem that the Convention had to face was the so-called double office held by Ciriaco De Mita, who was both Secretary of the Party and Prime Minister of the Italian government at the same time. Until a few months before the Convention opened, Italian journalists were continually reporting statements, summaries of meetings and interviews with political leaders belonging to the different factions in the Christian Democrat Party, sending out messages to each other and trying to arrive at the Convention in agreement or at least in a position of strength on the main question, the election of the new Secretary.

The fourth intermediating function of political communication is *the defining of alliances and of the contractual power of the individuals participating in them*. Many messages have the objective of seeking new forms of collaboration and giving notice that new alliances or previous ones are being formed or broken. The contractual power of those involved is therefore changed as is their capacity to determine the final result of the negotiation. Again the Christian Democrat Convention of February 1989 provides an example taken from debates preceding it: Giulio Andreotti, historical leader of a large faction of the Christian Democrat Party, intervened at different times in negotiating the choice of the future Secretary with interviews released by *Sabato*, a periodical published by 'Comunione e Liberazione'.[11] This choice was not casual: he probably wanted to notify Christian Democrat leaders that he could count on the support of 'Comunione e Liberazione', which controls an important area of the Catholic world with numerous votes within the Party, and could therefore determine significantly the outcome of the coming Convention.

Finally, there is one last negotial function of political communication: *to launch messages to test the reactions of adversaries or allies*. Again the last Christian Democrat Convention offers significant cases: at the end of the Neapolitan Convention of the Party, journalists spoke about an agreement on the future Secretary of the Party between the retiring Secretary, De Mita, and Scotti, one of the leaders of the Christian Democrat Party in Naples. The news, which was almost certainly groundless, was launched by De Mita's entourage to test the reactions of the Party's opposing factions to a possible agreement between the two leaders.

This intense and articulate debate, usual in Italian political life, is carried out almost exclusively in the newspapers, magazines and on television. The media, therefore, provide the different political groups with places and occasions for communication and perform a function of intermediation. The complexity of the coalition system along with a complex party system entail a long process of continuous negotiation and renegotiation of agreements. Often there is no room for this process in institutional seats because the agreements precede access to these seats by the political forces involved. The mass media system, which works, as we have seen, according to principles, routines, professional models and linguistics not far from those applied in politics, offers instead an opportunity for the political process to be carried out, and indeed in a public arena which, in a certain way, states its importance, official nature and public relevance, also putting into effect mechanisms of sanction.

Here we touch on a rather important problem. Most members of the Italian press and television news services are not capable of representing issues independently nor are they equipped with the credibility or authority which are necessary for influencing citizens' attitudes and behaviour. There is, moreover, a different public opinion stimulated by what may be defined as an 'elite' press which has rapidly and effectively developed in recent years and exercises a not unimportant power of defining what is relevant for public debate and sanction: we refer to such papers as *La Repubblica*, *Il Giornale*, *Il Corriere della Sera*, *La Stampa*. In particular the first two, *La Repubblica* and *Il Giornale*, are 'opinion' dailies that in just a few years have become a new and significant factor in Italian political journalism. For them too, however, what has been stated above applies, as they are only partially equipped with the power to construct an independent agenda of public discussion, and, more often than not, are limited to reporting and commenting on proposals received almost completely from the political system. Nevertheless, these papers express judgements on political negotiations and are endowed with sufficient credibility and public legitimation not just to influence people's opinions, but essentially to define the agenda of the discussion among the political, cultural and business elite. In this sense the debate that takes place within the public sphere assures its actors and their proposals the public relevance that would otherwise be lacking with contacts outside the scrutiny of the journalistic system and that otherwise would not be congenial to the historical evolution of the relations of 'parallelism' that exist between the press and politics.

In Italy the mechanism of public 'sanctions' and 'judgement' is therefore assured regarding the proposals put forward and the statements released, and this only further institutionalizes the process we have described.

SOME EMPIRICAL INDICATORS

The picture given up to now has certain consequences involving structure, content and form that also represent the empirical data produced by numerous studies which have inspired our discussion (Grossi, Mancini and Mazzoleni 1985, Marletti 1985, Cheli, Mancini, Mazzoleni and Tinacci Mannelli 1989).

In Italian political and above all electoral communication, *political issues traditionally dominate over policy issues*. By the first we mean all the more specifically political questions such as alliances, coalitions, government formulas, etc., while policy issues include the concrete problems on which it is necessary to make political decisions: inflation, pollution, drugs, etc.[12] The 1983 and 1987 election campaign data fully confirmed this tendency: in 1983 newspaper coverage of the election campaign was strongly focused on political issues; on the other hand, party propaganda focused also on subjects related to policy issues as a result in particular of the pressure and provocation from private television networks, even if political issues were prevalent (Grossi, Mancini and Mazzoleni 1985). In the election campaign of 1987 the political issues accounted for 37.5 per cent of the subjects dealt with in broadcasts organized by public and private television with the participation of politicians and journalists, while policy issues accounted for 21.1 per cent[13] (Cheli, Mancini, Mazzoleni and Tinacci Mannelli 1989).

As we have said, the predominance of political issues characterizes all Italian political communication even though it is even more evident during elections when the main questions almost always concern the make-up of the future government coalition, and political messages focused on concrete questions and their proposed solutions seem inappropriate. Solutions will rather be the subject of mediation among the participants of the future coalition and it is therefore unnecessary to become involved in projects and proposals which would certainly be modified during long and fatiguing negotiation. This is a characteristic shared by all proportional electoral systems in which the vote determines the strength of party representation and not the nature of the electoral programmes. It is significant that insistence on political issues is not limited to those active in the political system; journalists, too, propose these issues as the main topics for discussion at press meetings, interviews, etc. Politicians and journalists alike act according to established practices within a common symbolical universe which is focused essentially on the themes that should be negotiated among the many and different individuals and groups who will then form the coalition.

Those who receive this political message are the same ones active in the political system or, as we say in Italy, those who move within the 'palazzo' ('palace', establishment). When the reporter writes his piece, he knows it will be addressed to another member of the establishment: the statement or press release his article is based on is produced by the original political party source so that it might arrive, be received and interpreted by someone who is almost always another player in the same coalition political system. Almost thirty years ago Enzo Forcella, an expert on mass media and today an editorialist for *La Repubblica*,[14] wrote an essay titled 'Fifteen-hundred readers', some lines of which are quoted here:

> a political journalist in our country can count on about fifteen-hundred readers: the ministers and undersecretaries (all), the members of Parliament (some), the party leaders, union leaders, high prelates and a few industrialists who want to show they are informed. The rest don't count, even if the paper sells three hundred to a thousand copies. First of all there's no certainty the ordinary readers read the front pages of the papers and in any case their influence is minimal. The entire system is organized around the relationship between political journalists and the group of privileged readers.
>
> (Forcella 1959: 451)

Thirty years later the number of readers has grown[15] but the attitude, morals and the approach to understanding the work and functions of journalism have not changed. As a rule, the main interlocutors of the political press are still the same actors in the political system: they are the *source* and *target* of journalism (Blumler and Gurevitch 1986) and they are also the *privileged recipients*, and this characterizes the relationship between the media and politics in Italy. This is confirmed not only by the low number of copies of newspapers sold every day, but also by the results of the research already cited on the television campaign for the 1987 elections. During appearances by politicians from all the parties, at which a journalist was almost always present as an interviewer, moderator, etc., discursive strategies of attack and defence were more common than 'sales' strategies.[16] While the latter are usually addressed to the electorate to whom programmes and ideas are proposed for voting and acceptance, the former are addressed primarily to the other political interlocutors one is confuting or defending oneself from. In the latter case, the debate, while carried out before a vast television audience, remains primarily within the dynamics, questions and practices of the party system. This in effect confirms that the 'palace' members are the sources, subjects and recipients of the political communication as well as the journalists' intervention.

But there is a further reason why the so-called 'sales' strategies are little used: if we refer to another of the theories proposed by Gurevitch and Blumler, it is not difficult to find in Italy the figure of the political *gladiator* who uses the media essentially for playing his cards before his adversaries, allies and potential friends. In fact Gurevitch and Blumler wrote:

> when the political parties control the means of communication, the role of the gladiator will be adopted more often by the political spokesman, and the role of editorial guide will be adopted by the media personnel; this will exert pressure on the public to adopt the role of party factionists.
>
> (Gurevitch and Blumler 1980: 244)

From this point of view, the Italian television viewer is certainly a factionist; the prevalence of affiliation voting means more often than not that the audience has already made its choice and in general all it wants is a political communication confirming its beliefs. The members of the audience wait for signs in which they can recognize themselves. Both politicians and journalists alike know how to address such a public which is already familiar with the linguistics of politics and only want their favourite to win a clear victory over the opponent. The viewers or readers who are familiar with the system of politics understand and even accept the negotial use of political communication, even though it will not include them among its privileged recipients. The public seems to know and accept that this is what the game of politics is about and will in any case feel strongly involved and close to a party even when the party excludes such subjects from the list of privileged interlocutors.

CONCLUSION AND FUTURE PERSPECTIVES

In the picture we have drawn, journalists perform an important role in the negotial use of political communication; they are not intermediaries between the 'palace' and the citizens, as stated in the traditional literature on journalism which we referred to at the beginning, but rather among the different members of the same 'palace'. It does not seem imprudent to state that the same role can be found in other national situations having the same variables as the Italian political system. I refer in particular to some European countries in which, even though their historical evolution has been different, some of the characteristics described can be found.[17] Here one defines space for a public sphere in which journalistic information is called upon to perform a function of intermediation essential for the functioning of the political system itself and for the life of the social elites to which it offers channels of publicly relevant communication. The journalists are not only collectors and disseminators of information, they also guarantee a forum for the public debate essential to the functioning of the social order (Garnham 1986). As already suggested many years ago by Seymour-Ure (1969), in the Italian political sphere the major function of political communication is to connect horizontally various elite groups rather than connect vertically the elite and citizens as stated in the classic handbooks of journalism.

This appears to be a stable picture in which some signs of change are related to the advent of the mass-media market system. The birth of private television networks, for example, has begun to change some of the constants of the relationship between the media and the political system; it has changed the degree of state control over mass communications, thus determining space for different journalistic functions.[18] So too, the birth of some independent newspapers and the resulting growth in this field of commercial competition has changed press information in that journalists are beginning to raise issues and set agendas and are assuming a role of intermediation no longer limited only to the negotial use of political communication but performed between the political system and the citizens.

But, as stated at the beginning, these are 'weak' signals which only partially change the picture of persistencies in the functioning of the public sphere. The recent Italian evolution demonstrates that it is not enough to omit one of the 'constants of relationship' between the media system and the party system (I refer to the end of the public television broadcasting monopoly, since it has only partially involved television news services) for there to be substantial change, if the other dimensions of the relationship between media and political institutions remain unchanged. For example, the degree of mass-media partisanship has not changed nor has the degree of media–political elite integration. But most important there is not yet empirical evidence concerning the possibility of different structures and functions in the public sphere in relation to a political system whose constants seem to determine and limit the field of possible variations. There is not, that is, any empirical evidence concerning the fact that even though the constants of relationship are completely revolutionized, no different public sphere and no different political communication are created in which the journalist absorbs those functions, indispensable for correct democratic development of an intermediate dialectical body confronting the political system. Lacking this, the entire political system appears 'blocked', making turnovers in government leadership more difficult and excluding any expressions capable of applying influence, independent of party expectations.

On the contrary, for the moment, the fall of the public broadcasting monopoly and the consolidating of competition between newspapers have only further complicated the public sphere. Some papers (*La Repubblica, Il Giornale*, etc.) have in fact overlapped their independent political issue-raising with the traditional, still in effect negotial use of political communication, thereby becoming active in perpetuating it.

I think that the subject developed up to this point demonstrates the complex nature of the problems between the media system and the political system which excludes the possibility of a single reading, showing, on the contrary, that it is essential to consider the subject of the public sphere as a field requiring study by scholars in different sciences, and in this regard the universalization of a single model would be wrong. At the same time this study does not yet offer answers to many questions. The concept of public relevance and how it differs from the processes of legitimation has still to be clarified, and it is probably within this problem that the role of the common reader, faced with methods and subjects of communication which do not consider him as the main recipient, can be explained, even if such methods and topics take into account his political beliefs.

The discussion which followed the presentation of this paper during the seminar on 'Journalism and the Public Sphere in the New Media Age' (Dubrovnik, 8–12 May 1989) helped me very much in writing the final draft. I therefore thank all those who took part in it. I am equally grateful to Jay Blumler and Michael Gurevitch who gave me important suggestions.

NOTES

1 By 'protected' I mean that the life and the functioning of these circuits of communication are assured by the organization of the political parties and their interpersonal networks.

2 This definition comes from a particular interpretation of Habermas's concept of public sphere.

3 In communication exchanges in the public sphere, not only political communication but also economic information, labour news, etc. are included.

4 As for journalistic information, the public monopoly has not been affected by the birth of commercial or privately owned television networks which are denied the right to broadcast live, a privilege essential to effective coverage of current events.

5 The same definition is used by Carlo Marletti who intends it to refer essentially to the dynamics established between majority and opposition (Marletti 1987). More precisely, political scientists distinguish between the majority electoral system, which permits defining the government make-up at the time of voting, and the proportional electoral system, which is the Italian one, which determines the distribution of party seats in Parliament and delegates to the parties the formation of alliances.

6 The centre and centre-right governments involved Christian Democrats, the Liberal Party, the Republican Party, plus other minor groups. In the centre-left governments the Socialist party also had a primary role. However, over the years, these formulas have not remained unchanged and have often seen the exclusion of one of the above parties and the inclusion of another. Significant in this regard were the short-lasting so-called 'national solidarity governments' which in addition to the support of the centre-left parties were backed by the Communists as well.

7 This is the case of the so-called 'left-wing administrations' governed by coalitions of the Communist and Socialist Parties which are, instead, proud adversaries at the national level.

8 The current government majority is sustained by the Christian Democrats, the Socialists, Republicans, Social Democrats and Liberals.

9 Many political scientists blame the proportional electoral system for

coalition governments and the complexity of the Italian political system.

10 The interview was interpreted by most journalists to be part of the Socialist leader's plan to break off the government alliance with the Christian Democrats since it would be advantageous for him to do so, as was borne out by the election results.

11 'Communione e Liberazione' is an organization of Catholic fundamentalists which has recently gained in power and is capable of monopolizing and guiding a good number of Christian Democrat votes.

12 These definitions are taken from Patterson (1980) who more exactly speaks of policy issues and campaign issues.

13 To the 37.5 per cent of the policy issues must be added 26.3 per cent of the campaign issues which cover all those subjects more strictly related to the election campaign, such as the reasons for dissolving Parliament ahead of time, the question of the 'relay' or alternating governments, etc.

14 *La Repubblica* is the most widely circulated daily in Italy.

15 In Italy, however, newspaper sales are still low. Sales have only recently exceeded 6 million copies a day.

16 For a definition of the different strategies of debate, see M. Martell (1983), *Political Campaign Debates*, New York: Longman.

17 Similar operations can be found also in the United States: such newspapers as the *New York Times* and the *Washington Post* carry out the important role of circulating information and debate among different political and cultural elites.

18 As already stated, this is only partially true because private networks may not broadcast information live in the national territory.

REFERENCES

Agostini, A., Fenati, B. and Krol, S. (eds) (1987) *Annali della riforma*, Turin: ERI.

Blumler, J. and Gurevitch, M. (1975) 'Towards a comparative framework for political communication research', in S. Chaffee (ed.), *Political Communication: Issues and Strategies for Research*, Beverly Hills: Sage.

Blumler, J. and Gurevitch, M. (1981) 'Politicians and the press: an essay on role relationship', in D. Nimmo and K. Sanders (eds), *Handbook of Political Communication*, Beverly Hills: Sage.

Blumler, J. and Gurevitch, M. (1986) 'Journalists' orientations to political institutions: the case of parliamentary broadcasting', in P. Golding, G. Murdock and P. Schlesinger (eds), *Communicating Politics*, New York: Holmes & Meier; Leicester: Leicester University Press.

Cheli, E., Mancini, P., Mazzoleni, G. and Tinacci Mannelli (1989) *Elezioni in TV: dalle Tribune alla Pubblicità*, Milan: Angeli.

Forcella, E. (1959) 'Millecinquecento lettori', *Tempo Presente*, no. 6, pp. 451–8.

Garnham, N. (1986) 'The media and the public sphere', in P. Golding,

G. Murdock and P. Schlesinger (eds), *Communicating Politics*, New York: Holmes & Meier; Leicester: Leicester University Press.

Grossi, G. (ed.) (1984) *La RAI sotto analisi*, Turin: ERI.

Grossi, G. and Mazzoleni, G. (1984) 'Per un'interpretazione del rapporto tra Parlamento e sistema informativo: analisi ed indicazione di ricerca', in Camera dei Deputati, *Informazione e Parlamento*, Rome: Camera dei Deputati – Ufficio Stampa e Pubblicazioni.

Grossi, G., Mancini, P. and Mazzoleni, G. (1985) *Giugno 1983: una campagna elettorale*, Turin: ERI.

Gurevitch, M. and Blumler, J. (1980) *I mezzi di comunicazione di massa e l'istituzione politiche: l'approccio sistemico*, Bari: De Donato.

Habermas, J. (1962) *Strukturwandel der Oeffenlichkeit*, Neuwied: Hermann Luchterhand.

Kocher, R. (1986) 'Bloodhounds or missionaries: role definitions of German and British journalists', *European Journal of Communication*, vol. 1, no. 1, pp. 43–65.

Lippman, W. (1965) *Public Opinion*, New York: Free Press.

Mancini, P. (1984) 'La prima volta degli spots politici', *Problemi dell'informazione*, no. 1, pp. 7–33.

Mannheimer, R. and Sani, G. (1987) *Il mercato elettorale*, Bologna: Il Mulino.

Marletti, C. (1985) *Prima e dopo*, Turin: ERI.

Marletti, C. (1987) 'Agenda politica e giornalismo di élite in Italia', *Problemi dell'informazione*, no. 1, pp. 23–45.

Parisi, A. (ed.) (1980) *Mobilità senza movimento*, Bologna: Il Mulino.

Parisi, A. and Pasquino, G. (1977) 'Relazioni partiti-elettori e tipi di voto', in A. Parisi and G. Pasquino (eds), *Continuità e mutamento elettorale in Italia*, Bologna: Il Mulino.

Parisi, A. and Pasquino, G. (1984) 'La centralità del Parlamento nel sistema istituzionale come causa ed effetto della sua rilevanza informativa', in Camera dei Deputati, *Informazione e Parlamento*, Rome: Camera dei Deputati – Ufficio Stampa e Pubblicazioni.

Patterson, T. (1980) *The Mass Media Elections: How Americans Choose Their President*, New York: Praeger.

Seymour-Ure, C. (1969) *The Press, Politics and the Public*, London: Methuen.

Siebert, F., Peterson, T. and Schramm, W. (1963) *Four Theories of the Press*, Urbana and Chicago: University of Illinois Press.

Chapter 7

Musical chairs? The three public spheres in Poland

Karol Jakubowicz

INTRODUCTION

Following Jürgen Habermas, Nicholas Garnham (1986) defines the public sphere as the network of media, educational, knowledge and opinion-forming institutions within civil society whose operation is conducive to the emergence of public opinion as a political power. Of those, the mass media are today perhaps the most powerful element of the public sphere. Peter Dahlgren (1987) makes the point that the components of the public sphere (including prominently the production of news, views and ideas in public circulation) derive from, mediate and serve to reproduce the existing social order. The more a society is integrated and united around the fundamental values of the existing social order, the more likely it is to have just one public sphere. The more divided it is, the greater the likelihood of the various groups within it creating institutions of will- and opinion-formation constituting different public spheres, taking fundamentally different stands on the legitimacy of the prevailing social order, and the desirability of its continued existence (cf. Negt and Kluge 1983; Downing 1984, 1988).

The moot question here is how large the group has to be and how extensive an institutional network with what social reach (or impact, which can be far greater, though more difficult to conceptualize and study) it has to generate for the purpose of opinion-formation and expression to be recognized as a full-fledged separate public sphere. Also, it can be assumed that apart from the question of the social order, ideas circulating within the different public spheres are likely to overlap to some extent. So, how much overlap can there be without the different public spheres merging into one? Our remarks can provide only some pointers in these respects.

The foregoing suggests one perspective of looking at the situation in the Polish public sphere and system of mass communication. Another, equally fruitful perspective can be derived from the debate on the relationship between the media and society in the process of social change. Rosengren (1981) distinguishes four types of possible relationships, depending on one's view of whether it is the media that influence society (i.e. are the first mover and mould change), or vice versa (media mirror change), or whether the influence is mutual, or there is no influence either way. With regard in particular to the political process Peterson, Jensen and Rivers (1966: 120) point out that the media usually serve to strengthen the status quo (i.e. mirror the social order), but can also be used to oppose (i.e. mould) it; which of the two tendencies is stronger depends on the degree of stability or instability in society. This would suggest that while out of Rosengren's four possibilities that of 'interdependence' captures the essence of the relationship best, it should be modified by recognition of the *non-equivalence* of the media and society in that relationship, with macrostructural social factors influencing the media's role. The following discussion should shed some light on this question.

And finally, it should contribute to an understanding of the linkages between the mass media and politics. Gurevitch and Blumler (1983) point out that the central issue in the relationship between media and political institutions revolves around the media's relative degree of autonomy and to what extent and by what means it is allowed to be constrained, fixing their position on the subordination–autonomy continuum and crucially affecting their role in society. This seems to reinforce the thesis of the non-equivalence of the media *vis-à-vis* the macrostructural social determinants. As we will see, this issue is central to any discussion of the Polish mass media.

SUBVERTING THE APPARATUS OF COGNITIVE CONTROL

The Stalinist model of social organization made no provision for the existence of a civil society or of a public sphere, especially one defined as a 'space for rational and universalistic politics distinct from both the economy and the state' (Garnham 1986: 30), or as a situation in which 'all voices [would] hav[e] equal access to a neutral public sphere, where their unfettered rational discourse would culminate in the articulation of popular will' (Dahlgren 1987: 25). The power structure sought to subsume and assimilate the totality of culture, i.e. by fixing the media's position firmly on the subordination pole of the continuum. They were quite literally supposed to serve as State Ideological Apparatuses. More specifically – as a means of attempting to maintain what might be called *cognitive control*. As Adam Michnik, a leading opposition thinker, has put it,

> The communists who arrived [in Poland] at the end of the war succeeded in imposing false solutions because they succeeded in imposing their language . . . *most of our society* lost its language.
>
> (Michnik 1981: 67; emphasis added)

In the sphere of social communication this resulted in a situation in which

> the rules of the political game, the grammar of political language are so constructed that they automatically reproduce and per-petuate th[e] party's domination . . . [it is a] language which ha[s] no grammatical rules for concept-formation separate from the activity of the communist party.
>
> (Bauman 1981: 51)

In general terms, the institutions of the public sphere were to serve the purpose of introducing into social circulation only information, views and ideas functional in terms of the goals pursued by the power structure (with others to be suppressed by other, non-ideological and non-media means). This endeavour was successful in the early fifties, but has been a failure ever since.

'All political systems generate principles derived from the tenets of their political cultures, for regulating the political role of the mass media' (Gurevitch and Blumler 1983: 282; cf. also Smith 1979, McQuail and Siune 1986). Application of these principles depends on a number of factors:

– on how great the need is for the media to perform a normative and integrating role in society (Alexander 1981);
– on the public definitions of the media (McQuail 1987) and functions assigned to them, including especially on whether their content bears directly on questions related to the social order;

– and on the social reach and impact of the particular media: the greater they are, the more rigorous regulation is likely to be.

In Poland, as elsewhere, this general rule has been applied in a selective fashion. Broadcasting has been regulated more strictly than the press. Moreover, the authorities have long been unable fully to regulate the political role of all the print media, with some evading governmental control altogether.

A time of strife, of political turmoil, conflicts and social upheavals, dissent, a sense of injustice and being discriminated against, the flare-up of discontent over a particular issue – all these, together with lack of freedom of speech and of the press, have the effect of radicalizing and politicizing groups and individuals. This prompts them either to become communicators in their own right, setting up media as close as possible to the autonomy pole of the continuum, or information seekers, eager to seek out media giving expression to their views and experience. This helps explain why the apparatus of 'cognitive control' has almost never been leak-proof in Poland.

HOW MANY PUBLIC SPHERES IN POLAND?

We believe that in addition to the *official* public sphere, Poland has had, since at least 1956,[1] a second, *alternative* one, connected to the Roman Catholic Church. In 1976, they were joined by an *opposition* public sphere, since 1980 connected chiefly, but by no means exclusively, to Solidarity. We confine our analysis here to their media aspects.

The *official public sphere* was not designed to serve an unfettered rational discourse culminating in the articulation of popular will. Nevertheless, with different factions and tendencies within the broadly understood power structure using different newspapers and radio and television programmes to voice their views, the media of that sphere *have* served as a forum of political and ideological debate. Interestingly, internal bulletins and periodicals published at times of crisis and power struggles by local party committees, testifying to the need for additional outlets for the expression of opinion, have been defined as 'alternative media' within the official public sphere (Pisarek 1982).

Poland has some fifty newspapers and periodicals (including one daily) published by the Roman Catholic Church or by Catholic organizations, with a total circulation of some 2 million copies (cf. Koźniewski 1987). Other churches and denominations also have their own periodicals, though on nothing like the scale of the Catholic press.

Newspapers and periodicals in this category have always been a major forum for voices from outside the system, which is why we regard them as part of the *alternative public sphere*. Many of them deal with a wide range of political, economic and social issues, providing a channel for the expression of dissident views on all matters of importance to the Polish people, and in many cases offering an outlet for former establishment journalists. For example, during the period of martial law, some 1,200 journalists from the official media who had been active Solidarity members, were purged in a political vetting process conducted in 1982. Some left journalism altogether, but many others moved to Church, underground or fringe periodicals. Also, some journalists from the alternative public sphere later made their mark in the Solidarity press.

Since 1976, Poland has also had an *opposition public sphere*, consisting, as far as its media are concerned, of underground periodicals and books. This public sphere came into the open during the Solidarity period in 1980–1, in the form of about 1,000 Solidarity periodicals (ranging from mass-circulation national and regional weeklies to factory and college bulletins). They

> sought to undermine the foundation of the government's claims to legitimacy, and to spread the view that the existing social and political system did not serve the attainment of goals and values [of the socialist system – K.J.] internalized and accepted by society. The blame for this was laid at the door of the political system and of the power elite, busy pursuing its own interests and feathering its own nest.
>
> (Łabędź 1988: 43)

Before the emergence of Solidarity and especially after its dissolution in 1982 (during the period of martial law), thousands of clandestine, underground periodicals (some ephemeral, others with great staying power) have appeared all over the country. It is estimated (cf. Szarzyński 1989) that since the introduction of martial law in December 1981, a total of 2,077 titles of underground periodicals of various description (from national and regional periodicals with a circulation of up to 50–80,000, to factory or even secondary school newspapers) have appeared in the country. At the beginning of 1989, a total of nearly 600 such periodicals were published in forty-six out of Poland's forty-nine provinces, by Solidarity or one or another underground organization active in the country (for a detailed examination of the Solidarity press, cf. Jakubowicz, forthcoming a).

As for books, it is estimated that since 1977 clandestine publishers have brought out some 4,500 books and pamphlets with a circulation of between 1,000 and 7,000 copies (or up to 10,000 copies in exceptional cases) each, which works out at one copy for every two adult Poles (cf. Szarzyński 1989). Since the introduction of martial law, some 500 underground publishing houses have released over 3,000 books (cf. also Gajewski 1988).

In trying to describe the media of the opposition public sphere, Piotr Szarzyński (1989, p. 1) wrote at the beginning of 1989:

> [They] are committed to fighting the Communists to a different degree. Some openly call for a confrontation 'here and now'; others publish works of fiction not directly connected to the political struggle. Some have adopted a clearly defined and comprehensive political programme; others rarely go beyond a blanket rejection of every aspect of contemporary reality and are interested mainly in 'socking it to the Commies'.

Thus, there were few basic differences between the alternative and opposition public spheres in general orientation and attitude. However, the former has been prevented by censorship, and probably by the policy of the Church itself (oriented as it is to long-term survival and expansion), from openly questioning the fundamental tenets of the system or advocating its overthrow. The latter has sought to draw up a blueprint for a new socio-political system for Poland. We believe that this is a difference not of degree but of kind.

The three public spheres could be represented as in Figure 1.

Figure 1 The three public spheres in Poland

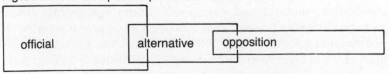

The audiences of the media forming part of the three public spheres are not mutually exclusive. Therefore the audiences of the three public spheres can be represented as in Figure 2.

Figure 2 The audiences of the different public spheres

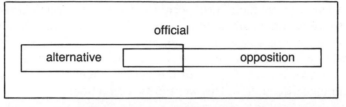

Both the alternative and opposition media can be said to have actually assumed that most of their readers would also follow the official media and to have concentrated on the kind of content which could not be found elsewhere. And so, for example, in 1980–1, items and articles on previously taboo historical issues took the second largest amount of space in Solidarity periodicals.

Of course, these are schematic representations. The other two public spheres do not begin to compare with the official one in terms of size and social reach, but nevertheless were and remain powerful instruments of opinion- and will-formation.

THE OLD POLITICAL SYSTEM COLLAPSES

An attempt to describe the choices facing Polish broadcasting and mass communication in general yielded the following forecast:

> Polish broadcast media may be said to have fallen behind the times. To catch up and satisfy predominant social expectations they would need to democratize, pluralize and decentralize. If any predictions can be made at all this is likely to happen in one of two situations: when the authorities become convinced that abolition of the broadcasting monopoly will not destabilize the social situation, or when the social costs of maintaining monopoly begin to outweigh the benefits – whichever comes sooner.
>
> (Jakubowicz and Jędrzejewski, 1988: 107)

Like most forecasts, it extrapolated the existing state of affairs into the future and in particular assumed the permanence of the country's political system, including especially the dominant role of 'the authorities', i.e. the country's power structure, and its ability to control the situation.

For a while, the forecast could be seen to be coming true. In 1988–9, the top political authorities sought to find a way to resolve Poland's internal conflict and dissent, and to head off the challenge to their own position which later came anyway. To this end, they embarked on a programme of reform designed expressly to encourage the emergence of a *civil society* and a *socialist parliamentary democracy* in the country. Obviously, this had to involve a redefinition of the public sphere and a change of communication policy. This went in two directions:

– loosening the power structure's grip on the media and allowing some opposition media openly and legally to compete with the official one for the attention of, and influence on, the population;

– reforming the official media so as to enable them to regain credibility and have at least a sporting chance in this competition.

As we will see below, these policies began to be put into effect. However, then the unimaginable happened. At a stroke, the whole political alignment became transformed and from a system of Communist Party hegemony Poland changed into a parliamentary democracy, with Solidarity as the senior partner in a new ruling coalition. This, however, did not so much invalidate the forecast as extend it much beyond its original compass: the social costs of maintaining not only broadcasting monopoly, but also the monopoly of power, had become unacceptable. Change was imperative and unavoidable – and it happened. At the time of writing, the new Solidarity-led government has yet to be appointed and only the first glimmers of change in the public sphere can be discerned. Below, we will look primarily at the situation as it has been so far, but will also try to divine the directions of change in the future.

THE OFFICIAL MODEL OF THE NEW PUBLIC SPHERE

New communication policy

This is summed up in a policy document published by the Party in May 1989. It said that freedom of speech coupled with respect for the law bolsters civil liberties. So, all forces active in the country's social and political life have 'an inalienable right' to the expression of their views and political standpoints, as well as to receive comprehensive, fair and objective information. Therefore they should be free to publish their own newspapers and periodicals and to have clearly defined access to what the document called 'the organizationally uniform state system of broadcasting'. As was stated in another official announcement, broadcasting was to 'perform general social functions in the nation with its considerable variety of views and standpoints' ('Konferencja prasowa . . .', 1989: 6) – meaning that it was meant to play an integrating, centripetal role in society.

This approach prefigured the outcome of the media debate during the round-table conference between the ruling coalition of political parties and other forces on the one hand, and the opposition on the other, in the spring of 1989. There, the government's monopoly of broadcasting and the party's near-monopoly control over the press came under heavy attack from all sides, including also parts of the political establishment.

The conference decided that the Press Law would be amended so that anyone, including a private individual, could start a newspaper without the need for a special licence. Accordingly, Solidarity is able to publish a growing number of its newspapers legally. Underground publishers and periodicals were invited to come in from the cold and operate legally. Censorship has been liberalized to a considerable extent.[2] Newsprint allocation will end in 1990, and newsprint will be available on the open market.

Even before the conference, the law had been changed so as to make possible the emergence of a licensed and supervised private and/or commercial sector in such areas as book publishing, film production and distribution, etc., and legal and technical conditions are being created for the inflow of new media content into the country (this concerns mainly video and satellite television).

So, in line with the principle formulated above, it is media with relatively limited social reach, including newspapers and periodicals (as well as satellite television, available, for financial reasons, only to very few viewers) which have been liberalized. The broadcast media are a different story, however. At the conference, the official side insisted on retaining both monopoly and unchanged institutional structures, while allowing a degree of access to airtime.[3] It saw broadcasting as the 'main lever' of building social consciousness and so was determined 'resolutely to defend [its] political cohesiveness' (Urban 1989).

Polish sociologist, Stanislaw Ossowski (1967) has distinguished three general types of social order:

– order of 'collective ideas', where social life is based on social customs and regulated by traditional behaviour patterns;
– polycentric order, where social life is based on interaction and is a result of non-coordinated actions by various decision-making centres, certain rules being common to all;
– monocentric order, where social life is regulated by centralized decision-making, with an institution supervising the observance of such decisions.

The new communication policy outlined above was clearly designed to counter what the authorities perceived as a threat that Poland's social system would become so polycentric (i.e. will represent what Karpiński (1985) calls 'atomized polycentrism') as to become unmanageable and uncontrollable. It sought, at a minimum, to use the broadcast media to define the rules common to all and extend the area covered by those rules as much as possible. The most that can potentially be achieved in this way would be combining the polycentric order with that of 'collective ideas' and thus creating *a polycentric order of centrally defined 'collective ideas'*. The Polish power structure seemed to hope that it would be possible to do just that, and in this way to preserve, or reintroduce, stability, and exercise a requisite degree of control over social life.

Stealing the opposition's thunder

The power elite also recognized that the emergence of a polycentric political system and the disappearance of practically all barriers to information flows required a new 'philosophy of propaganda'. According to one proposal, it should:

– remove the doctrinal shackles on propaganda;
– use objective information well combined with interpretation so as skilfully to suggest the desired attitude to the news;
– take a clear stand on each issue (adding up to a well-defined image of the social order for which the audience's support is sought), including engaging in open polemics with opposed views;
– clearly enunciate the political and ideological identity of one's own side;

– adapt the message to the audience, i.e. involve specialization and decentralization of the media;

– favour long-term consistency in propaganda instead of its erstwhile subordination to political expediency as well as short-term drives and campaigns;

– rely on the agenda-setting and -building and cultivation functions of the media, rather than on direct persuasion (Rosiecki 1989).

Old habits die hard, however, and so the most noticeable aspect of this new information policy is not so much the subtlety implied by this approach, but the lifting of the many politically motivated restrictions on what can be said in the official media. There are very few taboos left: everything (with very few exceptions) is fair game – and is criticized with relish.

It has been pointed out, however, that

[such] criticism may breed a sense of hopelessness and inure the readers to the abnormal situation surrounding them. In these circumstances, criticism of the crisis becomes a factor of its continuation, for either the absurdities being criticized are unavoidable, or they stem from the nature of the system itself, or finally there is no system of authority strong and intelligent enough to eliminate them – and in consequence the listener or reader concludes that he/she must learn to live with them.

(Szczepański 1987: 8)

In her perceptive study of *glasnost* in the Soviet Union and media liberalization in Poland, Jane Curry (1988) goes further and says that whatever the intent behind these policies, the messages that the populations of those countries actually 'hear' from media content include:

– *the propaganda of failure*: the economy is a disaster, workers are immoral and irresponsible, workers and their bosses are ineffective and besotted with social ills, managers and intellectuals are incompetent and corrupt, the system is inefficient and incapable of delivering on its promises, prospects for improvement are bleak.

– *the propaganda of power*: the system can do the unthinkable and its subjects are powerless to respond; individuals are ultimately powerless subjects of the system; however widespread the opposition, it cannot change or frighten the leadership; in short: 'We won, you lost, we control.'

– the propaganda of distance: mature communism with *glasnost* added is creating not a sense of involvement and mobilization but of so great a distance between rulers and ruled that politics has come to be based on the ascriptive stances and particularistic values of premodern and non-participant societies.

Also another aspect of the new information and propaganda policy of the official media is open to different interpretations. It is, of course, a sign of their new-found openness that:

– a special weekly radio programme composed of extracts from the programming of Polish-language services of Radio Free Europe, the Voice of America, the BBC, etc., was introduced some time ago;
– extensive use is made in Polish Television programming of footage from western satellite television channels reaching Poland, e.g. by arrangement with CNN or Sky Channel;
– opposition spokesmen are encouraged to appear on Polish Radio and Television.

However, this policy can also be read as serving the purpose of co-opting some aspects of the alternative and opposition public spheres and sources of information. And indeed, clandestine publishing houses, for example, are suffering now that official ones publish previously banned books (cf. 'Skreślanie z indeksu', 1989). However, much more is at stake here. The official Polish media clearly seek to copy the methods used by western media in imposing hegemony, whereby the 'definitions of reality' favourable to the power structure come to constitute the primary 'lived reality' for the the majority of society, in part because the power structure

> strive[s] and to a degree succeed[s] in *framing* all the competing definitions of reality *within [its] range*, bringing all the alternatives within [its] horizon of thought.
>
> (Hall 1983: 333)

This signifies a major change of strategy, from one of mind-management and full cognitive control to one of *limited cognitive control*. As we have said, previously the power structure sought to prevent the emergence of any genuine public sphere, or at least to preclude the position of the official media from being challenged. Now, bowing to the inevitable, it was prepared to give its own media much more latitude and let them move away from the subordination pole of the continuum, and recognize the existence of the other public spheres (with their own 'definitions of reality') wholly autonomous in relation to itself. It did, however, hope to be able successfully to pursue its new strategy, based on the 'all important insight that to be effective, hegemony in the public sphere need not be absolute, merely dominant' (Dahlgren 1989: 31). After all, despite access to many media outlets, most people still used the official media, and especially television, as their main source of news.

NEW INFORMATION ORDER

Defining the new order

'Observance of the constitutional principles of freedom of speech and publication' featured prominently on the list of demands addressed to the government by shipyard workers in Gdańsk in August 1980 during the strike which gave the first impetus for the birth of Solidarity. The agreement subsequently signed with the government called for the introduction of a new, liberalized law on censorship (which went into effect in 1981); it also laid down the principle that the media should express a diversity of views and standpoints, and should be accountable to the public.

Solidarity's First Congress in 1981 demanded the abolition of what it called the state administration's monopoly of broadcasting; announced that it would fight to win access to, and establish genuine social control over, the broadcast media, and announced that in addition to its own press it would also set up a wide array of other media outlets. It also supported the journalists' right to a say in the running of the media and initiated the process of drafting a new broadcasting law, which was interrupted by the introduction of martial law.

Thus began the effort, launched by Solidarity aided by the Association of Polish Journalists, to define the principles which should govern the new information order in the country.

The key concept here is *socialization*, meaning direct social control over the media operating in the interest of society. A second major concept is *access*, understood broadly enough to be almost equivalent to 'the right to communicate'. 'Social access to the media' is a widely used phrase, meaning that the media should be at the disposal of society for the purpose of free, untrammelled and pluralistic communication. Hence a determination to abolish all monopolies in this sphere. Thus, what used to be a system of top-down, unidirectional and univocal communication would become one of horizontal, participatory communication ('society talking to itself').

As can be seen, in terms of the communication democratization debate, these ideas are not really new ones, not even in Eastern European debates on democratization of communication (Jakubowicz 1987). However, they place special emphasis on one aspect of communication democratization which deserves special attention here.

Scannell (1989) speaks of 'communicative entitlements' which presuppose 'communicative rights' (the right to speak freely, for example). However, in the British system of representative democracy to which Scannell is referring, it is the role of the broadcasters, acting 'on behalf' of the public, to 'entitle' it to speak and serve as gatekeepers in the process. It is thus a system in which 'power accrues to the representatives, not to those whom they represent' (Scannell 1989: 163). In the sphere of broadcasting, exactly the same approach has been proposed by the power structure in Poland. As part of the new strategy outlined above, it was accepted that the broadcast media should serve as channels of 'bottom-up' communication; but it was the media themselves which were supposed to serve as 'spokesmen' for the masses and 'express' their views and feelings.

The ideologues of the new information order in Poland reject this approach. They see communication as *empowerment*, as the exercise of a right, and satisfaction of the need, to communicate by 'speaking with one's own voice', without the need for spokesmen and intermediaries. In general social terms, this approach springs from what might be called a *substantive* understanding of democratic communication as an element of 'communicative democracy', seen as an integral element of political democracy and an essential part of the process of democratic governance.[4]

In this approach, therefore, communication as empowerment strongly ties in with the notion of *subjectivity* in its philosophical, political and social sense (cf. Poprzeczko 1988) – itself an often used term (which denotes a right to mastery of one's own fate, to individual or group identity in the broadest meaning of the term, as well as to self-determination and self-government) to describe the goal of change being promoted by Solidarity. In view of the nature of Poland's political, social and economic system, working-class protest in August 1980 involved a very clear desire to reform the social system so as to make sure that society and its members would be in a position to perform their role as subjects. Hence Solidarity's goal of transforming Poland into a 'self-governing commonwealth'. Thus, in this approach communication as empowerment combines both respect for the right to communicate as a basic human right and a way of satisfying a fundamental human need, and a view of participatory communication as satisfying a fundamental *social* need, as a prerequisite of democracy and self-government.

Building the new order

Let us begin with broadcasting where progress has so far been slowest.

During the round-table conference, Solidarity submitted a three-stage plan for the socialization of broadcasting. In stage I, Solidarity editorial departments would be set up within Polish Radio and Polish Television, with guaranteed amounts of airtime at their disposal; right of reply (encompassing elements of the American Fairness Doctrine) would be observed in radio and television programming; representation of all the nation's major political and social forces in the governing bodies would be ensured. In stage II, one nationwide radio channel and one nationwide television channel would be turned over to social groups and forces and under new laws anyone could set up regional, local or community radio or television stations, cable systems, etc. In stage III, a National Broadcasting Council, a non-governmental body with a representation of all major political and social organizations, trade unions, associations, communities and minorities, would be invested with policy-making and supervisory powers over broadcasting.

As we have seen, these ideas came to naught. However, in July 1989 Solidarity demanded control over news and current affairs programmes on the second national television channel and a change in the composition of the Polish Broadcasting Authority, reflecting the division of seats in Parliament, as well as the transformation of broadcasting to a state-owned system, supervised by Parliament. In addition, Solidarity organizations in major cities are moving to establish their own radio stations. In June 1989 a 'Foundation for Social Communication' was set up in Kraków. It aims to operate its own radio and television stations, a telematics network covering Kraków, a publishing house specializing in books on broadcasting and informatics, a record company, etc., and also to set up professional training courses for broadcasters.

As for the print media, the barriers preventing change are partly administrative (the existence of a huge press and publishing concern controlled by the Polish United Workers' Party) and partly financial. To overcome the former, it is proposed, among other things, that the concern itself be changed into a holding, giving particular newspapers and periodicals much more independence; also that some papers should be separated from the concern and be published by a new house, with a board of directors composed of representatives of various forces, including the opposition. Leaders of the Association of Polish Journalists call on local communities and enterprising individuals to set up new newspapers, treating their establishment as a business proposition which can be sure to recoup the initial investment and make a profit.

Most importantly, however, the number of Solidarity newspapers is growing and many other new newspapers and periodicals approach social issues in quite a new way. The process is sure to gain momentum.

WHAT NOW?

If the situation caused by Solidarity's entry into government lasts, it will have far-reaching consequences for all aspects of the social order, if only by upsetting old divisions between the power structure and the establishment in general on the one hand and the opposition on the other.

This can set in train one of at least three processes:

1 If a national consensus on the shape of the new social order can be worked out and if that new order proves both durable and effective in meeting the nation's material and non-material needs, then the reasons for the existence of different public spheres will no longer apply. Audience research studies in Poland show that even now the broadcast media's credibility and appreciation indices soar whenever there is social peace,

stability and a relative sense of well-being. So, the opposition public sphere will wither away, or will be marginalized. The Church media will remain and even no doubt grow stronger, but they will not be voices from outside the system, and even less will they constantly challenge it. The media system will be pluralistic, also in political and ideological terms, but in the main will proceed from a fundamental acceptance of the social order which in turn will enable it to accommodate and accept that pluralism.

2 If the new order proves as divisive as the old one, then at least two public spheres – the official and the opposition one – will emerge out of the present process of change. However, this can hardly happen by way of a straight swap, with old opposition media becoming the new official ones and vice versa. For one thing, it is hardly likely that Solidarity newspapers or new radio and television stations will now become straight government media. However, the irony of the situation is that having been developed partly by former journalists from the establishment media, they will now themselves represent the new establishment, alongside, for example, the media controlled by the Polish United Workers' Party which, too, will be part of the new ruling coalition. For another thing, in addition to broadcasting (a government agency, but so far run by the party's Central Committee) and the Polish Press Agency, the Polish government has so far directly controlled just one (!) newspaper. A great majority of newspapers and periodicals are published by the above-mentioned publishing concern controlled by the party. So, the government's ability to develop a new official public sphere speaking directly for itself (assuming that it will want to do so) will be limited, at least at first. In addition, it is likely that new legislation will transform broadcasting into a public corporation accountable to Parliament and not to the government. Also the publishing concern may be broken up. Accordingly, new lines of division will appear in the media world, depending on how the political situation develops.

3 The new order may – for a time at least – enjoy popular support, but differences of opinion concerning the best ways of overcoming Poland's crisis will run so deep, and dissatisfaction with the government's – *any* government's – inability to end

it quickly will be so strong, that they will feed the continued existence of different public spheres. In that case, we may see the emergence of a dominant one, revolving around the existing social order, and strong subsidiary ones, speaking for various dissenting groups.

In any case, the Polish situation seems to confirm both the 'interdependence' model of society–media relationships and their non-equivalence in those relationships. What this means is that while the media *can* play an active role in promoting, accelerating or slowing down change, the impetus which decides what role they will play, and what processes they will promote, comes from outside the media system, and their effectiveness in moulding change is also decided largely by external factors. In line with the view advanced by Peterson, Jensen and Rivers (1966), as long as Poland's political system was relatively stable, the opposition public sphere was less of a threat to its continued existence. Its growing instability, ineffectiveness and all-encompassing chaos made them into a much more potent force.

The Polish situation also confirms that the political process is a major, and perhaps even *the* major macrostructural determinant of the media scene. The official public sphere was obviously shaped by political considerations and designed to serve primarily political goals. The motivations behind the establishment and growth of the opposition public sphere were also predominantly political. And it was the fundamental change in the country's political system that made Poland into such a laboratory for the study of the public spheres and the relationships among them.

One day, when society does become integrated and united around the fundamental values of the transformed, democratic and prosperous social order, Poland may end up having only one public sphere to speak of.

It will not be a moment too soon.

In a small way, this paper reflects the pace of change now sweeping Poland. It was originally written in the spring of 1989 and presented at the seminar on 'Journalism and the Public Sphere in the New Media Age', Dubrovnik, 8–12 May 1989 under the title 'A delicate balancing act: co-opting dissident public spheres and journalists in Poland'. Then, at the beginning of August, it had to be substantially revised and updated to be submitted for publication in Media, Culture and Society under the title 'Poland: a clash of public spheres'. Just a month later, Poland's political system was changed so radically that the entire frame of reference within which the

earlier two versions were written no longer obtained. Accordingly, it had
to be rewritten once again.

NOTES

1 However, there was underground publishing also in the years 1944–9
(a total of some 300 periodicals and several dozen pamphlets), when
there was still active opposition to the introduction of the communist
system in the country and prior to the imposition of the full Stalinist
regime which crushed all opposition and eliminated all opponents.
Under Nazi German occupation during the Second World War,
the various factions and organizations in the Resistance movement
brought out some 2,000 periodicals and 1,500 books. In territories
incorporated into the Soviet Union under the Molotov–Ribbentrop
pact, there appeared in the years 1939–41 and 1944–6 several
dozen periodicals and books published by the Polish underground
(Turnau 1989).
2 The government actually offered to abolish pre-publication censorship
altogether. However, the opposition had no choice but to reject this
idea, pending the eventual abolition of censorship. With prices of
newsprint rising sky high, confiscation of the entire press runs of
a couple of issues of any opposition newspaper as a result of post-
publication censorship would bankrupt such a newspaper and force it
to fold.
3 It was agreed at the round-table conference that during the campaign
before the June 1989 general election, all parties and movements
would receive regular time slots for the presentation of their candidates
(Solidarity received 23 per cent of airtime allotted for that purpose).
Once the election had been held, that form of access was stopped.
However, also in line with round-table agreements, journalists and
broadcasters representing the opposition have continued to broadcast
weekly programmes on radio and television (45 minutes in each case).
It was also stated that the same opportunity might be offered to
journalists and broadcasters representing other political, social, trade
union and denominational organizations. It may perhaps be significant
that the Roman Catholic Church was the first after Solidarity to win
regular access to (more) airtime several times a week on both national
radio and television (in addition to the holy mass already broadcast
on the radio every Sunday), and to two regional television services,
under an agreement signed with Polish Radio and Television in July
1989 (Dębecki 1989).
4 This conceptualization is developed more fully in Jakubowicz (forthcoming b).

REFERENCES

Alexander, J. C. (1981) 'The mass media in systemic, historical and
comparative perspective', pp. 17–52 in E. Katz and T. Szecskö

(eds), *Mass Media and Social Change*, London and Beverly Hills: Sage, pp. 17–52.

Bauman, Zymunt (1981) 'On the maturation of socialism', *Telos*, no. 47, pp. 48–54.

Bratkowski, S. (1989) 'SDP a środki komunikacji społecznej', *Most*, no. 21, pp. 135–40.

Curry, J. (1988) *Glasnost: Words Spoken and Words Heard*, prepared for the Kennan Institute, 'The Gorbachev Reform Program', 20–22 March, mimeo.

Dahlgren, P. (1987) 'Ideology and information in the public sphere', in J. D. Slack and F. Fejes (eds), *The Ideology of the Information Age*, Norwood, NJ: Ablex Publishing, pp. 24–46.

Debęcki, R. (1989) 'Pierwszy program już w sierpniu. Audycje religijne w radiu i TV – wypowiedź biskupa Adama Lepy', *Dziennik Bałtycki*, 17 July.

Downing, J. (1984) *Radical Media. The Political Experience of Alternative Communication*, South End Press.

Downing, J. (1988) 'The alternative public realm: the organization of the 1980s antinuclear press in West Germany and Britain', *Media, Culture and Society*, vol. 10, no. 2, pp. 163–82.

Gajewski, J. (1988) *Poza zasięgiem cenzury 1982–1986*, Kraków: Oficyna Literacka.

Garnham, N. (1986) 'The media and the public sphere', *InterMedia*, no. 1, pp. 28–33.

Geremek, B. (1989) 'W stronę gabinetu cieni', *Gazeta Wyborcza*, 27 July.

Gurevitch, M. and Blumler, J. G. (1983) 'Linkages between the mass media and politics: a model for the analysis of political communications systems', in J. Curran, M. Gurevitch and J. Woollacott (eds), *Mass Communication and Society*, London: Edward Arnold, pp. 270–90.

Hall, S. (1983) 'Culture, the media and the "ideological effect"', in J. Curran, M. Gurevitch and J. Woollacott (eds), *Mass Communication and Society*, London: Edward Arnold, pp. 315–48.

Jakubowicz, K. (1987) 'Democratizing communication in Eastern Europe', *InterMedia*, no. 3, pp. 34–9.

Jakubowicz, K. (forthcoming a) '"Solidarity" and media reform in Poland', *European Journal of Communication*.

Jakubowicz, K. (forthcoming b) 'Stuck in a groove, or why the 60s approach to communication democratization will no longer do', in S. Splichal and J. Wasko (eds), *Communication and Democracy*, Norwood, NJ: Ablex Publishing.

Jakubowicz, K. and Jędrzejewski, S. (1988) 'Polish broadcasting: The choices ahead', *European Journal of Communication*, no. 1.

Karpiński, J. (1985) 'Ossowski i Tocqueville. O rodzajach ładu społecznego', in E. Mokrzycki *et al.* (eds), *O społeczeństwie i teorii społecznej*, Warsaw: PWN, pp. 263–74.

'Konferencja prasowa rzecznika rzadu' [The government spokesman's press conference] (1989) *Rzeczpospolita*, no. 57.

Koźniewski, K. (1987) 'Przewodnik po prasie katolickiej', *Polityka*, nos 32, 34.

Łabędź, K. (1988) 'Prasa NSZZ "Solidarność" w latach (1980–1)', *Zeszyty Prasoznawcze*, no. 4, pp. 35–54.

McQuail, D. (1987) *Mass Communication Theory. An Introduction*, London, Beverly Hills, New Delhi: Sage.

McQuail, D. and Siune, K. (eds) (1986) *New Media Politics: Comparative Perspectives in Western Europe*, London, Beverly Hills, New Delhi: Sage.

Michnik, A. (1981) 'What we want to do and what we can do', *Telos*, no. 47, pp. 66–77.

Negt, O. and Kluge, A. (1983) 'The proletarian public sphere', in A. Mattelart *et al.* (eds), *Communication and Class Struggle*, vol. 2, *Liberation and Socialism*, New York, Bagnolet: International General, IMMRC, pp. 92–4.

Ossowski S. (1967) 'O osobliwościach nauk społecznych', in S. Ossowski, *Dzieła*, vol. IV, Warsaw: PWN, pp. 125–318.

Peterson, T., Jensen, J. M. and Rivers, W.R. (1966) *The Mass Media and Modern Society*, New York, Chicago, San Francisco, Toronto, London: Holt, Rinehart & Winston.

Pisarek, W. (1982) 'Raport o komunikacji społecznej w Polsce. Sierpień 1980 – grudzień 1981', *Zeszyty Prasoznawcze*, no. 3, pp. 17–28.

Poprzeczko, J. (1988) *Podmiotowość człowieka i społeczeństwa*, Warsaw: PWN.

Rosengren, K. E. (1981) 'Mass media and social change: some current approaches', in E. Katz and T. Szecskö (eds) *Mass Media and Social Change*, London, Beverly Hills: Sage, pp. 247–64.

Rosiecki, W. (1989) *Warunki wzrostu efektywności pracy propagandowej*, paper presented at the 3rd National Theoretical and Ideological Conference of the Polish United Workers' Party.

Scannell, P. (1989) 'Public service broadcasting and modern public life', *Media, Culture and Society*, vol. 11, no. 2, pp. 134–66.

'Skreślanie z indeksu' (1989) *Polityka*, no. 14.

Smith, A. (ed.) (1979) *Television and Political Life. Studies in Six European Countries*, London and Basingstoke: Macmillan.

Sparks, C. (1988) 'The popular press and political democracy', *Media, Culture and Society*, no. 2, pp. 209–24.

Szarzyński, P. (1989) 'Oficyny bez adresu', *Polityka*, no. 9.

Szczepański, J. (1987) 'Od diagnoz do działania', *Rada Narodowa*, no. 3 (special issue), pp. 3–9.

Turnau, S. (1989) 'Pięć lat bibuły', *Tygodnik Solidarność*, vol. 2, no. 13, p. 13.

Urban, J. (1989) 'Główne dźwignie świadomości', *Antena*, no. 19, pp. 1–2.

Williams, F. *et al.* (1985) 'Gratifications associated with new communication technologies', in K. E. Rosengren *et al.* (eds), *Media Gratifications Research. Current Perspectives*, Beverly Hills, London, New Delhi: Sage, pp. 241–55.

Zapotrzebowanie widzów na różnego rodzaju programy telewizyjne (1989) Warsaw: OBOP, mimeo.

Chapter 8

Discourses on politics: talking about public issues in the United States and Denmark

Ann N. Crigler and Klaus Bruhn Jensen

INTRODUCTION

Coping with the currently available amount of politically relevant information represents a major challenge for anybody conceiving of themselves as participants in national, much less international, political processes. Today, citizens who wish to exercise their political rights find themselves in a new and complex environment of communication. The new media age may imply a redefinition of the public sphere from the perspective of the audience.

The strategies by which people cope with this information environment have been studied using a number of different methodological and theoretical approaches. Several scholars have suggested that in-depth, qualitative approaches are particularly suited to examine the public's orientations towards and experience of political life (Graber 1984, Jensen 1986, Lane 1962, Morley 1980, Van Dijk 1988). For this article, we draw on recent empirical studies in two different cultural settings – the United States and Denmark – to propose a set of thematic conceptualizations which citizens employ to make sense of political issues. The emphasis is placed on a secondary analysis of the findings in each study with the aim of generating explanatory theory, which, in turn, may be used to design further comparative research. There are important differences as well as similarities between the two countries that are reflected in the themes which citizens use to discuss political topics. We suggest that a theoretical analysis which is grounded in the qualitative, empirical data (Glaser and Strauss 1967) establishes dimensions of politics that cut across cultures.

The analysis primarily seeks to accomplish two objectives.

First, we present a methodological argument for the relevance of qualitative approaches to political cognition; in-depth interviewing is the common methodology of the two studies. While in-depth work is a necessary complement to quantitative surveys, it is suggested below that current research based on schema theory, while relevant, tends to reduce the complexity of political understanding. For contrast, we point to the active role of political subjects in reconstructing and making sense of political information.

Second, in the discussion of findings, it is suggested that the characteristics of political information-processing in the two countries have implications for the definition of politics and of political participation and efficacy. The public's access to, use and understanding of information have traditionally been seen as constitutive elements of a public sphere. In comparing and contrasting the conceptualizations of political issues in the two settings, the discussion identifies differences between political cultures and considers changes for the organization of political communication in each country.

METHODOLOGIES

The American case

The American study was conducted in November 1987, and consisted of loosely structured, in-depth interviews about four political issues: the Strategic Defense Initiative (SDI), apartheid in South Africa, drug abuse and Acquired Immune Deficiency Syndrome (AIDS) (Crigler *et al.* 1988). Twenty-eight people participated in the interviews: eleven men and seventeen women. All were white and ranged in age from 18 to 75.

The interviews focused on the interviewee's general understanding of, opinions about, sources of information for and interest in the four issues. The oral interviews were conducted with the intention of 'empowering the respondent' (Mishler 1986). Each interviewer had six general questions to stimulate discussion and was instructed to probe and follow up on ideas mentioned by the interviewee. The interviewers sought to make the respondents feel as comfortable as possible by conducting the interviews in a living-room setting, by offering refreshments and by opening conversation on non-study related topics. The interviews, which lasted from one to two hours, were tape-recorded so that distracting note-taking was avoided. Upon completion, the interviews were transcribed to aid in the analysis. As the richness of this method lies, to a great extent, in the respondents' own words, the analysis entailed reading for themes that emerged from the data, rather than searching for predetermined categories. To ensure 'inter-reader' reliability in this method, two reading teams read each interview aloud, discussed the themes that arose within each interview and listened to the tapes for validation of the transcripts. This process was repeated for each interview, after which both teams compared results. The themes were virtually identical across the two teams.

The Danish case

The Danish study (Jensen 1987, 1988) explored the way in which television viewers reconstruct the meaning of political and other social information that is presented in news programming. The empirical material consists of one half-hour news program from the fall of 1985 and thirty-three in-depth individual interviews. The broadcast was selected randomly; the respondents represent a range of socio-demographic profiles.

The interviews were conducted in the respondents' homes on the day following the broadcast, focusing on its ten stories. In each case the respondent was asked to recount the content of the story, which was identified by the interviewer with a cue word; only then did the interviewer begin to ask for particular items of information given in the story. After verbatim transcripts had been prepared of all the interviews, as well as of the news program, a linguistic discourse analysis of all the transcripts was performed. While the analysis examined the characterization of political figures and institutions in news and interviews respectively, as well as their discursive structure, special attention was given to themes, that is, the unifying concepts which could be said to summarize each story from either the journalists' or the viewers' point of view.

In both studies, the themes that were employed by a substantial portion of the respondents were of a particularly general kind, being only remotely associated with the specific issues of politics as they are communicated in journalism. In sum, we identify a number of themes, which may be thought of as common denominators mediating between the discourse of politics and the discourses of everyday experience.

Themes of politics

In order to account for processes of political understanding, we elaborate the notion of themes as it applies to the two data sets. Themes are distinguished from the schemata and scripts of cognitive psychology, which have been the framework of some recent research in political communication (Graber 1988, Lau and Sears 1986, Van Dijk 1983). The schema approach tends to work from the top down, initially formulating hypotheses concerning general cognitive procedures or rules which are then applied to individual thinking through experimental or survey data. One underlying assumption is that schemata present subjects with hierarchical structures consisting of information that subjects tap to understand or act on the political world which they encounter. While not all types of schemata are sequential or stereotyped scripts (Abelson 1981), the theoretical assumption is that political cognition follows certain predefined patterns. This theoretical framework is analogous to the algorithmic model of a computer and fails to integrate or account for the affective, context-dependent and interest-driven nature of human understanding (Dreyfus 1979), particularly in an area such as politics.

In contrast, then, we take as our point of departure the specific understanding of politics which interviewees voice in an informal, conversational context, thus moving bottom-up from the data. Both studies worked from the assumption that political sense-making needs to be studied in terms which are grounded in the respondents' own discourses (Glaser and Strauss 1967). An important aspect of politics is people's conceptualization of events and issues about which they are regularly asked to hold 'opinions' and make voting decisions. We suggest that this is a complex process, which is influenced by background knowledge and political context as well as by particular strategies of understanding that may be more or less specific to individuals, social groups or cultures. Hence, we define theme as a translating mechanism used by individuals to make sense of public issues and events to which they are exposed, either through the mass media, interpersonal communication or direct experience. In discourse-analytical terms, themes are entailed by (follow from) and sum up the propositions employed by a respondent to characterize or discuss a particular political subject matter. Themes derive from various agents and processes of socialization, including mass communication. Thus, themes may serve to mediate between the discourse of politics and the discourses of other social forms of experience.

In establishing themes in the interview transcripts, the two studies employed different systematic, analytical procedures. While in the American study two groups of researchers discussed and compared emergent themes, the Danish study performed a linguistic discourse analysis of the interview transcripts. Moreover, one characteristic feature of the American sample was that themes were used by several respondents across several issues, whereas, in the Danish study, such a conceptualization across issues was not as manifest as the use of particular themes concerning particular news stories by several respondents. This may be due to the media-centered design of the Danish research, which emphasized the viewers' understanding of specific stories. And, this design may similarly explain why some Danish respondents recounted specific items while others relied more extensively on generalized themes. From a theoretical perspective, however, the interesting common feature of the samples is the nature of the themes, which are at once generalized yet concrete, practice-based concepts that appear to derive from everyday experience. It is this theoretical perspective which is explored further below.

Finally, we would like to emphasize that the findings do not represent a comparison of two political cultures in any empirical sense. The purpose of the chapter is rather a theoretical analysis and discussion of the explanatory categories which emerged in two different studies of political communication. Initially, one might expect to find few relevant similarities. There are fundamental differences between the political systems, ideological spectra, size and global roles of the United States and Denmark. In addition, the studies focused on current political issues generally (US) and on particular news stories (Denmark), and the purposes and disciplinary frameworks of the analyses were different. Nevertheless, we submit that the themes point to important structural as well as substantive similarities in the political understanding of the two samples. These findings, above all, suggest the need for more comparative studies of political conceptualization.

FINDINGS: FOUR TYPES OF THEMES

Powerful others

Talking about public issues provides an important context for people to see themselves in a social perspective, relating to what Mead (1934) described as the generalized other. The interviewees suggest that other social agents may not just be the source of role models and norms, but may often be thought of in terms of power or control over the individual. These are powerful others with some political role. Four sources of power or control are referred to in the interviews; frequently the individual's own lack of control is emphasized.

Government/state

The specific roles of government, or – in a European terminology – the state, may be understood in terms of either oneself or various political or social institutions being in control to varying degrees. In the Danish sample, the state is particularly conceived of as a rather distant yet powerful force, whether for better or for worse, regulating environmental protection, business practices, education and the economy. For example, in several stories the state comes across to the interviewees as a source of (creating) employment, and it is singled out for criticism because it (the National Bank) lays off people from coin production and moves the Royal Mint to West Germany:

> . . . it's terrible. They are closing down a place of work, you know, and moving because they want it to be cheaper, you know, and leaving a lot of people unemployed, and that seems crazy – that people who have been happy with their job for many years suddenly haven't got anything.
>
> (My translation, *passim*, K.B.J.)

In the American sample, a lack of personal control was expressed and often followed by mentions of others who could exercise some control or power. Government is one source of control having power over people: sometimes, it was personified in 'Ronald Reagan', other times it was seen as a more amorphous force, against which it would be difficult or impossible to fight. 'You can't fight city hall,' offered one woman. Another interviewee focused on Reagan and his power to place SDI on the national agenda:

> I think it's just an idea that Reagan has planned up in his head and I think he's gonna go ahead on it, and the public be damned, just like Bork . . . I don't think Reagan can accept a position from the American people, or anything. I think he's gotta have it. We're gonna have it, because he wants it. He's gonna ram it right down our throats.

Government as powerful other is not restricted to American government. When talking about apartheid in South Africa, one female respondent said:

> The government is really – (*pause*) I see it as a gigantic foot, just stepping on them and keeping them down.

God

In the American interviews, God was seen as quite powerful, especially with regard to AIDS. God was seen as punishing and correcting the evils of man. 'I think that the good Lord is doing this to stop all the living – the way people are living today,' said one 65-year-old man. A woman admitted, 'I think that, I hate to say this, but maybe God decided to bring it to scare people with their loose morals.' A young woman said that 'someone told me once that it's God's way of controlling the population. If they control AIDS, He's just going to throw something else out, so it's never going to end.' The Americans using this theme accepted the relative powerlessness of man especially in relationship to an omnipotent God. Although God and religion were not themes used to describe news stories in the Danish study, nature and the environment were seen as powerful, controlling agents.

Environment/nature

Whereas the environment is not an individual or institutional social agent, it emerged in the Danish sample as a major factor affecting people and their quality of life. The environment may thus be thought of as a powerful other in that it represents relatively fixed natural limits to social enterprise and existence. While the environment was certainly on the journalistic agenda in two stories about a recycling plant and about Danish environmental policy respectively, some respondents further introduced the theme when talking about a nuclear test by France at Mururoa and a story about east–west relations in general. Environmental pollution may be both related to and comparable with war in its implications. Moreover, some viewers talked at length about their own experience with shortages and recycling during the Second World War, thus pointing to the environmental theme as a relevant means of understanding several types of public issues.

Class

One noticeable feature of the Danish sample is a number of references to class as a powerful other. This occurs with reference to two stories about geographically and culturally distant events as well as in a feature item on a historical subject matter, which may suggest that class difference is a familiar aspect of experience that is mobilized to account for unfamiliar topics. Class difference is referred to, for example, as an explanation for a turn of events in El Salvador, where, among others, President Duarte's daughter who had been taken hostage by the guerilla resistance was exchanged for imprisoned guerillas. One interviewee had the following explanation for why this particular exchange came about: 'when it's people high up, things can always be arranged.' Thus, in the Danish sample, class may be one level in the conceptualization of politics and society. It is interesting, if not entirely unexpected, that this conceptualization is not as prevalent in the American sample.

Class as a powerful other was alluded to in the American case through the mention of wealthy people having more say in government:

> You can't fight city hall. You can't get at those, uh, the big money people. You cannot get at those big money people. This is something we all talk about – all these big issues, but, uh, when it comes right down to it, there's just a few that have a, a lotta say.

While the references to class are outweighed by the powerful others of government and God in the American sample, it would be most relevant for further comparative research to examine the specific conceptualizations of economic and political power structures in different national contexts.

Economics

In the American sample, economics was one of two themes that did not appear as separate conceptualizations in the Danish interviews; the other American theme addressed human impact in various respects.

Many interviewees in the American sample used an economic theme to discuss one or more of the issues. The economic theme was expressed in terms of costs, profits and in connection to the US or world economy. The American respondents often remarked on the economic utility of an issue: was it worth the money, would our money be better spent elsewhere? For example, one respondent noted the link between the cost of SDI and the current health of the US economy:

> Well, I think as a dollar and cents issue, it's sort of important. Because, if we don't spend the money on it, we have the resources to maybe reduce the national debt and allay the fears of future inflation.

Also when asked to comment on how the media portrayed the four issues, several respondents used an economic frame and suggested that the media's main concern was ratings and profits:

> I just think that they want to make a buck. You know? . . . So they want to get the mass population watching their show, which is what they have to do, in order to appease their sponsor, who pays a lot of money.

Not surprisingly, the Americans in this study did not talk about economics in terms of class difference or a conspiracy among the wealthy. Rather, they tended to focus on more particularistic and cost-benefit types of arguments.

Human impact

The human impact theme was used by American interviewees to discuss the issues in terms of the effects they have or do not have on people. This theme had a very strong affective component as it was marked by feelings of caring, worry, compassion or disregard for others.

The human impact theme can be divided into concern for people in three different spheres. The first includes the individual respondent as 'self'. The second sphere consists of societal groups to which the respondent belongs: family, friends, community, the United States and even the world. The third sphere is made up of groups to which the respondent does not belong, but with whom s/he can empathize. Often respondents would speak of two or three of these spheres to arrive at a coherent understanding of the four issues confronting them.

The human impact theme reflects primarily a personalization of issues: the interviewees tended to discuss the issues with reference to people. Sometimes, the human impact theme expressed a distance between the individual and the issue under consideration:

> But I can look at it as like, almost like I'm on another planet (*pause*) and I can look at it and say, well, almost draw a fence around myself and . . . isolate myself from these other problems that are going on like cocaine and AIDS . . . I don't equate myself with 10,000 people with AIDS, because I believe it's so far away from me and it will never touch in my life.

For the most part, however, the human impact theme reflected a caring and worrying for others:

> When David was dying from it, my friend saw him a month before he died. And he said, 'How are you feeling, David? How are things going?' He said, 'Great. Everything's going great.' You know, he's one of those . . . If he had said, 'Well, they gave me like 3 weeks to 2 months to live', you'd be like, 'Oh, my God.' You know what I mean. And people would feel bad for him. He didn't want that. He wanted people to treat him how they usually did, so he didn't say anything. And then when he died, it was kind of a surprise to everyone. But I feel worse for his mother, because David died and two weeks later his father died of a brain tumor. So that poor mother had to sit there and watch her husband and son die slowly (*pause*) another thing that I speak from experience in. It's not like I'm just reading out of a book, because I know someone who died of it.

While in the Danish sample the sorts of human impact referred to are rather specific, centering around unemployment, the Danish respondents also tend to discuss this in terms of an impact on individuals, and sometimes social groups, to which they belong or with whom they can empathize. As already mentioned, unemployment is linked with the intervention of the state, or lack thereof, but the economic mechanisms involved are not elaborated by the interviewees. Instead, also in a story about a recycling plant which had just opened, some of the Danish respondents focused strongly on the workers who were interviewed on the news, and who were happy about their new jobs in times of unemployment.

Center–periphery

In the case of international news, it appears that the different roles of Denmark and the United States in global politics may account for the respective conceptualizations of international issues in the two samples. In the American case, interviewees tend to understand the issues from center stage, aligning themselves with their country and positioning the United States in relation to other players of international politics, with whom the US is, furthermore, polarized. The us/them positioning of the United States versus other nations is most evident for the issue of SDI, and it is often expressed in a general discussion of the role of the US *vis-à-vis* other governments. There tends to be an unstated assumption that the US must play a central role in world affairs; the explicit conversation revolves around a questioning of that role. In some cases, American intervention into the internal affairs of other countries is addressed. One respondent wanted to see a decline in the role played by the US in supporting various leaders, referring to the Shah of Iran, Battista in Cuba, Franco in Spain: 'They're all gangsters. They're all dictators, and we protect them.' Other respondents were concerned with America's vulnerability and displayed mistrust not only of the Soviet Union, but also of some smaller foreign powers:

> I don't know what we're doing in Nicaragua, I don't know what that Iran-Contra was all about, it was such a mess. I think our own enemies are some of the smaller nations that, like Iran, Iraq, possibly some of the smaller than Russian countries that can bring in small nuclear weapons and small planes or something.

The Danish interviewees, on the other hand, repeatedly understand international conflicts as involving forces that are quite distant and sometimes unidentified. While war and other military action could affect them, interviewees may not align themselves with a particular party to a dispute, instead contrasting 'us' with a 'them' which includes, for example, both superpowers. Summarizing a story about east–west relations, an elderly man said:

> It had to do with their Star Wars and all their militarization, and that's something which comes up every day, so after a while one shunts it aside, it isn't something we are very involved in . . . it's high politics, so it really isn't something for us.

Collapsing different types of conflict, several Danish interviewees refer to east–west tension overall as well as more localized conflicts such as those in Argentina and El Salvador in similar terms, indicating a sense of distance from both types of conflict. In the understanding of a possible nuclear conflict, threatening their existence, the interviewees' sense of distance may turn into a sense of impotence: 'we can't do anything, you know, we'll be destroyed.'

DISCUSSION: DIMENSIONS OF POLITICS

Some of the observed differences in the two samples may be accounted for by cultural factors. As already suggested, individuals may understand political information with reference to powerful others, which range from religious to parliamentary-political agents. It appears plausible, for example, that the relatively more secularized nature of Danish culture would explain why religious aspects were not introduced by the Danish respondents, in contrast to the US sample. This is despite the fact that one news story took up undertakers and their business practices, which might reasonably bring to mind the religious aspects of death.

Moreover, there emerge some interesting conceptualizations of the political and economic spheres of society. While some Danish interviewees draw on the theme of class to make sense of a variety of news stories, the American respondents conceive of economic relations not in terms of class power or powerful others, but in more specific, monetary transaction terms. The role of government is also articulated in different ways. Whereas some American interviewees do refer to government when discussing their lack of personal control, government is only one of several powerful others. On the other hand, Danes tend to emphasize the responsibilities of government for the social and economic welfare of individuals. Moreover, the emphasis on individuals and personalization in the American human impact theme may certainly reflect the classical liberal tradition noted by so many political observers of the United States (De Tocqueville 1974, Hartz 1955, Huntington 1968), but further research is needed to explore this aspect of American culture. The attention to class and to human impact in the context of government unemployment policies is more characteristic of a Danish social democratic tradition. What seems to emerge is thus a cultural difference in the discursive construction of society, respectively highlighting market capitalism and the welfare state.

Finally, it appears that an awareness of the position of one's home country in the center–periphery structure of the world contributes to specific ways of discussing political information. It is plausible that whereas Danish television viewers observe most world events from the sidelines, Americans conceive of international events as involving the US as a central agent. This does not imply that Americans, when debating international issues, necessarily endorse particular positions or policies, but only that their taking of positions occurs within a culturally specific perspective. Thus, the Danish and American respondents begin to situate different international agents along a dimension of centrality or influence.

Several perspectives on political issues may thus underlie the specific variations in the themes. First, the interviewees' reconstruction of international issues highlights the relationship of center and periphery in world politics, implying differences of global perspective. While the perspective of the American sample on global politics is that of an interested party or agent, the Danish perspective is that of a marginal player in world affairs. This pattern, however, might be complicated in the eyes of these or other respondents if they were to consider the role of international alliances as well as of economic and technological co-operation. In further research, it will be particularly relevant to examine the conceptualization of developing nations as well as of the east–west relationship by individuals in different cultural contexts.

Second, the interviewees identify a perspective of power, a vertical relationship which places individuals in a systemic perspective and points to the authority or dominance of powerful others over individuals. The sources of power range from a ruling class to God, and do not constitute any pure or logical taxonomy. The common concern, however, is with the control exercised by powerful others; the individual is, from this perspective, primarily an object of control. This suggests one question for further research: what is the perceived scope for action by individuals within a social, natural and/or religious order as it currently exists? It would be of special relevance to examine further, in addition to the perceived relationship between different powerful others, whether respondents assign similar roles to themselves as compared to other individuals or social groups in those power relations.

Moreover, the theme of economics, as found in the American sample, calls for further exploration. On the one hand, it may be a way of seeing social issues generally in a monetary perspective, which is indicative of a concern with the allocation of monetary resources. On the other hand, this conceptualization may also imply an emphasis on enterprise and competition as structuring forces of society, thus de-emphasizing the power structures assumed under such concepts as class and state.

Third, the theme of human impact suggests that personalization may be an important strategy for understanding political information by placing social issues in a personal perspective. This may involve either looking for information that has ramifications for oneself or understanding information in terms of analogies from one's own experience, which may make some form of identification possible. It is a common assumption of psychological as well as literary research that much understanding either has the structure of or draws on narratives centered around individual characters, even though, as suggested in this chapter, the forms of understanding may be less determinate than has been assumed in some previous research.

Fourth, the interviews contain some suggestions that it may be relevant to explore a perspective of social distance in further research. People bring a sense of social belonging or identity to the understanding of political information, a sense of being a subject among other social subjects; exposure to political communication is one occasion for considering individuals in social perspective. One relevant question is how people conceive of their own position in the social structure when confronted with specific public issues. For an answer to this, we again point to further research.

While the conceptualization of politics in the two samples exhibits similarities as well as differences, it is important to bear in mind the overall differences between the two studies.

For example, in the Danish sample, the many references to the environment may be accounted for, in part, by two stories on pollution and recycling, even if the theme was generalized and applied to other stories. Similarly, the discussion of the state as a powerful other in the question of (un-)employment may be prompted by several interviews with workers during the program. In the American sample, the prevalence of human-impact and religious considerations may, in part, be due to the moral aspects of drug abuse, AIDS and, perhaps, apartheid. We suggest that the themes identified in each sample revolve around a set of shared perspectives, which are articulated in culturally specific forms in each sample.

Finally, it appears that the perspectives may intersect in the understanding of a particular issue or news story. A powerful other such as the state may be seen as responsible for unemployment, whose impact may, furthermore, be conceived in personalized terms. However, we do not suggest that the perspectives make up an integrated structure which might predict the understanding of a given issue. Indeed, both studies support the conclusion that people perform an active reconstruction of politics while drawing on a variety of themes. A better understanding of how this reconstruction takes place is important not just for the analysis of politics as an aspect of everyday life, but also for empowering people in contexts other than research.

CONCLUSION

Political information, as reconstructed by individuals and social groups, may become a resource for political debate and action. This is an important premise of the public sphere as an agent of representative democracy. In this light, the apparently widespread thematic understanding of politics may be a mixed blessing. Themes are certainly useful mechanisms for translating the discourse of politics into other discourses of human experience. However, unless the reverse translation process – from the experience of the human impact of, for example, particular economic policies or of class difference, into specific courses of political action – is promoted by the institutions and processes of political communication, the legitimacy of the political process is compromised. Perhaps this is most clear in the case of the news stories from Danish television, which pertain to concrete decisions being implemented, but the implications for political participation are of a general nature.

The public sphere should be conceived of, not just as a set of social institutions, but as a collective, communicative process through which people engage in political life. Citizenship must be enacted in social practice if it is not to remain an abstract, static bill of rights. The present studies suggest that research on political conceptualization and reception is necessary for the understanding of how and to what extent the public sphere works from the perspective of the individual citizen. Depending on the specific, social and cultural context, such studies can lead to debate about the conditions of political communication, and may imply changes in the journalist's presentation of political information, in civic education and the place of media literacy in the curriculum and ultimately in the institutions of legislative politics.

Research may support such deliberations in several respects, even if much of the effort of necessity remains concentrated on basic research. To develop a framework of explanatory theory, more comparative studies of a variety of political cultures are needed. Furthermore, variations in the thematic conceptualizations, especially according to gender and socio-economic status, should be examined in depth, and projects should be developed in order to study the stability of themes over time. A variety of sources of political socialization need to be considered to account for the development of thematic conceptualizations. The fictional genres of mass communication and the stories and jokes of interpersonal communication may have been under-researched as aspects of political communication and understanding. Also in these areas, qualitative methodologies will be an important complement and corrective to survey research in the attempt to explain how themes of political understanding relate to the formation of opinions and the exercise of political rights.

In conclusion, this comparative secondary analysis of political conceptualization in two nations allows us to see more readily the context in which individuals process political information. While several similar themes were used by interviewees in the two studies, the themes were articulated from different contextually bounded perspectives. The themes included: powerful others, economics, human impact and center–periphery relations. The perspectives of control/power, personalization, social distance, money and the global roles of the two countries framed the discourse on political issues differently in the US and Denmark. More focused comparative research on these perspectives of political conceptualization offers a promising avenue for a better understanding of how people make sense of politics.

REFERENCES

Abelson, R. (1981) 'Psychological status of the script concept', *American Psychologist*, vol. 36, no. 7. pp. 715–29.
Crigler, A., Just, M., Neuman, W. R., Campbell, D. and O'Connell, J. (1988) 'Understanding issues in the news', paper presented to the 1988 annual conference of the American Association for Public Opinion Research.
De Tocqueville, A. (1974) *Democracy in America*, New York: Schocken Books.
Dreyfus, H. (1979) *What Computers Can't Do*, 2nd edn, New York: Harper & Row.
Glaser, B. and Strauss, A. (1967) *The Discovery of Grounded Theory*, New York: Aldine.
Graber, D. (1988) *Processing the News*, 2nd edn, New York: Longman.
Hartz, L. (1955) *The Liberal Tradition in America*, New York: Harcourt, Brace & World.
Huntington, S. (1968) *Political Order in Changing Societies*, New Haven, Conn.: Yale University Press.
Jensen, K. B. (1986) *Making Sense of the News*, Aarhus, Denmark: Aarhus University Press.
Jensen, K. B. (1987) *Seernes TV-Avis* (The Viewers' TV News), Copenhagen: Danish Broadcasting Corporation.
Jensen, K. B. (1988) 'News as social resource: A qualitative empirical study of the reception of Danish television news', *European Journal of Communication*, vol. 3, no. 3, pp. 275–301.
Lane, R. (1962) *Political Ideology*, New York: Free Press.
Lau, R. and Sears, D. (eds) (1986) *Political Cognition: The 19th Annual Carnegie Symposium on Cognition*, Hillsdale, NJ: Lawrence Erlbaum.
Mead, G.H. (1934) *Mind, Self, and Society*, Chicago: University of Chicago Press.
Mishler, E. (1986) *Research Interviewing*, Cambridge, Mass.: Harvard University Press.
Morley, D. (1980) *The 'Nationwide' Audience*, London: British Film Institute.
Van Dijk, T. (1983) 'Discourse analysis: its development and application to the structure of news', *Journal of Communication*, vol. 33, no. 2, pp. 20–43.
Van Dijk, T. (1988) *News as Discourse*, Hillsdale, NJ: Lawrence Erlbaum.

Part III

Journalistic practices

Chapter 9

The global newsroom: convergences and diversities in the globalization of television news

Michael Gurevitch, Mark R. Levy and Itzhak Roeh

The ideal of the 'informed citizen' has always been regarded as central to the functioning of democracies. An informed citizenry is considered to be a prerequisite for full citizenship for at least two principles, central to a democratic system of government: first, because in a democracy, those who govern should at all times be held accountable to the governed; and second, because democracy is based on active participation by citizens in the social and political life of society. Clearly, both principles are predicated on citizens being informed about the activities of government and the affairs of society (for a recent discussion of the relations between communication and citizenship see, for example, Murdock and Golding 1989). It is because of this that the mass media, primarily in their 'information function', have been hailed, cliché-style, as 'the lifeblood of democracies', pivotal for the functioning of healthy and vibrant democratic systems.

While citizenship has traditionally been conceptualized in terms of membership in a given society, over the last few decades the concept has taken on a global dimension. The notion of 'global citizenship' received considerable impetus from post World War II attempts to structure a new world order, a vision powerfully expressed in the symbolism associated with the establishment of the United Nations Organization. 'Global citizenship' implied the possibility of a supranational, global identity. These aspirations were greatly enhanced, first by the visions, and eventually by the development, of new technologies of communication that held the promise, for the first time, of a truly global communication system. Instant global communication, it was felt, offered the possibility of the emergence of a 'global village' – a global community, in which all citizens had access to the same informational and cultural resources – the foundation of a global citizenship.

Like many other utopias, this one too foundered on the harsh realities of the post WWII world, riven by cultural differences and conflicts, political and ideological antagonisms and immense economic inequalities. The information and knowledge resources on which a global citizenship must be based – free speech and free access to information, the capacity to process, comprehend and 'negotiate' such information, a sense of having a stake in the global flow of information, of being fairly represented in it and of the relevance of that information to one's interests, concerns and aspirations – were never evenly distributed around the globe, either at the level of the production of that information, or at the level of consumption.

Nevertheless, the technological precondition for the emergence of a global community – the development of a communication technology capable of creating a global communication system – has, indeed, been fulfilled. For the past decade or so, a global communication system based on communication satellites has been in place (Wallis and Baran 1990). We may inquire, therefore, what implications flow from this global communication system for the development of a globally knowledgeable audience.

This chapter attempts an initial examination of that question, by focusing on one aspect of that global system, namely the convergences and diversities in news events and news stories broadcast by different television news organizations, who are participants in a cross-national news exchange system. Two aspects of these convergences and diversities are examined; the topics, or events covered, and the meanings given to these events, as conveyed in the stories broadcast in different countries. The contribution that a news exchange system might make toward creating shared perceptions of the world across national boundaries is then discussed.

'THE SKY IS FULL OF STUFF'

We begin with a familiar observation. Every day, hundreds of miles above the earth, images that become the substance of television news span time zones, continents and cultures; images of social unrest, of peaceful political change and of natural and man-made disasters; vignettes of human triumph, suffering and folly; pictures of an increasingly interconnected world. 'The sky is full of stuff,' says one American news executive. 'We just take it down from the satellites' (Small 1989: 27). As a result, viewers of television news around the world might see the same, or similar 'stuff' on their evening news programs. McLuhan's hyperbolic 'global village' appcars to have arrived, courtesy of a satellite-based global television news system.

But in what sense is television news becoming 'global'? True, viewers around the world may see the same, or similar pictures, and witness the same events, but are they told the same 'story', or do they indeed decode those stories in similar or diverse ways? Moreover, in what sense is the globalization of television news a truly new phenomenon, deserving our attentions in new ways?

Claims concerning the globalization of the news media are not, of course, new or even recent (see, for example, Schramm 1959 and Hachten 1987). The printing press crossed national and cultural boundaries long before television. The international news agencies have been in the business of disseminating news materials around the world for almost a century and a half (Boyd-Barrett 1980, Fenby 1986). Radio and films were oblivious to national boundaries almost since their inception. Yet the advent of satellite technology, facilitating the instant transmission of visual materials around the world, may be argued to have ushered in a qualitatively new stage in the glohalization of news.

On what grounds do we make this claim? Our reasons are two-pronged. First, we would argue that the institutional arrangements for transmitting and exchanging television news materials, spawned by the availability of satellite technology, have transformed the global structure of news dissemination around the world, toward a greater decentralization of the system. Second, we argue that the differences between the flexibility and degree of 'openness' (see, for example, Fiske 1987) of verbal vs. visual texts render the dissemination of visual materials qualitatively different from the 'old' system of news transmission by the wire agencies. Let us elaborate.

THE GLOBALIZATION OF TELEVISION NEWS

The globalization of television news is the product of the har-nessing, in the service of news production and dissemination, of the new technologies of recording and transmitting visual materials. The introduction of satellite technology into the global dissemination of television news has not only extended the reach and increased the speed with which visual news materials are transmitted around the globe, but has also spawned new institutional arrangements dedicated to the international dissemination of television news materials (Sherman and Ruby 1974, Kressley 1978, Fisher 1980, Eugster 1983, Lanispuro 1987).

At least three 'arms' of that system need to be identified here:

1   The international television news agencies Visnews and WTN (Worldwide Television News), outgrowths of the 'traditional' news agencies Reuters and UPITN, distribute television news materials around the clock to television news organizations around the world.
2   International satellite-delivered news services, such as the US-based CNN and the British-based *Super Channel* and *Sky News*, provide fully shaped television news programs via satellite to clients in Europe and around the world.
3   Systems of television news exchanges have been set up under the umbrellas of a number of regional broadcasting organizations, such as the European Broadcasting Union, the Asian Broadcasting Union, Arabsat and Intervision, based in the Soviet Union and Eastern Europe. The news services of these organizations are linked to each other as well as with the news organizations of the US television networks. The following discussion applies primarily to the news exchange system.

Collaboration between these organizations forms the basis of the global news exchange system. Through a constant flow of telex messages and daily telephone conferences between specially designated 'news co-ordinators' and news liaison personnel based in the broadcasting organizations in different countries, an ongoing exchange of information is maintained about the availability of, and interest in, visual materials of news events (Lantenac 1975, Lindmuller 1988). The news exchange services and agencies also provide the technical support arrangements for the electronic sharing of these news materials. The relatively small group of 'news co-ordinators' and liaison personnel perform a primarily 'gatekeeping' function, albeit on a global basis. Hence the metaphor of 'The Global Newsroom'.

These arrangements have important implications for the traditional argument about 'media imperialism' - i.e. the view, popularized in the late 1960s and early 1970s, according to which western media institutions and interests dominated the global media system, and served as the back door for the reintroduction of western economic and cultural influences into Third World countries (e.g. Tunstall 1977, UNESCO 1980).

Our impression, based on observations of the operations of the Eurovision News Exchange system conducted during 1987, and of the relationship between Eurovision and other regional news exchange organizations, is of a rather decentralized and mutually dependent system. During our observations, for example, we noticed a considerable degree of interaction between the European and the Asian systems, characterized, we thought, more by a peer relationship than dominance and subordination. Admittedly, our evidence is impressionistic, yet it seems that the era in which two or three global news agencies dominated the flow of world news from bases in London, Paris or New York is, perhaps, gradually being superseded by one in which Tokyo and Kuala Lumpur (the co-ordinating centers for Asiavision) play a role more on a par with the one played by the centers of the EBU news exchange system in the various European capitals.

CONVERGENCE, DIVERSITY, DEPENDENCE

The impact of the global newsroom can be studied in part by examining some of the patterns of story usage by the national services which participate in the Eurovision News Exchange. Among the appropriate questions to ask in this regard are:

1   Considering all the national services which air stories from EVN feeds, how much diversity and how much convergence do we find in patterns of usage across services?
2   Focusing on individual national services as the unit of analysis, how dependent is each service on the Eurovision News Exchange for its 'foreign' news footage?

The data reported here come from a content analysis of television news stories which aired during the main evening newscast of eighteen different television news services and from an examination of official EBU documents reporting story use for the thirty-six national broadcast services which are regular and associate members of the Eurovision News Exchange. Videotapes of eighteen different main evening bulletins were collected for a two-week period (weekdays only), 16–20 February and 15–19 June, 1987. Newscasts examined ranged from *ABC World News Tonight with Peter Jennings* to *Heute* on ZDF to the Arabic language broadcasts of Jordanian television.

A total of 2,569 different news stories were coded by trained graduate students at the Hebrew University of Jerusalem and the University of Maryland.[1] Coders were fluent in the language of the newscasts they coded. Each story was initially given a multi-word descriptor which told what the story was about. After preliminary coding, each story about the same persons/events was given the same, short 'name'. In addition, coders also recorded, among other things, the amount of time the story received and whether it could be classified as 'foreign' news from the perspective of the country on whose broadcast it aired (for a discussion of the problematic nature of classifying news as 'foreign' and 'domestic', see Levy and Barkin 1989).

We begin our analysis of diversity and convergence in usage patterns with Table 1, which reports on the extent to which the news stories transmitted on the Eurovision News Exchange actually appeared on any news program of the Eurovision member nations. Based on a day-by-day examination of EVN usage reports for June, it appears that the most heavily used story of any day was seen on a minimum of thirteen to a maximum of twenty national services.[2] Similarly, the second most heavily aired story of any given day during the sample week was used by anywhere from eleven to seventeen national services.

Table 9.1 Most frequently used EVN stories by day

Day	Story	No. of services airing
June 15	Korea unrest	19
	Italy vote	17
June 16	Reagan speech	20
	Korea unrest	15
	M. Rust flies into Red Square	15
June 17	Corsica terrorism	13
	Subway vigilante sentenced	11
	Korea unrest	11
June 18	Korea unrest	13
	Bardot auction	12
June 19	Korea clashes	19
	Spain bomb blast	19

For example, on 16 June, EVN footage of President Reagan's televised speech in which the President discussed a laundry list of items including the economic summit, tensions in the Persian Gulf, talks with the Soviet Union and the US budget deficit, appeared on newscasts of twenty national services. That multi-subject story was the most widely used EVN story of both the day and week.

By contrast, later in the week (18 June), only thirteen national services carried EVN-derived footage of student unrest in South Korea, but that was still the day's most commonly aired story from the Eurovision News Exchange.

While the most frequently used EVN stories tended to be hard, often-breaking news, occasionally soft or feature news is also widely aired. Several Eurovision news co-ordinators told us that stories about animals (pandas, whales and water-skiing squirrels) often received wide 'play'. Similarly, celebrity news too was sometimes widely used. On 18 June, for example, an item about an auction of film star Brigitte Bardot's personal effects was the second most widely used story, airing on eleven different national services.

Overall, the data in Table 1 demonstrates that for some 'big' stories of the day, there is substantial, but not complete, convergence of coverage across the thirty-six services we examined. Indeed, this less than complete convergence is further illustrated in Table 2, which shows that no story appeared on all thirty-six national services or even on twenty-one out of the thirty-six full and associate members of the Eurovision News Exchange.

Only one story during the June sample week (Reagan speech) was used by twenty national services, while three out of seven (42.7 per cent) of all stories transmitted on an EVN feed were used by four or fewer national services and 87.2 per cent of the week's EVN stories were not used by two-thirds of member services. However, every story transmitted was aired by at least one national broadcast service.

What is one to make of this pattern of convergence on the 'top' stories of the day, coupled with substantial diversity on any day's lesser news? First, it is clear that since television news is a picture-driven medium, the sheer availability of news footage undoubtedly makes it more likely that a story will be broadcast by any news service if it contains pictures. Thus, the existence of the global newsroom increases the likelihood that different news

Table 9.2 Percentage of EVN stories used on different numbers of national news services

National services	Percentage of EVN stories	
0	0.0	(0)
1	1.8	(2)
2	12.9	(14)
3	15.7	(17)
4	12.3	(13)
5	5.6	(6)
6	5.6	(6)
7	7.4	(8)
8	9.3	(10)
9	1.8	(2)
10	8.3	(9)
11	3.7	(4)
12	2.8	(3)
13	4.6	(5)
14	0.9	(1)
15	1.8	(2)
16	0.0	(0)
17	1.8	(2)
18	0.0	(0)
19	2.8	(3)
20	0.9	(1)
Total	100.0	(108)

programs in different countries will have the same or similar news.

Second, the convergence of coverage we observed also implies a measure of *shared professional culture*, a certain commonality in news values and news judgments, across all national services. At the same time, the diversity of judgments on lesser items also suggests that this sharing of news values is not complete and that national social and political differences, as well as differences in journalistic norms between nations, also play a part in shaping patterns of news coverage. Finally, these data point to considerable 'slack' in the influence of the Eurovision News Exchange on national news coverage. Viewed collectively, at least, the behavior of the national television news services does not appear to reflect a system in which Eurovision plays a strongly dominant role.

However, if one shifts the level of analysis away from collectivities or systems and focuses instead on individual national services, a significantly different picture emerges. Table 3 examines

Table 9.3 EVN dependency for selected main evening bulletins

National service	EVN dependency 1[a]	EVN dependency 2[b]
BRT (Belgium–French)	42.5%	88.3%
TVE (Spain)	16.3	51.9
ARD (Germany)	12.8	40.0
IBA (Israel–Hebrew)*	10.5	66.7
TF1 (France)	6.1	41.3

Notes: [a]EVN dependency 1: Number of EVN stories aired/Total number of stories aired.
[b]EVN dependency 2: Number of EVN stories aired/Total number of foreign stories aired.
*Data for the Israel Broadcasting Authority are based on only three days' reports, since the network was shut down for two days during the sample week by a strike.

the degree to which five national broadcast services depend on EVN materials for their main evening news bulletins. Data presented in the table were derived by comparing videotapes of those bulletins with videotapes of EVN feeds for the June week. The bulletins were chosen from a geographically diverse group of large and small countries.

The percentages reported in Table 3 represent two types of 'EVN Dependency': 'EVN Dependency 1', defined as the ratio of EVN-generated stories used in the main evening bulletin to the total number of stories appearing in the bulletin, and 'EVN Dependency 2', defined as the ratio of EVN-transmitted stories used in the bulletin to the total number of foreign news items aired. Thus, EVN Dependency 1 is a measure across the entire newshole, while EVN Dependency 2 assesses the impact of EVN materials for all foreign news coverage.

At the level of main evening bulletin there is considerable variation in EVN dependency by national broadcast service. The French-language service in Belgium, for example, depends on EVN materials for three-sevenths (42.5 per cent) of its total newshole and a very substantial 88.3 per cent of its foreign news coverage. By contrast, none of the remaining four main bulletins examined depended on EVN for more than one-sixth of their total stories, but all did depend on the Eurovision News Exchange for roughly half of their foreign reports, a significant degree of dependence.

THE PRODUCTION OF MEANINGS: VISUAL VS. VERBAL TEXTS

The second major theme of this chapter is based on assumptions about the relative 'openness' or closure of visual and verbal texts. By 'openness' we mean the extent to which these different kinds of texts constrain the meanings embedded in them or, alternatively, allow for multiple decodings of their meanings. Thus, it can be argued that verbal texts (e.g. news stories in the printed press) are relatively 'closed' (i.e. they constrain the range of interpretations or meanings of the events they report) since *any account of an event necessarily defines its meaning*. On the other hand, 'pure' visuals (i.e. visuals unaccompanied by a verbal caption or text) are relatively 'open', as they are susceptible to a wider range of interpretations or 'stories' based upon them. Let us illustrate with an anecdote (albeit perhaps not of a typical incident), related to us by a member of WTN's bureau in Tel Aviv. During an especially cold winter spell in Europe a few years ago, a cameraman on the bureau's staff suggested a story that could appeal to freezing European television viewers. He went to the Tel Aviv waterfront and shot some footage of bathers splashing in the sea (thus attempting to illustrate the different, milder climate). The footage was duly sent to WTN's headquarters in London, and from there was transmitted to WTN's clients. WTN's bureau chief in Tel Aviv, who regularly monitored the news on Jordanian Television, was surprised the following evening to see their footage on Jordan Television's news broadcast, used to illustrate a story about the decline of tourism to Israel. The pictures did, indeed, show a rather sparsely populated beach.

Intriguingly, the visuals exchanged through the Eurovision news exchange system are sent primarily in the form of 'raw materials', that is, unedited footage, including only 'natural sound'. The task of editing and shaping these materials into news stories remains in the hands of news editors in the different broadcasting organizations. Thus, while the same visual materials might be used by editors in different countries, the final shape of the stories they are telling, their narrative and thematic structures, and the meanings embedded in them remain in the hands of editors working with different national audiences in mind.

For students of television news this offers a very useful opportunity to compare the meanings in stories of the 'same' event, and thus to examine comparatively whether and how such diverse meanings are constructed. Indeed, we are thus provided with a 'live laboratory' in which to explore the process of television's 'construction of reality'. Such comparative analysis is especially important in an era characterized by increasing globalization of television news, for it offers an important antidote to 'naïve universalism' – that is, to the assumption that events reported in the news carry their own meanings, and that the meanings embedded in news stories produced in one country can therefore be generalized to news stories told in other societies.

Our basic assumption, then, is that different societies tell themselves – on television and elsewhere – different stories, coherent narratives that serve particular purposes, and that particular cultural settings would account for this diversity. Note that the diversity of the stories told, even about the 'same' events, is our point of *departure*, rather than a *'finding'*. It is precisely the richness of the spectrum of narrative variation that we find fascinating. It is through this diversity and variation that the question of the production of meaning can be best addressed.

COMMONALITIES AND DIFFERENCES

For the purposes of our comparative analysis we identified in the materials we gathered (two weeks of evening/nightly broadcasts from eighteen services in twelve countries) those stories which dealt with the 'same' event and were broadcast on eight or more of the television services studied, typically on the same day. Stories dealing with the 'same' event could be of two kinds: first, they could be stories reported by special correspondents of the different news organizations, using their own visuals, filmed by their own crews; or, second, they could be based on visual materials taken, in part or in whole, from the news exchange system. These stories may be narrated by a reporter or an anchor/newsreader in the studio or by a correspondent in the field. We shall discuss two examples, one for each kind: first, a scene-setting story about the elections in Ireland in 1987, as told by three correspondents, for the BBC, Belgian television (RTBF) and the American network CBS; then, the coverages of Gorbachev's speech at the 'Peace Conference' convened in Moscow in June 1987.

Before we proceed to discuss these examples, let us briefly present two themes that emerged from our analysis, that is, the ways we attempt to explain the commonalities and the differences in the stories. We labelled the first 'the domestication of the foreign', whereby we argue that 'foreign' news events are 'domesticated' and told in ways that render them more familiar, more comprehensible and more compatible for consumption by different national audiences. The second theme addresses 'the stability of narrative forms', that is, the ways in which accounts of news events are couched within the framework of 'stable' narratives, i.e. narratives that are already stored, as it were, in the collective memory of different societies and cultures.

Domesticating the foreign

One of the consequences of a highly developed news exchange system is the erosion of the 'traditional' priorities accorded by television news to 'domestic' and 'foreign' stories. Depending in part on the availability of 'dramatic' footage, news events of potentially global interest, e.g. a presidential election in the US, an earthquake in Armenia, a soccer tragedy in England or the rescue of three whales trapped underneath the Alaskan ice (Rose 1989), have become staples of television news services around the world. Thus, 'foreign' news stories are often accorded the airtime and prominence more commonly reserved to stories of domestic interest. In a picture-driven medium, the availability of dramatic pictures competes with, and often supersedes, other news considerations.

But the globalization of television news has not diminished the uniquely national character of news programs in different countries. In fact, one of the more salient impressions emerging from an examination of our materials has to do with the ways in which television news simultaneously maintains both global and culturally specific orientations. This is accomplished, first, by casting far-away events in frameworks that render these events comprehensible, appealing and 'relevant' to domestic audiences; and second, by constructing the meanings of these events in ways that are compatible with the culture and the 'dominant ideology' of the societies they serve. Thus, for example, US television coverage of recent events in Eastern Europe has been consistently couched in the terminology of the triumph of 'freedom' and 'democratization', thus conveying a sense of America's triumph in the cold war. (CBS's report from the Berlin Wall, showing pictures of East Berliners returning home from their shopping spree in West Berlin carrying colorful plastic bags filled with their purchases, prompted CBS's anchor, Dan Rather, to describe the returning shoppers as carrying 'the fruits of freedom'. 'Freedom' has thus become the 'freedom to shop'.)

But the significance of the 'domestication' argument goes further. It serves to counter uncritical assumptions about the globalization of the media. Indeed, the tendency to 'domesticate' news stories may be regarded as a *countervailing force to the pull of globalization*. Thus, the convergence of different news services on the 'same' set of stories should not necessarily be viewed as leading to a 'homogenization' of news around the world. Indeed, if the 'same' events are told in divergent ways, geared to the social and political frameworks and sensibilities of diverse domestic audiences, the 'threat' of homogenization might have little basis.

The stability of narrative forms

Our analysis is also located firmly in the perspective of news as story-telling. This approach borrows its concepts and strategies from literary criticism, and proposes that specific news stories should be examined as related, in the same way as documented historical facts and incidents, to one or another myth or super-story or cultural theme, as these appear in different cultures. The meaning of a concrete news story is always produced in the public space of culture, and in the framework of a relevant family-of-stories, already familiar to the members of a given society. Indeed, it can be argued that for an event to be judged 'newsworthy' it must be anchored in narrative frameworks that are already familiar to and recognizable by newsmen as well as by audiences situated in particular cultures. The events are then narrated in ways which invoke these familiar, stable frameworks, thus also contributing to the stability of that culture. Moreover, not all human stories are, or must be, culture specific. Indeed, many themes are universal. Let us illustrate. A recently published book describing television's coverage of the 'rescue' of the three whales trapped under the Alaskan ice attributes the global reach of the story to the proximity of the event to a satellite dish. But the universal appeal of the story may also be explained through its basic, universal theme, which could be defined as 'the plight of the innocent'. Perhaps that is why television news editors everywhere are so enamored of 'animal stories'. The universal appeal of these stories is immediately apparent.

TWO ILLUSTRATIONS

Let us turn now to our two examples. First, a story from Dublin. On 16 February 1987, the day before a general election in Ireland, 'scene setting' stories about the election were broadcast on the BBC, CBS, RTBF (Belgian television) and TF1 (French television). Unlike the raw materials disseminated through the news exchange system, these stories did not come from the same source. Rather, they were produced and narrated by the broadcasting organizations' own correspondents in Dublin. Nevertheless, there are interesting similarities – and differences – between the BBC's and CBS's stories on the one hand, and the Belgian and French stories on the other.

Both the BBC and the CBS stories focus on Ireland's economic problems, and more specifically on the high rate of unemployment among Irish youths. Both correspondents describe attempts by these young unemployed to secure a better economic future outside Ireland – primarily in the United States. The similarities between the stories are, in fact, quite remarkable. Apart from the correspondents' accents and the occasional phrase (e.g. the reference by CBS reporters to the 'Irish sport of hurling – which looks like hockey played like baseball on a football field') there are hardly any differences between the stories. For American viewers, however, the story may evoke memories of the 'potato famine', thus invoking a recognizable theme in American culture.

On the other hand, the stories on French and Belgian television 'domesticate' the story by focusing on the role of the Catholic Church in Irish politics. Images of multi-children families, and of young mothers pushing baby-strollers, serve as a background for a discussion of the resistance of the Church to contraception and abortion, and more generally, the political powers of the Church. The choice of that issue by the correspondent suggests an attempt to present the Irish election story in ways that would resonate among the viewers at home, who might be similarly preoccupied with the issue of the relationship between church and state.

TF1 (French television) also focuses on the religious aspect, but on a Catholicism that is 'different from ours'. The story exhibits an ambivalence toward the 'innocent' Irish, who are loved because of their wish to preserve their Catholicism, while paying a heavy price for it: youth unemployment and painful immigration, due to the restrictions on contraception and abortion. Amongst us, says the French reporter, even hard times do not result in immigration. The story implicitly contrasts the Irish and the French positions on limiting the size of families. Throughout, the story weaves pictures and text to produce a rhetorical contrast between the 'authenticity' of Irish society's preservation of traditional values (rural scenes; an old couple dressed in authentic village clothes, with an accordion playing in the background) and images of young unemployed struggling in a hopeless labor market.

The coverage of Gorbachev's speech at the 'Peace Conference' in Moscow raises different questions. Unlike the previous example, the visual materials here are either very similar or identical. By and large, the stories are narrated by the news organizations' own correspondents in Moscow, although some of the less affluent services are fully dependent on the news exchange for their visuals, and narrate the story from the studio, based, presumably, on wire services dispatches.

In spite of the near-identity of the visual materials, however, the event is presented differently to American and British audiences. This is not to say that the American and British versions are totally disparate. In fact quite the opposite. All the stories share the same five narrative elements: (1) the growing openness in Soviet society, as seen in Gorbachev's emphasis on human rights; (2) the presence of Andrei Sakharov in the audience; (3) the approval of Gorbachev by his celebrity audience; (4) Gorbachev's criticism of the arms race and the 'star wars' program; and (5) uncertainties about the release of the dissident Joseph Begun.

But while the choice of story elements may be 'global' (i.e. shared by all), the American and British news stories present different, culturally specific *themes*, using the same elements. This is reflected initially in the *order* in which the different elements appear in the stories, as is seen in Table 4.

The differences in the order of the elements in the American and the British stories indicate that the 'production of meaning' in the news is a complicated and multidimensional process, with no two agencies agreeing completely with each other. However, underlying the differential ordering is a considerable thematic unity

Table 9.4 Story elements by selected national news services

Elements	ABC	CBS	NBC	ITN	BBC
Gorbachev's efforts	1	1	2	1	2
Arms reduction	2	4	4	2	1
Begun's release	3	2	5	3	–
Sakharov's presence	4	5	1	4	3
Impressed participants	5	3	3	5	4

within the American stories on the one hand, and the British stories on the other. Let's turn to the American stories first.

There are a number of related themes running through the American coverage of the event. The dominant leitmotif is skepticism, both about Gorbachev's motives and intentions and about the significance of the 'Peace Conference' as a whole. This is represented in a number of ways. CBS's story begins with a tabloid-like pun, suggesting that Gorbachev is combining an 'arms offensive' with a 'charm offensive', and pointing out immediately that 'his latest move to be taken seriously and sincerely by the west may have been blunted by his own KGB secret police'. His deceit is implicit in that while he is all smiles, 'his' secret police continue their dirty work. Begun is introduced early as the foil to Gorbachev. Following Dan Rather's introduction, CBS's Moscow correspondent Wyatt Andrews prefaces Gorbachev's statement on nuclear arms with a warning that this is an 'unusual speech, full of flowery language . . . as if he wanted to convince the world that he means it when he says he wants no nuclear weapons'. The dubious character of the speech, already established by Rather, is thus restated by correspondent Andrews. After the clip showing Gorbachev's speech, Andrews makes the transition from the intent of the conference (the Gorbachev ruse) to its effectiveness (the suckers in the audience). Gorbachev, he tells us, was speaking to a 'collection of one thousand of the world's most influential writers, businessmen and scientists' and 'If Gorbachev was working on impressing them, he succeeded.' In fact, Rather had set up the function of this audience with his very first words: 'A star-studded group of international movers and shakers was in Moscow today.'

After the intent of the conference is made clear, its authenticity is further questioned by inserting the story about Joseph Begun's continued imprisonment. 'Mr Gorbachev's speech concludes a week of contradiction,' Andrews tells us. While there have been releases of political dissidents, Begun is still not free. The implicit conclusion is that things have improved but not improved enough. As Andrews concludes, 'Gorbachev seemed to be fighting hard for the respect and understanding of his powerful audience. In short, trying to earn from one thousand influential private citizens what he has not earned from the Reagan administration.'

Evidence that the CBS story is driven by shared American narrative frameworks can be seen in its commonalities with the NBC and ABC stories. Like the CBS story, NBC and ABC are skeptical of Gorbachev's motives. NBC calls the conference a 'master stroke' by Gorbachev, raising images of motives not quite straight. It orients the viewer to one more example of American perceptions of Gorbachev as a trickster/magician who continuously pulls new rabbits out of his hat. While it incorporates the Begun story towards the end, the NBC story is heavily skewed in its content towards coverage of Andrei Sakharov. This, of course, is not incidental. It ties in with the function that Sakharov plays in the narrative. Sakharov is introduced by NBC's Moscow correspondent Stan Bernard with a great deal of dramatic import: 'In the *grand* Kremlin palace, the *presence* of this man *startled*. Andrei Sakharov, the Soviet Union's most famous dissident.' Throughout the NBC story Sakharov gets as much airtime as Gorbachev. The unique qualities of the conference shift from Gorbachev to Sakharov in a subtle way. Gorbachev is seen as a consummate politician who made the conference possible, but Sakharov implicitly is the superior of the two. Sakharov becomes the symbol not only of Gorbachev's achievements but, by personal contrast, of the differences between the two. Clearly, Gorbachev is no Sakharov.

In addition to being a foil to Gorbachev, the focus on Sakharov is crucial in how it mediates the story. Like Begun, Sakharov functions as an instrument of the narrative's aim of distrusting Gorbachev's intentions. Both Sakharov and Begun play the same narrative function. They are thematically equivalent. They serve to invoke another staple of American narratives of the Soviet Union, namely, the representation of opposition to communism and to the Soviet government by a heroic and creative person, to whom is attributed the essentially American notion of the commitment to freedom and democracy. At an even more fundamental level it might be argued that Sakharov also represents the fundamental American empowerment of the individual, who single-handedly, heroically, fights oppression and big government.

The ABC story is briefer than the two other American stories, but thematically it echoed their concerns. Sakharov and Begun are presented midway through the narrative, immediately after Gorbachev has said his piece. The story ends by attesting that the 'public figures attending . . . were impressed by the new Soviet thinking, but there were skeptics'. The story does not make clear, however, who those skeptics were.

We turn now to the two British stories. Unlike their US counterparts, both British stories are essentially appreciative of Gorbachev's policies and of his leadership, and critical of the American response. According to ABC, Gorbachev 'renewed a plea for an end to the arms race'. In contrast, the BBC begins its story with the statement: 'Mr Gorbachev has accused the United States of making a secret move at the Geneva arms talks which, if true, breaks a promise made to both the American congress and the NATO alliance.' The reference to the scrapping of the ABM treaty is framed in bold, accusatory terms against the United States. In the American stories the ABM accusations were given little or no play.

The focus on America's role in the arms race serves as the lead-in for the two intertwined themes in the narrative of the British stories. Gorbachev's efforts – the dominant element in the story – are portrayed approvingly, in contrast to the skepticism and distrust in the American stories. The other theme – criticism of the Reagan administration – does not even feature in the American stories. The treatment of the issue of arms control and 'star wars' encapsulates both themes. In the BBC story, Gorbachev's initial accusation against the US is legitimated by a British general, present at the Moscow conference, who says that 'nuclear arms were no use as weapons'. The story also ends on Gorbachev's call for the need to dispose of all nuclear weapons. While the Soviet Union is 'willing to renounce its nuclear power status and reduce all other armaments to a bare essential', America's secret moves over the ABM treaty, and continued efforts on the 'star wars' project are seen as endangering the Soviet initiatives.

Throughout the narrative of the British stories Gorbachev appears to be the determinative presence. The role he plays is essentially a *creative one*, while in the American stories it is primarily *manipulative*. This is manifested, for example, in the lead sentence of the ITN story: 'Even by the standards Mr Gorbachev has himself set, this was a most extraordinary event', and in the characterization of the event:

> Five years ago, with Lenin's statue looking on, the idea of Leonid Brezhnev turning up for the same event as Gregory Peck, Kris Kristofferson and Andrei Sakharov would have been unthinkable. Yet that precisely is what Mikhail Gorbachev chose to do.

The American, and especially President Reagan's presence through the narratives is framed as passive, inept and retreatist. On the question of arms control, the Soviet proposals are met not only by continued American resistance but also by ignorance. Reagan's poor performance at Reykjavik is emphasized. The American negotiators are portrayed as clearly out of their depth in dealing with the magnitude of the Soviet proposals. The story goes on to illustrate the American incompetence in other examples of the performance of the US administration: disclosures about the Iran–Contra affair; the continued meddling of Nancy Reagan; Donald Regan's exposures, all add to the negative picture. The story winds up by saying that the only reason 'Reagan wants to talk to the Russians is to deflect attention from the Iran–Contra affair'. Gorbachev, however, has always wanted to talk and, in fact, in the whole superpower debate, he 'continues to make the running'.

The British stories also make different use of Begun and Sakharov. Sakharov's presentation in the stories is largely neutral and referential. He is not made the focus of the story. Both the ITN and BBC stories point out that he sat a few feet away from Gorbachev. This proximity emphasizes Sakharov's approval of Gorbachev, as in ITN's statement: 'the freed dissident, Andrei Sakharov, was there to applaud him.' Like Sakharov, the American actor Kris Kristofferson also represents an approving presence. His approval is seen as significant because, as ITN reminds its viewers, Kristofferson starred in 'what even America regards as the most vigorously anti-Soviet TV serial ever made', a serial (*Amerika*) that represents (like Reagan and the arms talks) the United States' continued reluctance to participate in the peace process.

European acceptance of Gorbachev's sincerity may not have come easily, but when it did it was reinforced by the long-standing irritation at the United States' apparent reluctance to budge from its cold war mentality. It is the framework of American–European relationships on the one hand, and European–Soviet relations on the other, that constitutes the narrative framework of the British stories.

CONCLUSION

What, then, are the implications of this analysis for the issue with which we began – namely, the contribution of the globalizing of television news to the emergence of a 'global citizenship'? At least two potentially major consequences of instant global communication could be hypothesized here. First, it seems plausible to assume that the opportunity afforded to television viewers around the world to become witnesses to major events in far-away places, often 'live', as these events unfold, is likely to have major shaping influences on the cognitive maps of the world that these viewers carry in their heads. While at this point in time we can only speculate what 'scratches' (Isaacs 1958) were left on the minds of viewers around the world as a result of the recent flood of images from, say, the Berlin Wall or from Wenceslas Square, it is tempting to hypothesize that these images, and some of their meanings, have become parts of a *shared* view of the world, and thus constitute a contribution to a *shared* global citizenship. Second, we should also consider the extent to which the eventual success or failure of large-scale social and political movements ought to be credited to the global publicity accorded to them by a global television news system. A revolution seen on 'live' television constitutes the global audience as participants, albeit distant and passive, in the social process unfolding on the screen, transforming it from a 'domestic' into a global event.

Whether or not these hypothesized consequences approximate 'real life' circumstances must, at this point, remain an open question. If anything, our analysis suggests a negative answer. Global events, we found, are shaped and reshaped by television news reporters and producers in ways that make them comprehensible and palatable for domestic audiences. Thus, while the images may have global currency, the meanings given to them may not necessarily be shared globally. Television news in different countries, feeding on an increasingly similar global diet, facilitated by a global system of distribution and exchange of news materials, still speak in many different voices. The Global Newsroom is still confronted by a Tower of Babel.

The research reported here is part of a larger investigation, 'The Global Newsroom' project, supported by the Smart Family Foundation Communications Institute of the Hebrew University, Jerusalem; the Center for Research in Public Communication of the University of Maryland; and the US–Israel Binational Science Foundation. The authors would like to acknowledge both Professor Akiba Cohen's original insight about the organization of international television news exchanges which led to this project, and his continuing, enthusiastic support for this study. We would also like to thank our research assistants Anandam Kavoori and John Cordes, coders and crunchers extraordinaires.

NOTES

1 No inter-coder reliability measures will be provided on the data reported here, because so many different coders, speaking so many different languages, and living in two geographically distant locations, were involved. However, given the nature of the coding scheme, we believe that the coding produced a highly reliable data-set.
2 From the official EBU usage reports, it is clear that coverage by the US networks, the BBC, ITN and occasionally other services of the biggest story of the day rarely included news tape provided by the Eurovision News Exchange. However, since the issue under discussion here is similarity of coverage, reports by these 'wealthier' national services on topics covered in EVN-fed stories are included in the totals presented.

REFERENCES

Boyd-Barrett, O. (1980) *The International News Agencies*, Beverly Hills: Sage.
Eugster, E. (1983) *Television Programming across National Boundaries: The EBU and OIRT Experience*, Dedham, Mass.: Artech House.
Fenby, J. (1986) *The International News Services*, New York: Shocken Books.
Fisher, H. (1980) *The EBU: Model for Regional Cooperation in Broadcasting*, Journalism Monographs 68.
Fiske, J. (1987) *Television Culture*, London and New York: Methuen.
Hachten, W. (1987) *The World News Prism*, 2nd edn, Ames, Iowa: Iowa State University Press.
Isaacs, H. (1958) *Scratches on Our Minds: American Images of China and India*, New York: Day.
Kressley, K. (1978) 'Eurovision: distributing costs and benefits in an international broadcasting union', *Journal of Broadcasting*, no. 22, pp. 179–83.

Lanispuro, Y. (1987) 'Asiavision news exchange', *Media Asia*, vol. 14, no. 1, pp. 46–52.

Lantenac, P. (1975) 'Live from the Eurovision newsroom in Geneva: a day like any other', *EBU Review: Programmes, Administration, Law*, vol. XXVI, no. 3, pp. 37–41.

Levy, M. and Barkin, S. (1989) 'Characteristics of foreign and domestic television news: selected findings', paper presented to the annual meeting of ICA, San Francisco, May.

Lindmuller, G. (1988) 'Eurovision news exchange', paper presented to the Television News Symposium, Hebrew University, Jerusalem, 16 June.

Murdock, G. and Golding, P. (1989) 'Information poverty and political inequality: citizenship in the age of privatized communication', *Journal of Communication*, vol. 39, no. 3.

Rose, Tom (1989) 'Freeing the whales: how the media created the world's greatest non-event', New York: Birch Lane Press.

Schramm, W. (1959) *One Day in the World's Press*, Stanford, Calif.: Stanford University Press.

Sherman, C. and Ruby, J. (1974) 'The Eurovision news exchange', *Journalism Quarterly*, vol. 51, no. 3, pp. 478–85.

Small, W. (1989) 'Network news: king of the mountain', *Washington Journalism Review*, no. 11 (May), pp. 26–8.

Tunstall, J. (1977) *The Media are American: Anglo-American Media in the World*, London: Constable.

UNESCO (1980) *Many Voices, One World*, Paris: UNESCO.

Wallis, R. and Baran, S. (1990) *The Known World of Broadcast News*, London and New York: Routledge.

Chapter 10

A tyranny of intimacy? Women, femininity and television news

Liesbet van Zoonen

In this chapter I shall explore feminist perspectives on journalism and the public sphere. A basic feminist requirement of news is that it should enable women (and men) to make sense of their own social and political circumstances in such a way that they feel empowered to criticize and change them. One might argue that news never enabled anyone, woman or man, to understand their own circumstances:

> How often does it occur that information provided to you on morning radio or television, or in the morning newspaper, causes you to alter your plans for the day, or to take some action you would not otherwise have taken, or provides insight into some problem you are required to solve?
>
> (Postman 1984: 68)

However, the customary feminist critique postulates that news has always been more alien to the socio-political concerns of most women than to those of most men. That critique is rapidly overtaken by changes in the subjects and styles of TV news, current affairs programmes and other forms of journalism, including among other things a growing attention to human interest subjects, an intimate and personal mode of address and the treatment of political behaviour and issues as though they are matters of personality. The label 'intimization' provides a convenient reference to these trends.

I hope to incite a reconsideration of feminist perspectives on journalism by analysing a seemingly marginal phenomenon: the predominance of women newsreaders in Dutch television news. Although their exact number may change with regularly occurring changes in personnel, women invariably occupy at least half of the anchor positions. This phenomenon fits in the context of a wider movement of women into various areas of journalism. For instance, recent figures about the composition of American newspaper staffs show that 35 per cent of the workforce is female. About half of the new workers are female (*Media Report to Women* 1989). A similar trend is said to occur in Britain (Sparks 1989). Can it be that women are conquering a once exclusively male domain? In the case of Dutch television news, women's increased visibility runs parallel with a conscious editorial policy to construct an informal and intimate relationship with the audience. Such intimization occurs in other countries and other areas of journalism as well. One might thus consider the female newsreader in the Netherlands, and the general increase of the number of women journalists, as no more than the embodiment of intimacy, signifying just another articulation of traditional femininity.

Feminism seems to have two options to evaluate recent developments in journalism. On the one hand one might contentedly conclude that journalism is no longer a male preserve, but on the other one might also claim more cynically that the increasing access of women to the profession is part and parcel of the intimization that seems to permeate most news. I shall elaborate these two positions in the following paragraphs and conclude that both are caught in the dead end of the 'sameness–difference' dilemma of feminist theory, (too) simply put as 'should women become the same as men and thus equal, or can women be different from men but still be equal?' I then go on to argue that the 'sameness–difference' dilemma is an inextricable product of the bourgeois concept of the public sphere which dominates contemporary evaluations of journalism in western democracies. The concept can be of no avail to a feminist perspective on journalism since it is philosophically and historically rooted in universalist concepts of gendered human nature and society, resulting in the restraints of a male public sphere and a female private sphere. In the final part of the chapter I suggest a more particularist feminist approach, which uses as a starting-point the way gendered audiences make sense of the news.

CONQUERING A MALE DOMAIN

Feminist approaches to the news have been relatively straightforward. Criticism centres not so much on how women are presented as on how they are not present at all. According to a global research review by Gallagher, in not one country does the number of women appearing in news coverage exceed 20 per cent (Gallagher 1980). The few times women are included, they mainly appear in human interest stories, in a domestic setting or to give emotional eye-witness accounts. A more recent study carried out in the EC countries by Thoveron (1986) observes some progress in that women are being shown more often in more significant roles, but concludes that among the journalists appearing on the screen there still is a severe under-representation of women. The role of newsreader is most common for women journalists: 28 per cent of the newsreaders were found to be women.

Women's exclusion from the news is often conceived as a result of their marginal participation in the public sphere in general. In such arguments the concept of the public sphere contains all non-private and non-domestic activities people might engage in, and is not limited to spaces and occasions in which people enact their political role as citizens. Thoveron (1986: 293), for instance, assumes that the people running TV channels 'cannot be held responsible for women's low profile in the political, industrial and economic world. Their programmes are a mere reflection of the actual situation.'

Others, however, argue that the male dominance among reporters results in news which reflects a male view of reality, leaving little room for feminist and women's achievements, or consigning topics and approaches that traditionally belong to the realm of women to special niches in the news, like human interest and lifestyle time slots.

No matter how one explains the exclusion of women from the news, there seems to be consensus about the fact that their professional and symbolic under-representation reconstructs the present division between a public male world and a private female world.

> The lack of coverage of women and the placement of what coverage there is has a clear potential to affect the news audience. Beyond the obvious effect that the audience will remain uninformed about women and women's issues, the implicit symbolic messages contained in the coverage largely serve to reinforce cultural stereotypes about the insignificance of women and their 'proper place'.
>
> (Pingree and Hawkins 1978)

Therefore feminists have argued for an increased number of female journalists as well as an increase in news items featuring women (cf. Gallagher 1984). One of the rationales behind such recommendations is the idea that 'as more women in television news succeed in positions of responsibility and high visibility, the way is paved for those who seek acceptance in traditionally male domains' (Gelfman 1976: preface). Others add that an increase in the number of women journalists would result in more balanced and less sex-stereotypical news (Butler and Paisley 1980).

Dutch television news presents an interesting test case for such beliefs. In 1965 the first woman newsreader of the 'Journaal', as the Dutch news bulletin is familiarly known, made her appearance. In the 1970s about one-third of the presentation teams consisted of women, but it wasn't until recently that anchor-women acquired a central role in the news. At the moment news bulletins are broadcast five times an evening and presented by seven alternating newsreaders. Five of them are female.[1]

At face value this dominance of anchor-women in Dutch television news can be said to mark an uncommon and positive development. Those newsreaders provide female audiences with positive sociological role models, quite rare in other programme types:

> Combining the tools of a journalist with the power of the television medium the on-air newswoman knows herself to be a role model for others. Positive role models for women remain remarkably rare in television, a medium that generally creates and reinforces the classification of the female sex as secondary.
> (Gelfman 1976: 168)

There is an equally important symbolic value to the appearance of women newsreaders. Paradoxically, the perceived objectivity of the news and its social status depend for a great deal on the perception of a presenter's personal reliability, credibility and authority. The suggestion that the presenters speak the 'objective discourse of truth' is supported by their discursive central location, materialized in their position behind the central desk in the news studio (cf. Fiske 1988: 288–9). The personality thus constructed embodies the viewers' need for a person who knows everything and who will explain the confusing and often unsafe world to them. 'This all-seeing, all-knowing, god-like person is, of course, male

and white. White women, and men and women of another race
. . . are left to the margins of the morning and the nightly news'
(Morse 1986: 64). In the Netherlands, however, for the greater
part our guides in experiencing the threatening modern world are
women. One is tempted to conclude that the appearance of female
newsreaders in the Dutch Journaal indicates that power, authority
and expertise are no longer features exclusively reserved for men;
it seems to indicate that 'woman' no longer automatically signifies
sexuality, submissiveness, domesticity and other usual forms of
televisual femininity. The high number of anchor-women in Dutch
television news might tell audiences that the public sphere, of which
the news is a constituent part, is no longer a male preserve, but an
appropriate place for women to reside too.

The Dutch case is not that simple, however. In the context of
recent changes in Dutch television news, the dominance of women
newsreaders presents another scenario. The increased number
of female newsreaders runs parallel with an 'intimization' of the
Journaal, among other things recognizable in its modes of address.
I will describe those changes below and argue that the dominance
of women newsreaders can also be seen as yet another articulation
of traditional femininity.

THE INTIMIZATION OF DUTCH TELEVISION NEWS

Dutch television news has undergone numerous changes since it
was first broadcast in 1956. The first bulletin looked more or
less like the newsreels shown in movie theatres. It went on air
only three times a week at 8 p.m. Due to technical limitations
and personal preferences the focus was on human interest stories
and ritual functions of news, labelled as 'story journalism' by
Schudson (1978). Newsreaders appeared infrequently in that
period, usually only by necessity when images to visualize events
were not available. They were thought to hamper the objective
character of the news.

If a newsreader were seen while giving the news, any change in
his visual manner, a smile or a lift of an eyebrow might, however
little this was intended, be interpreted as comment. The sacred
dividing line between fact and comment would be blurred.
(Holland 1987: 146)

Although newsreaders appeared ever more frequently on the screen, the uninvolved and detached mode of reading the news remained common practice until the mid-1970s. Personal traits and peculiarities were de-emphasized. As one TV critic ironically put it:

In the first place a newsreader, be it a woman or a man, must not be too attractive, and – although this is less relevant – not too bad looking either. Of course it is strictly prohibited to read bad news in any other way than good news. Objectivity would be endangered by it.

(NRC Handelsblad, 8 August 1975)

In the mid-1970s the appointment of a new executive producer led to a shift from story journalism to 'information' journalism. Under the new regime the Journaal would be no longer guided by the availability of interesting moving pictures: 'We will not do news that is fun to watch any more', the new producer said as he took the job (*Haagse Post*, February 1975). Instead the focus would be on politically and socially important issues.

Although the introduction of the autocue system made a more intimate mode of address possible, enabling the semblance of face-to-face conversation between newsreader and audience, the newsreader had to remain as detached, uninvolved and blank as possible, because the aura of objectivity had to be maintained. The Journaal acquired a reputation of being serious and objective but a little dull and uninteresting to watch.

In 1985 a new editor-in-chief was appointed, a former correspondent for the Journaal in Great Britain, Peter Brusse. He wanted to change the news into a popular television programme with natural transitions; into 'more than a dull listing of events'. The news should offer audiences opportunities to identify with events and personalities. Human interest stories therefore had to be a major ingredient of the news and newsreaders were urged to transform their serious mode of address into a more personal and intimate style:

Presenters should be more than people who merely read the news. They must inspire confidence. You must be able to trust them like you trust the neighbour next door, who is familiar to you and who keeps an eye on things while you are away. An authoritative person like Walter Cronkite, who explains which assaults are important and why.

(NRC Handelsblad, 2 February 1987)

Brusse became subject to heavy criticism from his own staff and from fellow journalists, especially from the print media. His attempt 'to make news entertaining by a light and populist appeal' was looked upon with contempt. His two-year regime was later characterized as a 'reckless period of experiments and failures' (*Parool*, 1 January 1988). He left the Journaal quite soon, disappointed with the possibilities of changing it. However, Brusse's efforts paved the way for his successor who managed to work out many of Brusse's ideas. Under his management the Journaal acquired its present style and format.[2]

Three teams of reporters and presenters are responsible for five daily news bulletins. The 8 o'clock news is still the most important news bulletin in terms of allotted time, energy and audience attention. It is aimed at a family audience and is supposed to have a smooth and informal mode of address. In line with its 'family appeal' this bulletin also features sport news. The bulletin is presented by a woman and a man, alternating each week. They are both experienced newsreaders who were assigned to this bulletin because of their popularity: 'Reliable, cosy and familiar' (*Parool*, 3 March 1988).

The other bulletins too have their own formula and are supposed to be distinctive news *programmes* appealing to different target groups. As an internal policy paper of the Journaal states: 'Attempts to produce a more inviting and personal Journaal have to motivate audiences to watch the news, and enlarge their pleasure in watching it' (NOS, 1987). As Brusse had already argued, newsreaders are now seen to be crucial in constructing a particular image for each news bulletin, and in establishing an intimate and stable relationship with the target audience. The audience must be able to identify with and relate to the anchor-person of his or her favourite news bulletin. 'We looked for journalists that can present a programme. As far as their appearance is concerned. . . they must look like ordinary people. They are not supposed just to read the news but to tell it from their own personal involvement' (*Parool*, 3 March 1988).

The intimization of Dutch television news is an example of how some values from the private sphere are transferred to the public sphere of the news. This is expressed partly by an increased attention to human interest subjects, but more telling is the way the relation between the audience and newsreader is constructed – through carefully picked personalities and intimate modes of address – as a matter of personal friendship or close family ties.

INTIMIZATION AND THE WOMAN NEWSREADER

This background sheds another light on the high presence of women newsreaders in the Dutch news. In theory, the intimization of TV news could have been achieved with an all-male anchor team. However, that would deny the gendered nature of private sphere values. It comes as no surprise then that the intimization of Dutch TV news coincides with a remarkably high number of women newsreaders.

At this point a disclaimer is necessary. The women newsreaders themselves will firmly deny that the supposedly superior capacities of women to sustain intimate relationships (in this case with the audience) is the main reason for appointing them. The women newsreaders and their superiors will rightfully refer to professional standards providing criteria for recruitment policies.

Without denying their professional performance, however, women can hardly be expected to come to the public sphere playing merely a professional role, in this case as a newsreader. Again that would deny the gendered nature of subjects, the gendered nature of cultural expectations and perceptions. 'Woman' inevitably signifies a whole cultural set of feminine values. Which of these come especially to the fore varies and depends on the particular context, as comparison between the women newsreaders of BBC news and Dutch TV news shows.

Writing about BBC news, Holland wonders:

> Is there some quality expected of newsreaders, which, despite the apparent contradictions, is turning this into a suitable role for women to play? . . . Is this role of mediation and management one that can be reconciled with the forms of femininity that have been constructed out of power relations between women and men?
>
> (Holland 1987: 142–3)

She argues that newsreading might become a 'woman's job' because the newsreader's task has become that of a performer.

For women 'the invitation to speak with the voice of authority may be nothing more but an invitation, yet again, to be a decorative performer' (Holland 1987: 149). Holland draws her evidence from public discourse about well-known British anchorwomen, in which their appearances and 'feminine' styles (often criticized as not 'feminine' at all) are continuously foregrounded. Holland concludes that the presence of women newsreaders in the BBC news expresses a common and well-known form of televisual femininity: woman as a pleasurable object for the voyeuristic (male) gaze: 'If we are not watchful we will find that once more, with the infinite flexibility of effortless power, women will have been put in their place again' (Holland 1987: 149).

In abstract terms her argument can be applied to Dutch television news as well. In the Dutch case too the high visibility of women marks another expression of traditional femininity, but there is a remarkable difference as to what element of femininity is exploited. As we have said, the number of women newsreaders increased when editorial policy led the Journaal to cover more 'human' aspects of the news. The former executive producer Brusse, whose arrival accelerated this trend, explicitly called this the 'women's touch' in the news. 'Men's news is to write on the front page that a fire happened, women's news is to write inside why the guy lit a fire for the third time' (*Journalist*, November 1986). During his brief period as editor, Brusse continually questioned the rationalistic underpinnings of the Journaal and emphasized the entertainment value and emotional qualities of news:

> One tear on TV tells you so much more than an ever so well described tear in the newspaper. Television made us communicate and participate in world affairs with tears. A Journaal without a tear is not a real Journaal and that has to be learned.
>
> (*Elsevier*, May 1988)

In Brusse's ideal Journaal, newsreaders are assumed to provide the audience with a stable point of identification with the news as *a programme* among the flow of competing TV programmes. The newsreaders are assumed to establish an intimate and personal relationship with the audience of their particular bulletin. 'Audiences must be able to identify with the people who tell them the news. They must derive a sense of stability from them' (*Volkskrant*, 1 November 1986). Assigning the same team of anchors to each news bulletin guarantees that audiences know who to expect and who to relate to. Consider – as a short sidestep – the common practice in most other European countries, where usually 'different individuals will read on different days so that the public does not come to associate the news with a single source' (Morse 1986: 58).

Thus the common conception of the anchor as the authoritative, wise and all-knowing (male) neighbour who guides you through a complex and confusing world does not seem very appropriate for the Dutch TV news. A comparison with the caring and never failing mother who tucks you in every night after a day of emotional arousal, seems more to the point. This characterization is underlined by the deliberately plain and ordinary appearances of the anchor-women. Once, one of the more popular women newsreaders was asked in a newspaper editorial:

> Why do you dress in such a dull and tasteless way? Colours that don't match, blouses and jackets that often look ludicrous on you. . . . Throw all the old stuff away. *Although you might want to look like a 'common' woman*, common can mean charming, feminine and stylish as well.
>
> (*Telegraaf*, 6 March 1988; my italics)

PRIVATE SPHERE VALUES IN A PUBLIC SPHERE CONTEXT

Feminists may express different views on the developments in Dutch television news. Some feminists might value the dominance of women newsreaders in Dutch television news as evidence of women conquering the once exclusively male public domain. Other feminists will argue that women again are chained to their 'feminine' roles, since a revision of editorial policy and styles of presentation has transformed the formerly 'masculine' role of the newsreader into one that is more in line with traditional femininity. A third group of feminists might add that the 'feminine' contributions of women newsreaders are necessary and praiseworthy adaptations of formerly detached, rationalistic and alienating news bulletins. This last argument is a customary legitimation in struggles for women's access to journalism in general. Increased access would presumably result in a reconsideration of the professional status of 'hard' and 'soft' news, less factual and more background information (cf. Neverla and Kanzleiter 1985).

All three perspectives derive their main ingredients – and take their main unresolved questions at the same time – from liberal feminist discourse. Liberal feminism ascribes the differences between women and men to the different roles they play in society. Women's roles are primarily acted out in the private sphere of family life, men's roles in the public sphere of paid work and politics.[3] The ultimate aim of liberal feminism is the integration of women in the public sphere. However, as women exchange their private for their public roles, they too might take on – be it gradually – the 'male' characteristics appropriate to that sphere. Although women and men would then be equal, the 'softer sides' of humanity would be lost in the process, an outcome that no liberal feminist desires. Thus, women should go public without forsaking their 'femininity'. What is argued for then is a recognition of private values as appropriate for the public sphere.[4]

There are several problems to this argument. On a theoretical level it assumes and reconstructs the public–private division. As a consequence it reproduces traditional gender identities (cf. Van Zoonen 1988). I will elaborate this point later.

More pragmatically, it seems a little naïve to assume that a simple transference of private sphere values to the public sphere will prove their appropriateness for it. As the professional and critical reception of the transformed Dutch television news suggests, transporting private sphere values to the public sphere is more likely to result in concerned discourses about the devaluation of the public sphere, which in the end reconstruct the gendered public–private division.

The intimization of the Journaal has met severe criticism from print journalists in particular, but from its own staff as well. The two major building blocks of the intimate news – human interest topics and an intimate mode of address – encounter most attacks. Under the headline 'Journaal on the decline' a Dutch TV critic laments 'the populist selection from possible news events with disproportionate attention for the obvious and the expected' (*Volkskrant*, 1 August 1989). Nor does this critic appreciate the 'snug domesticity' created by informal chats between anchor, correspondents and the weatherman.

Critical comments of journalists are hardly ever part of a well-formulated argument referring explicitly to the norms and values the Journaal is supposed to live up to. However, the underlying discourse can be reconstructed from the work of several authors (e.g. Bennet 1988, Elliott 1986, Meyrowitz 1985, Postman 1984).

They express genuine concern that the 'intimacy' of television news prevents an understanding of public life that is analytical, historical and critical. The invasion of the public arena by topics, values and actions once belonging exclusively to the private sphere is said to erode the adequacy of the public sphere and to endanger effective public discourse. Sennett (1974: 5), for instance, talks about the 'tyranny of intimacy' that transmutes political categories into psychological ones: 'As a result, confusion has arisen between public and intimate life; people are working out in terms of personal feelings public matters which properly can be dealt with only through codes of impersonal meaning.' Kress (1986: 397) argues that the operation of personalized language – letting the individual instead of the institution speak – assigns public events to the private sphere. 'It is to offer an account of that event which says that there is no account other than individual action and expression.' The viewer is positioned as an individual guided by common sense, while a public mode of address would position the viewer as a public citizen aware of the operation of institutional processes. Dahlgren (1981) entertains a similar argument in the assertion that although intimate modes of address can invite identification with media personalities such as politicians, they do deflect attention from the substantial issues concerned.

Such critical comments of journalists and intellectuals tend to re-construct rigid divisions between discourse appropriate for the public sphere (analytical and detached) and discourse appropriate for the private sphere (emotional and involved). Thus the transference of private sphere values to the public world of television news hardly modifies beliefs about the legitimacy of private sphere topics, values and behaviours for the public sphere, as liberal feminists would have us believe. The opposite happens instead: it is argued that because TV news is permeated with private sphere values it has lost its traditional social and political functions. The intimacy of TV news results in its discursive expulsion from the public sphere.

BEYOND THE BOURGEOIS PUBLIC SPHERE PARADIGM

The Dutch case suggests that feminist perspectives on journalism and the public sphere are caught in a two-faced trap from which there seems to be no escape. On the one hand, women can opt for full integration in the public sphere on present conditions: they thus become the same as men and equal. Some highly esteemed private sphere values will be lost in the process. On the other hand, women can choose to maintain their private sphere values in public sphere conditions, aiming in the long run at a modification of the public sphere. They will remain different from men.

This dilemma is another expression of the 'sameness–difference' debate which emerges recurrently in the feminist movement and feminist theory. Summarized in an almost intolerably simplified manner, it pertains to the question: are women essentially the same as men but 'made' different by culture and history, in which case 'only' a reversal of culturally and historically defined roles would be necessary. Or are women essentially different from men and oppressed by masculine culture and history, in which case a total revision of the existing social set-up would be needed. In other words, is femininity an essential or a cultural feature of women? (Note that both positions assume unambiguous and stable meanings of 'femininity', a point to which I will return later.)

The question whether women are 'simply' the same, or 'obviously' different[5] has driven much feminist theory into academically interesting but narrowly focused debates with sometimes only remote reference to acute and concrete problems (cf. Mitchell and Oakley 1986). Within the feminist movement it has often led to paralysing antagonisms, with respect to media strategies for instance expressed as: is the movement best served by creating its own media or by seeking integration in existing media?

Recently feminist political philosophers have suggested ways out of the suffocating grasps of the 'sameness–difference' dilemma by pointing to its historical specificity (Ehlstain 1981, Benhabib and Cornell 1987). They claim that the dilemma is a philosophical and historical product of bourgeois society's distinction between a public sphere populated by men and a private sphere inhabited by women.

Writing about France, Landes (1988:22) asserts that the eighteenth century marked a turning-point for women: 'Public–private oppositions were being reinforced in ways that foreclosed women's earlier independence in the street, in the marketplace, and, for elite women, in the public spaces of the court and aristocratic households.' She ascribes the genesis of the bourgeois public–private distinction to republican philosophies and policies rooted in a firm aversion to absolutist practices characterized among other things by stylized discourses and extreme mannerism. Elite women, through their position as *salonnières*, exercised a crucial role in shaping public speech and behaviour according to the conventions of the absolutist days. The republican complaint against the decadent and effeminate monarchy thus involved opposition to the public role of women as well: 'The metaphor of the "reign of women" signified the corruption of society at its heights' (Landes 1988: 27). Landes indicates convincingly that an important dimension of the bourgeois revolution pertained to the representational styles of the absolutist monarchy – the power of the *salonnières* and 'feminized' public life – by which bourgeois men felt emasculated. She analyses the work of Montesquieu and Rousseau to argue that the central categories of bourgeois thought – universal reason, law and nature – are embedded in an ideologically sanctioned order of gender difference. 'In their preferred version of the classical universe, bourgeois men discovered a flattering reflection of themselves – one that imagined men as properly political and women as naturally domestic' (Landes 1988: 4). The bourgeois revolution thus banished women to the home and called men to their natural fulfilment in political life. The 'natural' state of society – as opposed to the decadent and perverted absolutist monarchy – was restored through the revolution. Landes concludes that modern feminism is an inextricable product of the gendered structure of bourgeois society. Its prime dilemmas – sameness or difference – could only be articulated as a consequence, and within the limits of a public–private distinction rooted in the assumption of fixed gender identities. Most theorists and historians of the bourgeois public sphere, including Habermas in both his earlier and his more recent works, have failed to appreciate the gendered subtext of the concept (cf. Fraser 1987).

Feminism has been moderately successful in crossing some of the lines of the public–private distinction. Through the slogan 'the personal is political' feminists have ensured that issues formerly considered private, such as sexual and family relations, have become legitimate subjects for political discourse. Another achievement is that supposedly private and personal experiences are now recognized as legitimate moral bases for political activism. Especially the latter feminist efforts might fundamentally alter the gendered assumptions of the bourgeois public sphere model and eventually overcome the sameness–difference dilemma.

Young (1987) asserts that the bourgeois public sphere concept presupposes a civic public consisting of impartial moral reasoners standing outside the situation discussed, adopting a detached attitude. This civic public is not misled by particular ends and interests, but guided by universal rationality. The capacity of human beings temporarily to discard all non-rational aspects of their existence – affectivity, desire, feelings – is a necessary assumption in such deontological theory of reasoning. The ideal of universalist rationality theoretically and practically excludes women, and not as a mere accident. 'The ideal of a civic public exhibits a will to unity, and necessitates the exclusion of aspects of human existence that threaten and disperse the brotherly unity of straight and upright forms, especially the exclusion of women' (Young 1987: 59). Young concludes that the bourgeois concept of the public sphere is ultimately a totalitarian one for it eliminates otherness by ignoring the irreducible specificity of situations and the difference among moral subjects. As an alternative Young proposes a contextualized evaluation of public life which would appreciate specific discourses due to e.g. the particular experiences of women and ethnic groups.

To recapitulate the argument of this section: historically and philosophically the bourgeois public sphere model assumes and prescribes a universal distinction between rational public aspects of human nature and emotional private ones. Not coincidentally this distinction is interlinked with fixed gender roles and identities. This gendered subtext of the bourgeois public sphere model leads feminist evaluations of journalism straight into the tentacles of the 'sameness–difference' dilemma. Therefore I join feminist political philosophers who suggest replacing the universalist morality of the bourgeois public sphere model with more particularist and contextual evaluations of public life. I shall briefly address the question as to what such particularist and contextual evaluations of journalism would amount, in the final section.

WHEN WOMEN WATCH THE NEWS

Arguing for a contextual instead of a universalist evaluation of journalism raises the question as to which context should be taken into account. The bourgeois public sphere concept is very much focused on the institutional context of journalism, e.g. the theoretical and practical autonomy of news media *vis-à-vis* the political system, the professional performance of journalists, the democratic potential of commercially produced news media. In so far as the audiences or readers of the news ('publics') receive attention, they are often seen as mere aberrations from the ideal civic public, since much research shows that actual publics do not behave and react as ideal citizens are supposed to. People spend less and less time reading newspapers, are not highly motivated to watch the news, have a relatively brief attention span and forget the items presented in the evening news within minutes (cf. Graber 1988). Often, researchers are so concerned (sometimes even indignant) with publics *not* fulfilling their democratic duties as citizens, they forget to ask what people do with the news instead. I propose to take such concrete experiences as a starting-point for developing critical alternatives to the anachronistic bourgeois public sphere model. This would mean a shift from institutional contexts to reception contexts.

What would such a contextual and particularist feminist evaluation of the intimacy of Dutch television news amount to? I can only tentatively answer that question for Dutch audience research is minimal in this respect. Surveys carried out in other countries usually do not reveal great differences in the numbers of women and men watching news programmes but evidence from qualitative data does show gendered ways of relating to news and current affairs programmes. 'Masculinity is primarily identified with a strong preference for factual programs (news, current affairs, documentaries) and femininity identified with a preference for fictional programs' (Morley 1988: 43). Several reasons are offered for such a difference.

Some authors claim that the news doesn't provide women with knowledge that enables them to make sense of their own daily experiences. Consequently they will not feel much incentive to watch. Morley (1988: 45) illustrates this by the observation that women do watch local news programmes very attentively.

> They say that they don't understand what international eco-
> nomic news is about and, as it has no experiential bearing on
> their lives, they're not interested in it. However, if there has
> been a crime in a local area, they feel the need to know about
> it, both for their own sake and their children's sake.

A related reason for gender-specific reception of TV news might be found in the relevance of another social function that TV news can fulfil for its recipients. Jensen observed that for many male viewers TV news provides 'legitimation': 'an opportunity for the recipient to . . . feel part of a particular social order' (Jensen 1986: 227). Women, and other outsiders to the 'particular social order,' might not feel part of that order and might not see the need to keep up with it at all.

These kinds of observations might suggest that the intimacy of Dutch television news would appeal to women in particular, since its subjects and mode of address seem to be in close accordance with the discourse of their life-world. However, such a conclusion again reconstructs a gendered public–private distinction. The women that are referred to in the above-mentioned research are living (or assumed to be living) in traditional family situations. Women are more or less equated with isolated housewives, still confined to the private sphere. Aside from the theoretical problems such an analysis runs into – as discussed in the previous sections – few people still live in traditional family situations, and the 'isolated housewife' is hardly representative of 'the average woman' any more. More than half of the households in Amsterdam, for instance, consist of a single individual. The way women from different social and cultural backgrounds, with different intellectual and political predispositions and with a variety of public careers, relate to the intimacy of Dutch (TV) news and to recent trends in journalism in general, is yet to be explored, and should be an important part of the agenda for research in journalism. In many cases such explorations will result in contradictory evaluations of the feminist qualities of TV news and journalism, simply because of the increasing heterogeneity of 'woman' as a social and cultural category. But if we reject the universal and consensual bent of the bourgeois public sphere model for its exclusionary mechanisms and propose the recognition and appreciation of differences instead, we can hardly replace it with a new universal, be it feminist, norm for public life. We need to allow for contradictions within our own feminist public discourse as well.

I would like to thank my students Wiet van Hoorn and Connie van der Molen who collected material for this paper. The comments of my colleagues Joke Hermes, Pieter Hilhorst and Ien Ang on earlier drafts have been very useful.

NOTES

1   This figure is based on the August 1989 situation.
2   Refers to August 1989.
3   In most expressions of liberal feminist discourse the concept of the public sphere refers to all non-private or non-domestic instances. Elshtain (1981) argues strongly against such an inflation of the concept.
4   This argumentation is not reserved to liberal feminism. Elements of it can be found in other feminist discourses (e.g. radical, socialist) as well.
5   Note that this formulation constructs 'femininity' as deviant. Rephrasing the question as 'are men simply the same, or obviously different?' implies a whole different status quo.

REFERENCES

Benhabib, S. and Cornell, D. (1987) *Feminism as Critique*, Oxford: Basil Blackwell.
Bennett, W. L. (1988) *News: The Politics of Illusion*, New York: Longman.
Butler, M. and Paisley, W. (1980) *Women and Mass Media: Resourcebook for Research and Action*, New York: Hasting House.
Dahlgren, P. (1981) 'TV news and the suppression of reflexivity', in E. Katz and T. Szecskö (eds), *Mass Media and Social Change*, Beverly Hills: Sage, pp. 101–15.
Elliott, P. (1986) 'Intellectuals, "the information society" and the disappearance of the public sphere', *Media, Culture and Society: A Critical Reader*, London: Sage, pp. 101–15.
Elshtain, J. B. (1981) *Public Man, Private Woman*, Oxford: Martin Robertson.
Fiske, J. (1988) *Television Culture*, New York: Methuen.
Fraser, N. (1987) 'What's critical about critical theory: the case of Habermas and gender', in S. Benhabib and D. Cornell (eds), *Feminism as Critique*, Oxford: Basil Blackwell, pp. 31–56.
Gallagher, M. (1980) *Unequal Opportunities: The Case of Women and the Media*, Paris: UNESCO.
Gallagher, M. (1984) *Employment and Positive Action for Women in the Television Organisations of the EEC Member States*, Brussels: Commission of the European Communities.
Gelfman, J. (1976) *Women and Television News*, New York: Columbia University Press.
Graber, D. (1988) *Processing the News: How People Tame the Information Tide*, New York: Longman.
Holland, P. (1987) 'When a woman reads the news', in H. Baehr and G. Dyer (eds), *Boxed in: Women and Television*, London: Pandora Press, pp. 133–51.
Jensen, K. B. (1986) *Making Sense of the News*, Aarhus: Aarhus University Press.

Kress, G. (1986) 'Language and the media: the construction of the domains of public and private', *Media, Culture and Society*, vol. 8, pp. 395–419.

Landes, J. B. (1988) *Women and the Public Sphere in the Age of the French Revolution*, London: Cornell University Press.

Media Report to Women (1989), vol. 17, no. 4, p. 3.

Meyrowitz, J. (1985) *No Sense of Place*, New York: Oxford University Press.

Mitchel, J. and Oakley, A. (1986) *What is Feminism. A Re-examination*, New York: Pantheon Books.

Morley, D. (1988) 'Domestic relations: the framework of family viewing in Great Britain', in J. Lull (ed.), *World Families Watch Television*, Beverly Hills: Sage, pp. 23–48.

Morse, M. (1986) 'The television news personality and credibility', in T. Modleski (ed.), *Studies in Entertainment*, Bloomington: Indiana University Press, pp. 55–79.

Neverla, I. and Kanzleiter, G, (1985) *Journalistinnen*, Frankfurt: Campus Verlag.

NOS (1987) *Het NOS Journaal*, Hilversum: Kijk & Luisteronderzoek.

Pingree, S. and Hawkins, R. P. (1978) 'News definitions and their effects on women', in L. K. Epstein (ed.), *Women and the News*, New York: Hasting House, pp. 116–33.

Postman, N. (1984) *Amusing Ourselves to Death*, New York: Penguin Books.

Schudson, M. (1978) *Discovering the News*, New York: Basic Books.

Sennet, R. (1974) *The Fall of Public Man: On the Social Psychology of Capitalism*, New York: Vintage Books.

Sparks, C. (1989) 'Goodbye, Hildy Johnson', paper presented to the seminar 'Journalism and the Public Sphere in the New Media Age', Dubrovnik, Yugoslavia; reprinted in the present volume (Chapter 2).

Thoveron, G. (1986) 'European televised women', *European Journal of Communication*, vol. 1, pp. 289–300.

Van Zoonen, L. (1988) 'Rethinking women and the news', *European Journal of Communication*, vol. 3, pp. 35–53.

Young, I. (1987) 'Impartiality and the civic public', in S. Benhabib and D. Cornell (eds), *Feminism as Critique*, Oxford: Basil Blackwell, pp. 57–76.

Chapter 11

Tales of tellyland: the popular press and television in the UK

Ian Connell

INTRODUCTION

Much concern has of late been expressed about the quality of information on 'serious public affairs' available from the media. Briefly stated, the concern is that in a variety of ways informative, in-depth and investigative journalism is being marginalized not just in the tabloid press, but also in the broadsheets, as well as in television. In its place, there is an increasing volume of material on aspects of our lives that are thought of as largely unessential. As evidence, those who are concerned would cite the growing number of columns devoted to leisure, style and consumer affairs, to photographs rather than words, and not least of all to stories about those prominent in the entertainment industries, cinema, popular music and above all television. What we are said to be witnessing are essentially private matters being publicly paraded, while matters of broader, national and political relevance are gradually receding into the background. There is much about the present situation which seems to lock people into the private sphere and blocks a transition to the public one.

It has been proposed that the balance between this sort of material and informative, public affairs journalism has been tipped irretrievably in the former's favour, and that this has already had serious consequences for the UK's political system. There are those who see this tendency further weakening the majority's already weak involvement in the political system. In effect, those who see the developing situation this way assume that a plentiful supply of high-quality information is a precondition of effective participation in parliamentary democratic processes.

Cutting down on the supply of such information not only disenfranchises people, but runs the risk of cultivating political apathy, if not barbarism.

My main aim here is to review and to clarify by questioning some assumptions that have been made in debates about popular culture and the way it interfaces with political affairs. Is it useful, for instance, to continue to assume that many of the institutions of popular culture not only stand apart from official political forms and processes, but also cultivate a rather inchoate and disabling resistance to them? Resistance is, perhaps, too strong a term, since it suggests deliberate action against official political cultures and systems. The view more often adopted is that the state cultivated is more akin to surly, alienated passivity. I wish to explore such questions via a consideration of the relationship between the 'popular' or tabloid press and television. In so doing, I will also question some of the assumptions that are typically made about the tabloid press.

Between December 1988 and February 1989 I read and analysed a range of tabloid papers, including the *Sun*, the *Daily Mirror*, *Today*, the *Daily Mail*, the *Daily Star*, the *Daily Express*, the *Sport* and, when they existed, their Sunday equivalents. Not being a regular reader of any of them, I was struck by the volume of material they contained about the actors and presenters of television programmes. Apart from programme listings and television columns, there were on average about two items per day in each of the papers. In the *Daily Mirror*, there were often as many as seven or eight items. In addition to those on television there was an almost as abundant supply of similar material on figures in the music and cinema industries.

It was not just the volume of material on 'show business personalities' that was striking, but also its prominence. Such material was often featured as the lead item on the front pages of these papers. Public affairs stories, with which the broadsheets would have led on a given day, were often relegated to a brief mention on the front pages of the tabloids and/or to somewhat fuller treatment on other pages. In short, then, figures from the world of entertainment were featured extensively and prominently in the tabloid papers examined.

Another striking feature was the form of the journalism adopted. The majority of the stories I read were constructed in very different ways from those included in the broadsheets. Only very few had any of the attributes of serious journalistic styles. Equally few could be seen as serving an insider public with the information they needed to have an informed view of such matters as the evolving editorial policies of television or the ways in which the exploitation of different delivery systems might transform the structures of visual broadcasting. The general preference seemed to be for stories about scandalous incidents involving well-known personalities. Being more accustomed to, and probably more at ease with, the conventions of broadsheet journalism I found it difficult to understand this preference. What was newsworthy about these stories? Maybe very little. Maybe they were there, as many others have said, only to amuse, titillate and entertain readers. It was difficult to imagine they had any kind of informative intent.

What I was seeking was an answer to the question, 'why was there an abundance of stories about the scandalous affairs of show business personalities?' The volume of them might be satisfactorily explained in economic terms, but not the journalistic forms of representation they regularly employed. Moreover, while market studies might with reasonable success identify segments of the potential readership to be addressed, they could at best only hint at the modes and forms of address to adopt to attract and hold the attention of the desired segments. Clearly some form of linguistic cultural explanation would be needed, since the evolution and institution of these forms will have required some reading and interpretation of the particular structures of feeling and thought employed by the desired segments. That said, cultural explanation of the sort outlined above hardly seemed adequate.

Like any other stories, those told by the tabloid press about TV personalities almost imperceptibly articulated certain frameworks of understanding, interest and emotion. One of the things the analysis attempted was to describe what these frameworks were. As I do not wish to over-excite expectations, I have to point out that with the time and resources to hand, only the first steps to an adequate description have been possible. They were enough, however, to realize that these stories involved something more than the satisfaction of dodgy desires. There were additional features which suggested a moralizing tone and a considerable measure of condemnation of those involved in the scandals. Having noted these features, it was difficult then to see the stories as the means

by which the base desires attributed to their supposed readers could
be easily satisfied.

NEWSPAPERS OR NOT

It proved extremely difficult to read the tabloid papers I selected
as 'news' papers. In retrospect, it is clear that I was employing a
model of newspapers and a set of expectations derived from my
greater familiarity with broadsheets. As long as I did so, I could
not avoid comparing them unfavourably and viewing them as the
impoverished relations of the broadsheets. It is now clear that
to expect of the tabloid press articles that perform at least the
basic journalistic jobs of providing accurate information on, and
some measure of dispassionate analysis of, current 'public affairs'
is bound to lead to disappointment and frustration. Such material
is regularly granted, at best, only a secondary position in most of
the tabloids. On finding that there is very little such material in the
most prominent positions in tabloid papers some critics have been
quick to dismiss them as newspapers. Is their dismissal justified or
not?

The places where public affairs stories would be found in
broadsheets, were in the tabloids occupied instead by 'human
interest' stories and stories about personalities whose public visibility had been occasioned by some dubious behaviour, often of a
sexual kind. To illustrate, we can take the front page of the *Daily
Express* for Thursday, 2 February 1989. Immediately below the
paper's title, across the full width of the page were the following
elements:

ADULTERY INSIDE TODAY: THE MOST   An affair in
REVEALING STUDY YET   the office
                                         See Centre Pages

Between these announcements and directions was a passport-size
photograph depicting a man kissing a woman's hand as she is
conducting a telephone call.

Immediately beneath this section of the page was a photograph
of Cybill Shepherd smiling to camera with a baby in each arm (her
twin sons). This picture occupied two-thirds of the page width
and about half of its remaining depth. Superimposed on the top
left of the photograph was the caption 'Star Cybill walks out on

her husband PAGE 3'. A further caption, immediately beneath, stated:

> MOONLIGHTING WIFE: TV star Cybill Shepherd last night walked out on husband Bruce Oppenheim, the father of her twin sons

To the right of this picture and its captions, running the full length of the page, and of one column's width, was a report headlined 'Anne attacks charity cheats'. The report, set in bold, reported that Princess Anne 'yesterday attacked Third World countries that squander western cash sent to help the poor'. At the foot of the column was a directive to the effect that the remainder of the story could be found on 'Page 2 Column 1'.

At the foot of the page, framed by the Cybill Shepherd photograph above and the Princess Anne report to its right-hand side was another report with the headline LABOUR FIRE SKY TV MP. This referred to the 'dismissal' of the Labour Party's 'front bench spokesman', Austin Mitchell (pictured to the left with the caption 'Defiant: Austin Mitchell) on his acceptance of a presenter's job with the then about to be launched Sky TV satellite service.

With such a front page, not atypical of those to be found on other tabloids, it is tempting to suggest that these papers really cannot be treated as *news*papers. It is not simply that they do not lead with this or that story given front page prominence in one or other of the broadsheets, but rather that they elect not to use *any* stories of the kind used by broadsheets on the front page. If the essence of good journalism is about seriously reporting serious matters – those which have been accepted on to the state's agenda of acceptable controversies – then the tabloid papers must be seen as only vestigially newspapers. Given, for the moment, this qualification, it is not surprising that the tabloid press is judged to be debased, and to be set on a course which is lowering if not trivializing journalistic standards.

To render this judgement on the tabloid press is, however, to grant too much weight and authority to a particular set of journalistic traditions. There is another set of traditions as ancient as that upon which the present-day broadsheets in the UK draw. It has long been dismissed as trivial and scandalous, in part because of its continuing fascination for those private worlds which exist in the shadow of public ones. From within the official strata of the public world it has been and is strongly felt that the private should not be used for publicity, and it has as a consequence long been insisted that serious journalism must be conducted tastefully and decently. Popular journalism has, however, revelled in turning topsy-turvy the preferred order of these worlds. The 'invasions of privacy' that are now commonplace have not been, and are not, always waged by tabloid reporters against ordinary members of the public suffering some grief or catastrophe. Much more alluring are those situations where a 'respected' public figure has been caught out in some private affair which public morality condemns as a transgression. Even more alluring still are those occasions when a public figure's private actions flatly contradict his or her public pronouncements.

In reporting such affairs, tabloid papers have been denounced as squalid and distasteful. Often, it is perhaps not so much the reporting as the affair itself that is squalid, or the public hypocrisies which usually attend their 'revelations'. Condemnatory responses of the kind with which we are all familiar may be little more than an attempt by representatives of official, public cultures to prevent further public inspection of uncomfortable transgressions of codes of conduct by which they would have us all live. In such circumstances it does not seem inappropriate to suggest that the tabloid papers can be considered subversive. They can force into the open problems associated with liberalism's assumption that individual freedom will be tempered with responsibility in private matters, at least among those who can be regarded as civilized. Their revelations of improprieties, or, with the aid of telephoto lenses, of actions which have not been carefully cultivated and rehearsed, have the potential to puncture and disrupt the aura of respectability and authority which envelops those who hold public office. I said they can do so, because I am aware that they can sometimes reinforce authority by means other than the rites and rituals which attend certain public offices. So, the snatched images of the royals at play may reinforce their authority, rather than undermine it, by humanizing them. Nevertheless, there remain occasions when the invasions mounted by the tabloid press are not against private territory at all, but instead against the imaginary dimensions of the world of public figures. Then, they bring to public visibility disclosures every bit as sensitive as those leaked about the secret services or about MPs' undeclared commercial interests. These may have the capacity to shatter illusions, though not, perhaps, within the hallowed realms of the public sphere. At the very least, they can be reminders that 'they', public figures, are not always what they prefer, or allow themselves, to seem; that they are not above the earthiness of the everyday world; and that they are not the paragons of the virtues they may seek to promote in others.

Well, okay, this seems plausible, but what about some of the other material which finds its way on to the pages of the tabloid press. What are we to make of the prominent coverage of Cybill Shepherd's marital problems? What are we to make of such headlines as 'BOOZED BOTHAM NUTTED HOTEL GUARD' (*Sun*, 15 December 1988), or 'TARBY'S NIGHT WITH BLONDE' (*Sun*, 16 January 1989)? In some measure these stories may operate in a similar though more intense way. They frequently deal with figures whose talents have granted them wealth and privilege in measures that are beyond what most of us can hope for. They lead easy and seemingly glamorous lives which again sharply contrast with the lives most of us are able to lead. It may be that these figures have been granted rewards which, to many, may seem ill-deserved. The revelations of their troubles and tribulations may be the only means available to bring them down a peg or two.

Whatever the reasons for the attractiveness of such material to these papers, it cannot be dismissed as trivial. Contrary to what is usually assumed, these papers are not unserious. Those of us who have come to analyse journalism have perhaps allowed ourselves to define the serious in far too narrow a fashion. To be serious, journalism would appear to have to deal with only those matters which are already on the agendas of parliaments, major corporations, organized extra-parliamentary political groupings and various kinds of pressure groups. We have also tended to work with rather narrow conceptions of what is political. So, a matter is political only if we can detect some organized presence advocating a particular course of action and mobilizing support for it. We have forgotten that politics is about all and any manifestation of power, whether or not that manifestation assumes the dominant forms available within parliamentary democracies. There is a very real sense in which the stories in the tabloid papers are political. In their peculiar, brash and bawling ways they bring to visibility that which the variously powerful would prefer to ignore, would choose to consider 'by the way' or would dismiss as regrettable, loutish traits. They remind us that in the midst of sometimes quite desperate poverty and impotence, there are those with everything.

Nor can we forget that in dealing with the tabloid press we are dealing with a species of journalism. Much of the criticism which would deny these papers the status of journalism is far too rationalist. What I have in mind is the kind of criticism which would strictly separate entertainment from information, which finds the tones of the tabloid press too lurid and bombastic. This is a criticism which would have reporting concentrate on fact and analysis, unadorned by allegory, metaphor and allusion. Whatever such criticism might celebrate as an ideal, the fact is that it is very difficult to identify passages of journalism from broadsheets that are utterly devoid of such characteristics. No, the stories I shall be looking at in more detail from the tabloid press can be considered informative even although they do not read as scientific reports. And, moreover, they are newspapers in that they chronicle unfolding events just as much as their broadsheet relations. Where they differ is in the nature of the events they consider worthy of our note.

MYTHOLOGICAL PARTNERS

As was said above, the relation between the tabloid press and television which has been forged by the former's stories is, perhaps, best seen as a symbiotic one. There is mutual advantage in it. The form of the relation is complex in that it is multi-faceted. It is in part economic and in part also political, but not least of all, it is also cultural. It is with the cultural dimension of the relation that what follows is mainly concerned. What sort of cultural relations are there between the tabloid press and television, and how do they serve their mutual interests? To answer these questions, we must turn to the stories themselves to determine what they might signify about television, or more precisely the various categories of people who work within it. It should be stressed that, in the absence of a developed understanding of the transactions and transformations that occur in the reading of these stories, all that can be legitimately considered here is their *meaning potential*. The main task will be to describe how certain of television's performers are made to appear in the stories.

There were lots of stories from which to select. The main ones, those given the fullest and most spectacular forms of coverage, tended to feature 'TV stars in trouble' which most often arose from reported sexual encounters of an illicit kind. How might we begin to understand these stories?

Within the columns of the tabloid press, images of television are constructed and cultivated which lift it, and those involved with it, out of the ordinary, everyday world. The most useful way to regard these stories is as a species of fabulous writing. Usually, we tend to think of such writing as creating other, remote worlds that are peopled by marvellous characters possessed of awesome powers. They are, often, worlds which operate according to physical and social laws that are, in several ways, different from those of our own mundane or primary world. Something of the sort is present in the tabloid stories about television. The world they create – let's call it tellyland – is populated with characters who, if not marvellous, are certainly glamorous. There is little in the writing or illustration of the stories to suggest that these characters do many of the things which fill up the days of 'ordinary' people. It is true that they are sometimes made to experience some of the same sorts of grief or emotional crises as ordinary people, but on such occasions the experience is of a more intense quality. The attributes which really distinguish them as extraordinary beings are their capacity and apparent desire for pleasure.

In no small way the otherness of this world is created by having it operate according to mysterious social laws. What pleasures there are in the ordinary world are normally to be gained by social labour. In tellyland, however, social labour, in any of its familiar forms, does not seem to exist. We rarely see the main characters 'at work'. Instead we see them enjoying the trappings and pleasures that many might assume are rare treats. What is in the ordinary world rare, is in tellyland pretty close to being normal. When we see in photographs the characters of tellyland they are, usually, dressed as for an 'occasion' of some sort. Their lives seem to consist of little more than attending functions or parties. On rarer occasions, they are presented as recuperating from the effects of their socializing at health farms or 'drying-out' clinics. Both men and women are well turned out, the former in what appear to be well-tailored lounge suits or dinner suits, the latter in designer dresses and gowns. The majority smile, though there is from time to time one scowling at the camera (perhaps for invading the privacy of their pleasure). They look, in general, carefree and affluent if not wealthy. The means by which this happy state has been achieved are, however, rarely dealt with explicitly.

The stories not only have mythological properties but also moral ones. They seem to presuppose certain standards of respectable behaviour. The stories are usually triggered by some sort of failure to observe these standards, though there are some which celebrate their observance to an exceptional degree. The main infringements are alleged or reported sexual indiscretions, and sometimes villainy. Many of the stories are about adultery, one night stands, broken relationships, sexual potency and inventiveness (though sometimes also the lack of them), sexually exploited and then abandoned innocents. The majority of characters are granted sexual attributes which, by ordinary world standards, are awesome. They have voracious sexual appetites, incredible sexual capacity and an almost immeasurable sexual imagination. Their supernormal attributes are in tellyland just normal. This is highlighted by the inclusion, from time to time, of stories about stars who have failed to shine in these respects. Most of the time, then, the moralizing occurs when the narrator and/or their informants have perceived a misuse of their special sexual powers. But there is quite considerable ambiguity about the stars' use of these powers. Fascination and awe coexist with disapproval and even disgust, sometimes even within a single story. Contrary to what might be supposed, however, unqualified celebration is rare.

It would be misleading to suggest that all the tales of tellyland are concerned with sexual encounters and the problems following from them. Something of the range is indicated by the following list of the kinds of narrative action employed during the period when the papers were monitored. These include:

Rise to stardom by chance: as in the story 'FAITH THANKS HER LUCKY BOOBS – SPLIT DRESS SHOT ME TO STARDOM' (*Mirror*, 15 December 1988).

Demonstrating worthiness of a place among the stars: as in the stories 'I'M A PERFECT DAD SAYS RIK THE B'STARD' (*News of the World*, 12 February 1989) and 'I'LL BE BACK VOWS BRAVE MARTI' (*Mirror*, 16 January 1989).

Being seen doing star-like things: worthy deeds on behalf of less fortunate beings, such as contributing to charities or being photographed at charity functions.

Fortunate escapes: usually being let off minor misdemeanours such as fines for driving offences.

Revelation of sexual encounters, scandal or intrigue: as in the stories 'TARBY'S NIGHT WITH BLONDE – SECRET DATE IN COUNTRY HOTEL' (*Sun*, 16 January 1989) and 'TV'S MIKE ROCKED BY SEX SCANDAL TRICK OR TREAT EMPLOYS VICE GIRLS' (*Star*, 16 January 1989).

Revelation of unheroic qualities or 'secrets': as in the stories 'CABBIE KILLER DEN WAS KING OF THE NICK' (*Sun*, 16 January 1989) and 'THE FILTHY TRUTH ABOUT TELLY'S MR NICE' (*News of the World*, 12 February 1989).

Others included the expression of sympathy in the face of misfortunes of a personal kind, and celebration of reinstatement and success. One other category deserves rather fuller mention, and that is boundary transgression.

This occurred in several guises. Fundamentally, there were two broad classes, the one involving the hierarchical system of tellyland and its appropriate modes of behaviour, the other the place of tellyland in the wider social system. Examples of the former were the stories about minor stars putting on airs and graces, about them presuming too much about their standing in tellyland. Among the most vitriolic stories were those about stars of the upper strata spiralling down. There are a few stars whose actions normally trigger something pretty close to celebration. They are treated as paragons of the implicit virtues. They are perfect partners, faithful, generous in their charity and completely professional. Perhaps because they are willingly celebrated as such, when one of them goes off the rails little quarter is given. Often, their transgressions fall within the second class, and involve improper relations with those from other worlds.

The fabulous character of the tabloids' coverage of television should not be exaggerated for two main reasons. First, fabulous conventions are tempered with journalistic ones. The things which happen to, or involve, the heroes and heroines of the stories do so within a journalistic time-scale; they have either just happened or are in the processes of happening. The events or actions are reported, typically by sources close to the main characters or by witnesses. These sources include jilted lovers, outraged observers and friends or relations of injured parties. Though I have mentioned only two, the stories employ a sufficient number of journalistic devices to support the conclusion that they are best regarded as of a hybrid genre, what we might term 'fabulous reportage'. The primary function of this genre is to provide a diurnal chronicle of the troubles or other noteworthy events of tellyland.

Second, television is featured in a number of other ways. All the tabloids contained listings of and guides to programmes. The TV sections within which they are placed also include some editorial content by a named TV critic. This is usually an appraisal of selected programmes from the previous day, or of an actor's performance. Other editorial columns also provide some, more traditionally crafted, stories on television.

Editorial columns also provide a version of public affairs journalism with television as the subject matter. Such material is only infrequently provided and generally covered less extensively. There are no report-oriented 'media' columns of the sort now to be found in the broadsheets. During the monitoring period there were no news reports on such matters as broadcasting's changing pattern of industrial relations, nor on the changing relationship between broadcasting and government. Policy matters relating to television's much disputed cultural role did appear as the subject of news reports and in the form of moral issues. Just before Christmas 1988, several of the tabloids ran reports on the BBC's decision to issue guidelines on the appropriate use of 'four-letter words', depictions of violence and of sexual intercourse ('sex'), but the majority of items did not manifestly concern themselves with issues, but in various ways with the doings of TV personalities. Hardly a day passed during the monitoring period without the majority of the tabloids (the exceptions were *Today* and the *Daily Mail*) running personality items. There were several different kinds of personality items. The bulk of them can be classed as direct or indirect publicity or promotionals. The papers made fairly liberal use of copy which had probably originated with agents and promoters. Such items might consist of little more than a good-sized photograph with a caption or short paragraph about personalities attending some function or other. The 'photo opportunity' may have been arranged to promote either the personality, a new show, or both. Such coverage tended to be reserved for personalities of some standing. For those of lesser standing, there would be no photograph. The copy for them might be a paragraph of some twenty to thirty words, placed, usually, at the margins of a page. Such items were little more than fillers.

Items of content such as these were not the cardinal ones dealing with television. I identified as cardinal those which were prominently featured, and I assumed a functional relationship between prominence and importance. In short the more prominent an item, the greater its degree of perceived importance. As a rough-and-ready measure of prominence, I used a combination of such fairly obvious elements as location in the paper, position on the page, size and number of headlines, presence/absence, and size, of photograph and where appropriate whether or not colour was used. The most eye-catching were those that appeared on the first page, began in the top, left-hand quadrant of the page, had at least one headline in a large point size, were accompanied by at least one photograph of key participants and may have been continued on subsequent pages. Of perhaps equal, but certainly similar, standing were those billed somewhere at the top of page one, but presented across two pages elsewhere in the paper. Two examples of this were the *Mirror*'s serialization of 'The Bruce Willis Story' in January 1989, and the *Sun*'s 'Secret Life of Dirty Den', billed on page one as 'Another Exclusive'.

It was these cardinal items which took as their subjects the doings and misdoings of 'stars'. One of the striking features of the stories told was their presumption that the central characters were well known. I would suggest this was a presumption because few details were supplied to place them. Typically they would be named. Their status in tellyland was also provided as was the name of the show with which they were, or had been, associated. Apart from age, biographical details were not usually provided, an absence which could perhaps be seen as contributing to their appearance as beings from another world.

There would appear to be a relatively fixed set of nominal labels that is employed to refer to status in tellyland. Apart from the general one of 'star', others are more specific and indicate something of the roles with which the character has become associated. Sometimes 'top' is used, as in 'top comic Jimmy Tarbuck' or 'top TV chef Keith Floyd', to indicate standing.

At one level, it may seem as if this system of labelling tells us very little about the characters in the stories. At another, the labels may speak volumes. They are highly condensed points of reference, clues which are more than sufficient for those already in the know about who is doing what on television at any given moment. They are constructions which, in fact, presume readers who are indeed in the know and interested in the main characters. The character attributes are technically quite clever, employing puns and alliteration. No doubt written in the light of knowledge of what a figure has done, or is alleged to have done, they operate as pointers to the substance of the stories. The fact that they tend to be deployed in headlines, captions and the early paragraphs of a story, and that they are often printed in bold, reinforces the view that they are giving directions to readers about how to view the main character.

Having set characters in place the stories get down to the main business, which is to fill us in on what they have done. The actions with which they deal are of a quite different order from movements around the world of entertainment. They are actions taken from the 'private' lives of the stars.

I have said that stories of this sort belong to a hybrid genre that combines elements of fabulous and journalistic writing. They are sufficiently driven by journalistic imperatives to take an interest in events that are disruptive, unexpected or unanticipated. Those which were guaranteed pride of place dealt with just such events. The types of events which were of particular interest to the tabloids can now be further specified. They involved actions which were deemed unworthy, and unbecoming a member of the caste of television stars.

SOME CONCLUSIONS

Having spent some time with these newspapers, I have emerged with the strong feeling that research on the tabloid press has yet to provide an understanding of it which fully grasps its complexity. Academic discussion has rarely been able to go beyond its 'union bashing' in the context of major industrial disputes, its national chauvinism and its fascination with almost nude women. It has noted and measured the increasing volume of material devoted to the world of entertainment, and it has concluded that in conjunction with these other features the tabloid press does not serve its readers well as a source of information. Such a conclusion is based, I think, on too restrictive a judgement on what an information service in the public domain should be and how it should operate. Tabloid papers do not provide the service that 'quality' papers do, but this should not be taken as evidence that they have abandoned an informative mission.

⊘ I think too much of the critical judgement of the tabloid press is built upon a rather narrow understanding of politics and of the political role of newspapers. It has often seemed that the ideal political role for critically aware newspapers is to provide its readers with a daily run-down of the most recent instances of the effects of economic exploitation on the part of capitalism's major economic forces, along with a clear indication of the courses of action that the exploited should follow, and not least of all an equally clear indication of the alternative forms of social organization which the action taken would realize. When 'politically aware' critics have found little evidence that anything of the sort is done in either the tabloid or the quality press, they have concluded that since the press is not on the side of the exploited, it must be on the side of the exploiters. Within such a frame of mind it is not too difficult further to conclude that the tabloid's fascination with the world of entertainment and with the actions of the jesters to the court of capitalism is to add to their crimes by distracting potentially revolutionary groups – groups who, one suspects, are seen to be all too easy to distract.

There are many things one could say about such criticism, but I shall confine myself to its misunderstandings of the material which has been discussed here. It is undeniable that the tabloids give over a considerable proportion of their available space to the world of entertainment and those who people that world. It is equally undeniable that a good story about these people will, in most cases, be given priority over those about the debates and disputes of parliamentary political affairs. What is deniable is that this has anything much to do with distraction.

The examples of the tabloid coverage of tellyland which have been discussed here present those who people it as problematic. Though they do exist, there are considerably fewer examples of coverage which confines itself to promoting stars or celebrating their good deeds. There would seem to be a greater enthusiasm for items of content of the sort that has been discussed, and in addition, for candid photographs where stars are caught off their guard, often in far from flattering situations. Note should also be taken of the fact that among TV stars, just as much as among the royal family, there is a fair amount of hostility to the tabloid press's use of this candid photography. While to a certain degree the stories told valorize the main characters, it is more often the case that they do the reverse.

The material is such that it could be seen as performing a kind of cultural police work. Implied throughout all these stories is a twofold perspective on the proper conduct of stars. One aspect of this perspective is that stars, perhaps because of their status and associated lifestyles, are morally fairly wayward beings. Certainly there is an 'ordinary world' morality – or rather, a morality which is proposed as of the 'ordinary world' – by which only a few of these stars live their off-screen lives. The stories are not particularly interested in the moral codes by which stars do live their lives, but rather in demonstrating how far removed they are from the moral codes of the everyday world. The other aspect of this perspective is that stardom carries with it certain responsibilities as well as privileges. It is recognized that stars can lead sometimes spectacularly opulent lives. This opulence is accepted if, in return, the stars do what the stories require of them, namely that they accept the responsibilities of paragons, not just of their crafts, but also of moral virtues. What the papers' efforts of revelation focus on are those instances where stars have stealthily turned their backs on these wider responsibilities. So long as stars behave themselves, acknowledge their responsibilities and act in accordance with the mythology of stardom, their 'private lives' are comparatively safe.

The tabloid's revelations are not confined to stars of television alone. Any representatives of established public organizations are fair game if actions in what has been regarded as the private sphere contradict or contravene what the papers regard as proper moral conduct. They are even fairer game if those representatives have, either by their position or by their own pronouncements, lent their support to what the papers would regard as proper moral conduct. In hunting down their game, the tabloids have in effect contributed to a blurring of the distinctions that could once have been drawn between the public and private spheres. Certainly these papers are not willing to accept in all cases that the private is off limits. This raises difficult issues, only some of which have been publicly discussed. The tabloid's 'invasions of privacy' tend to have been discussed with reference to those depicted as either falsely charged by one or other of the tabloid papers, or as without the resources adequately to defend themselves against their unwanted inquiries. What have not been discussed are those instances where a public figure adopts and promotes as universally applicable a certain moral or legal position 'in public', which that figure then violates or contradicts 'in private'. As was said earlier, such situations have an almost magnetic pull on the tabloid press.

What do the tabloid papers' revelations amount to? At one level, they can be seen to impose a form of discipline. The papers can, as we have seen, turn nasty. Their publicity of 'private' wrongdoing is an ever-present threat to those contemplating actions which might be taken as deviant. The morality by which they target their 'victims' is, however, rarely spelled out. Much more work needs to be done to be able to say more definitely what this morality consists of. At this stage, we can say that, whatever the precise characteristics of the morality, it is held to be universally applicable. This is never stated explicitly, but it is presumed. On this score, the papers are open to criticism since the morality is not applied evenly across all their forms of coverage.

Some final remarks have to be made with regard to privilege. On this matter, the papers are deeply ambiguous. It seems too far-fetched to suggest that the papers express an aversion to the privileges of the stars. Nowhere was there evidence that these papers were suggesting on a regular basis that the stars, and the other types of public figure who were the subjects of their revelations, should be stripped of their privileges, still less that the privileges they possessed were a symptom of systemic inequality. Nevertheless, the characterization of some subjects as loathsome was often related to earnings and/or to lifestyles which depended upon considerable earnings. Perhaps behind such characterization there lurked a feeling that could not find adequate expression, namely that very few stars deserve the privileges that come their way. Whatever is to be concluded on this point, one thing is certain. The stories presented the privileges as questionable. They were not presented as attributes of stardom (or other public office) which could be taken for granted.

Speaking personally, I found reading these stories fun. Of course since I have to be analytically interested in them, I have to ask why, and moreover, why others might find reading them similarly or equally pleasurable. In my view, the pleasure comes from the acts of revelation as such. They engender a reaction of the sort – 'well, you'll never believe what I've just read about so-and-so'. But there was also a certain pleasure in seeing those who would set themselves above or apart from the 'rest of us' brought down by the revelations. I realize this is a complex, populist reaction with both negative and positive aspects, and this is not the place to start commenting on them. However, it might be worth exploring further at another time, since I think it would prove to be a fruitful point from which to begin to understand why such stories seem popular with so many different kinds of reader.

Index